CONFEDERATE ARKANSAS

BARUCH AWARDS
1927–1972

1927 Carpenter, J.T., *The South as a Conscious Minority 1789–1861*.
1929 Whitfield, T.M., *Slavery Agitation in Virginia 1829–1832*.
1931 Flanders, Ralph Betts, *Plantation Slavery in Georgia*.
1933 Thompson, Samuel Bernard, *Confederate Purchasing Agents Abroad*.
1935 Wiley, Bell Irvin, *Southern Negroes 1861–1865*.
1937 Hill, Louise Biles, *Joseph E. Brown and the Confederacy*.
1940 Haydon, F.S., *Aeronautics of the Union and Confederate Armies*.
1942 Stormont, John, *The Economic Stake of the North in the Preservation of the Union in 1861*.
1945 Schultz, Harold Sessel, *Nationalism and Sectionalism in South Carolina 1852–1860*.
1948 Tankersley, A.P., *John Brown Gordon: Soldier and Statesman*.
1951 Todd, Richard Cecil, *Confederate Finance*.
1954 Morrow, Ralph E., *Northern Methodism and Reconstruction*.
1954 Cunningham, Horace, *Doctors in Gray*.
1957 Hall, M.H., *The Army of New Mexico: Sibley's Campaign of 1862*.
1960 Robertson, James I. Jr., *Jackson's Stonewall: A History of the Stonewall Brigade*.
1969 Wells, Tom Henderson, *The Confederate Navy: A Study in Organization*.
1970 Delaney, Norman C., *John McIntosh Kell of the Raider Alabama*.
1972 Dougan, Michael B., *Confederate Arkansas: The People and Policies of a Frontier State in Wartime*.
1974 Wiggins, Sarah Woolfolk, *The Scalawag in Alabama Politics, 1865–1881*.
1976 Next Award and Biennially Thereafter.

CONFEDERATE ARKANSAS

The People and Policies
of a Frontier State
in Wartime

Michael B. Dougan

THE UNIVERSITY OF ALABAMA PRESS

University, Alabama

Library of Congress Cataloging in Publication Data

Dougan, Michael B.   1944-
    Confederate Arkansas.

     Bibliography: p.
     Includes index.
     1. Arkansas—Politics and government—Civil War,
1861–1865.   I. Title.
E553.D68   320.9'767'04   76-40053
ISBN 0–8173–5230–9

CONTENTS

For W.L.D.

FOREWORD

In summing up his Civil War experiences in the hospitals of the North, American poet Walt Whitman prophetically observed: "Future years will never know the seething hell and the black infernal background of countless minor scenes and interiors (not the official surface-courteousness of the Generals, not the few great battles) of the Secession war; and it is best they should not—the real war will never get in the books." The war, Whitman reminded us, "was not a quadrille in a ball-room."[1]

The single object of this monograph is to prove Whitman wrong by putting Arkansas's real war into a book. Over the years every campaign has been fought and refought. Battles have been studied, generals' lives have been written, and any number of interesting arguments about various phases of the war have been explored. Yet it has been fifty years since D.Y. Thomas wrote of the experiences of Arkansas in the great Civil War. Much new material has come to light, while some interpretations need revision. That is the justification for this book.

What I have attempted in these pages is to portray a state's life, a biography of Arkansas's fortunes as a political entity through thick and thin. Even in the industrialized and mobile twentieth century our states still maintain an identifiable character. In the nineteenth century, especially before the war, the individuality of the states was highly pronounced. State loyalty, though it often proved transient at best in frontier America, was nevertheless often a more real feeling than national loyalty. Sectional feelings, especially at the South, bolstered rather than weakened state ties. Finally loyalty to local communal feelings was especially strong in isolated rural areas like the Ozarks. Thus while the outcome of the Civil War was decided by national causes, the greater number of people within the Confederacy never looked beyond the state and local impact from these national events. It is somewhat ironic that State's Rights, the constitutional philosophy of the Confederacy and her raison d'etre, helped in undoing her valiant sons. State's Rights, moreover, was merely the tip of the iceberg of state loyalty, state feelings, and state needs. Nowhere were these considerations stronger than among the homefolk. The majority of Arkansans did not fight for either side; they were too young, too old, of the "wrong" sex, or the "wrong" race. Yet the Civil War was so nearly a total war that their sufferings, their victories, and their defeats deserve the recognition formerly bestowed only on the army.

To tell their story I have tried to treat Arkansas as an organic entity and use her records as a form of autobiography. Newspapers, letters, diaries, reminiscences, legal documents, songs, official reports, and a dozen other contemporary sources tell the story. My object has been to ferret out these sources and let them have their say. That is my apology, if one is needed, for the numerous quotations. The grammatically unwashed letter of a soldier boy away from home for the first time must rub shoulders with the brilliantly abusive newspaper editorial if the heart and mind of Arkansas are to be heard.

Of course events do not speak for themselves. They must be made relevant and meaningful through establishing relationships. I have not tried to write from any preconceived point of view. In my family both the blue and the gray were worn, dividing the family circle with brother against brother. My obligation as a historian is to evaluate events with understanding and explanation. I do not intend to create either villains or heroes. I have endeavored to present the facts as I understood them.

Finally I owe many a debt of gratitude in the course of my preparation. Professor Bell I. Wiley, then of Emory University, was the original inspiration for this work and bore up under the strains of guiding it through its preliminary stages as a dissertation. His advice, inspiration, and the example of his own many fine books have served me in more ways than he knows. Libraries throughout the South have helped me with materials. My own institution provided a research grant enabling me to collect some loose ends. Mrs. Margaret Ross of Little Rock read and criticized many of the chapters while sharing with me her own vast stock of Arkansas lore. To her and to the persons who shared precious private collections with me, I owe a debt of gratitude. More than that I owe to my wife, who in proofreading and editing has learned more about Arkansas than a Philadelphia girl wanted to know. The mistakes and opinions herein expressed belong to the author for better or for worse.

CONFEDERATE ARKANSAS

1)

Introduction: Antebellum Arkansas

"Every man left his honesty and every woman her chastity on the other side of the Mississippi, on moving to Arkansas."
—Governor Archibald Yell, quoted in the Little Rock *Arkansas Gazette*, August 14, 1844

Union soldiers nicknamed her Rackensack; the western geographer Timothy Flint said she was the "epitome of the world." Somewhere between these two different points of view lay the historical reality known as Arkansas.[1]

The state, which joined the Confederacy on May 6, 1861, contained four distinct types of people: mountaineers eking out a traditional subsistence in the hills and hollows of the northwest and southwest; yeoman farmers situated on the better farming land in the uplands and along the numerous streams; large slaveowning planters generally located in the best bottom land of the Red, White, Arkansas, and Mississippi Rivers; and the motley swamp dwellers, poor white trash, and hunters living on the periphery of the plantation economy. Contrary to the situation in most of the South, geography scattered these types in irregular profusion around the state. Thus a given county frequently contained townships radically different from each other in every conceivable way. Sectional rivalry, so evident in the history of most Southern states, appeared in Arkansas at the local level and reemerged on the state level in a crazy-quilt of subtle and diffuse patterns.

The Louisiana Purchase opened Arkansas for American settlement. In the place of the handful of French settlers present in 1803, the 1820 census revealed 12,482 whites and 1,617 Negroes. In 1819 "A Citizen" wrote in the *Gazette:* "Our territory is rapidly emerging from the sable gloom which so long shrouded and concealed its merits from the citizens of the states." Eighteen months later a Helena Fourth of July toast proposed: "Our territory must improve—our little towns thrive—our climate and soil good—our rivers fine—and all we want is the art of man."[2]

The reality, however, was depressing. Potential settlers headed off for Texas leaving behind unpaid bills at the *Gazette*. In vain did Judge S. P. Eskridge describe the inhabitants of Arkansas as "correct in their morals, kind and liberal among one another, and hospitable to strangers." Fruitlessly, editor William E. Woodruff of the *Gazette* reported every Texas atrocity story, and assured readers that "the rage for emigrating to Texas is beginning to subside." From the vantage point of Helena or Memphis, potential settlers heard great stories about Texas, and they saw hundreds of miles of formidable swamps in Arkansas.[3]

The greatest single drawback to fast development was the difficulty of travel. Contrary to what the natives always told travelers, the western rivers were navigable for no more than half the year. Without roads, communications were uncertain at best. On one occasion, the mail to Little Rock was lost when the mailman's canoe overturned and he was drowned. Residents of the city in 1824 had no mail delivery for two months.[4]

Agitation for a road developed early. Its construction was hailed as a cure-all. "When completed," wrote editor Woodruff, "this road will be of immense utility to the territory, and will be the means of adding greatly to the present rapid increase of our population." Work was begun, but the contractor ran into trouble. One of the surveyors admitted that the route was bad, but said he and his associates had gone ahead

> Knowing that an important interest in the territory depended on that report, and also, of the effect it would have to announce to the people that no communication could be had with the Mississippi by means of a road.

Traveler G. W. Featherstonhaugh reported that the surveyors, "following the example of the ancient Roman roads in England, [had] taken the shortest line to get to the top, and carried it up at about an angle of sixty degrees. Our horse, therefore, came to a dead standstill."[5]

Immigrants, however, braved the difficulties. On December 9, 1828, Woodruff reported arrivals to be four times as numerous as before, and "the press of wagons is so great at the ferry at Memphis, that many of them are compelled to wait several days before they can cross over." Little Rock served as a frontier entrepôt for travelers headed for the Red River valley or southwest Arkansas.[6]

But the road from Memphis was only a marginal success. On February 29, 1832, Woodruff reported that it had been twenty-one days since any mail had arrived, because of the "dreadful state of the road between this and Memphis." In early 1833, parts of the road were rerouted, but problems continued. On May 23, 1837, Woodruff noted that "emigrants continue to flock to this part of the country; but they do it at the risk and cost of passing the most disgraceful bogs, wilderness, and swamps that can be found."[7]

Nor was the problem confined exclusively to the eastern sections. William Etter, editor of the Washington *Telegraph,* located on the military road from Little Rock to Texas, observed in 1847: "There is no such thing as a regular mail." Six months later he reported: "Our mail communications with the east are little better than none when a summer shower will stop them for a whole week." In the north, eleven years later, M. S. Kennard, editor of the Batesville *Independent Balance,* complained: "Independence county has no roads sufficient to convey out of her limits a convict to the penitentiary." While planking and some improvements took place in the decade preceding the war, bad roads continued to be prevalent.[8]

Rivers were the other means of communication. It has been claimed that fifty-one of Arkansas's seventy-five counties are watered by navigable streams. None, except the Mississippi, were reliable avenues of communication. All were notable for great floods and extended low water periods. The curse of the Red River was a raft, a huge backup of driftwood, some hundred miles in length; a similar obstruction existed on the St. Francis. The Army Corps of Engineers, under Captain Shreve, undertook to cut a passage through the Red River raft, but this did not insure the stream's usableness. In 1855, 40,000 bales of cotton were stranded because the river failed to rise.[9]

The Arkansas River was equally unreliable. On January 2, 1839, the editor of the *Gazette* observed: "For the last eight months we have been nearly cut off from all intercourse with the civilized world, owing to the rivers being depended on for the transportation of the mails, while there was scarcely water sufficient to float a dug out." The Arkansas, a Civil War soldier wrote his wife, "is one of the changeablest rivers that I ever saw, it is rising one day and falling the next and has been so all of this winter."[10]

Periodic flooding was also a cause of much complaint. On June 23, 1823, editor Woodruff reported that the Arkansas River had flooded "almost every plantation in this neighborhood, and a large proportion of the crops in the bottom are destroyed or materially injured." The next year, White River struck Batesville twice, in February and again in March, rising to the height of three feet in the courthouse the latter time. But the flood of 1833 on the Arkansas was probably the worst.

> Thousands of acres of corn were swept off, together with the dwellings and out houses of citizens in the vicinity of the river. All plantations on the north side of the Arkansas for several miles above and below this place are under water.[11]

Rivers were perilous even when navigable. The Red River had the highest insurance costs of any American stream, and the Arkansas ranked next. Editor Etter noted, "With almost every issue of our paper we are called upon to record one or more disastrous accidents occurring upon our western rivers. To travel on one of our steamboats is equivalent to gambling ventures upon one's life." In 1861 a newspaper correspondent on his way to Little Rock wrote:

> The Arkansas is the graveyard of steamboats, I should say, from the number of wrecks we passed and places pointed out where others had perished. I noticed the wrecks of the *Frontier City, New Cedar Rapids,* and *Quapaw* standing in water to their cabin floors at various places, some considerable distance apart.

Lack of transportation kept the economy at a subsistence level in the northwest. Although planters imported their foodstuffs from Cincinnati, the northwest was perfectly capable of filling the market except for the inability to get the goods to the buyers. In addition, merchants could never be certain from one year to the next when or if their supplies would arrive. Possible manufactures were retarded.[12]

Moreover unlike most other states, the line of the frontier stopped at Arkansas's western boundary. To the west lay an undefined Indian Territory, whose continued existence, together with the migration of Indians through the state, had an unsettling influence best symbolized in the person of Judge Isaac C. Parker, the famous "Hanging Judge." Thus despite the strategic implications of Fort Smith and the thirty-fifth parallel route to the west, Arkansas could not be a Mother of the West as was Missouri. A combination of geographic and political factors resulted in the prolongation of the frontier stage of economic development, which in turn gave rise to an adverse impression of Arkansas.

Travelers returning to the East circulated reports that Arkansas was "peopled by a race of semi-barbarians, who would not hesitate to cut a Christian into shoe strings in the twinkling of a bed post, merely for the amusement it might afford them." "The very name," the Powhatan *Advertiser* noted, "conjures up to the benighted, misinformed stranger, the bloody bowie knife, assassins, cut throats, and highway robbers." G. W. Featherstonhaugh observed:

> Gentlemen, who had taken the liberty to imitate the signatures of other persons; bankrupts, who were not disposed to be plundered by their creditors; homicides, horse-stealers and gamblers, all admired Arkansas on account of the gentle and tolerant state of public opinion which prevails there.

Nor was the image improved when local writers Charles Fenton Mercer Noland ("Pete Whetstone" of the *Spirit of the Times*) and Alfred W. Arrington (*Lives and Adventures of the Desperadoes of the South-West*) drew on their Arkansas experiences for fanciful western tales.[13]

There was enough substance to the stories to lend credence to the wildest accounts. Violence was present from the start, especially as the yeomanry pushed on to the unsurveyed Choctaw line, where some of the most available good farming land lay, and came in conflict with the Indians sent there for a permanent reservation. Sporadic clashes occurred, and cries of "great alarm," calling for more military protection appeared in the press.

In the back country, and in out of the way places deep in the swamps, canebreaks, and mountains, horse thieves, robbers, and cattle rustlers abounded. Murder of unwary travelers in desolate places was, apparently, common, although some of the tales were no doubt merely western exaggerations taken at face value. Gamblers and prostitutes frequented the river towns. Editor Woodruff reported in 1828 that Little Rock was "notorious at home and abroad." On May 20, 1840, *Gazette* editor Edward Cole wrote:

> We regret to be obliged to state that frays, fist fights, and other breaches of the peace are becoming more common in our city, than at any time since our residence here—and when we first arrived here, the place had a name bad enough.

The other river towns, Napoleon, Hopefield (opposite Memphis), and Helena were just as bad, and in the case of Fort Smith, worse. In 1860 a Fort Smith editor wrote: "Murder, vice, and rowdyism stalk our streets by night and by day with brazen effrontery, confident in the feeling that there is no power to restrain them." Helena, Featherstonhaugh quoted a native as saying, was where "all sorts of 'negur runners,' 'counterfeiters,' 'horse stealers,' 'murderers and sich like,' took shelter 'agin the law.' "[14]

Attempts at law enforcement only contributed to the image of lawlessness. Escape to Texas, "that asylum of oppressed Republican humanity," was easy. Finding witnesses was frequently difficult. And since many fights involved, in some degree, self-defense, juries were reluctant to convict others of practices resorted to by themselves. The "better sort" sometimes set a bad example. During one session of the state legislature, the Speaker of the House left his chair, pulled out his bowie knife, and stabbed to death a member whose remarks had offended him. After being reluctantly brought to trial, he was acquitted and reelected. Duels, though illegal, were common.[15]

Thus the criminal element flourished. The mayor of Little Rock was the head of a vast organization of counterfeiters, and used his official capacity to the benefit of his gang. English visitor G.W. Featherstonhaugh reported that there were scarcely twelve men in Little Rock who ever ventured into the streets without being armed with pistols or a Bowie knife. Thus lynch law was too frequently the only way to combat crime. Editor Woodruff, a man of enlarged views, and rated by Feathers-tonhaugh as "one of the most indefatigably industrious men of the territory," defended it. A correspondent in the *Gazette* claimed for it "salutary effects." Woodruff noted with approval an instance of *ad hoc* justice done to an alleged murderer:

> After divesting him of some of his clothes, they applied the oil of hickory to his back and limbs with such effect, that in a few minutes he had but little whole skin left between the back of his neck and heels. Not satisfied with this, they proceeded to put a farther mark on him by shaving one side of his head, but in performing this operation, either through the awkwardness of the barber or the darkness of the night, they not only took off all the hair, but one of his ears with it. They put him into an old canoe without a paddle and cautioned him against ever setting his foot in Little Rock again.

Arkansas, said the *Gazette* in 1841, "is a place where no law is recognized but Lynch law, and no rights acknowledged unless maintained by brute force."[16]

Not all the violence involved criminals. In Marion County a feud between two families spread until the entire county was at war, and the governor had to call out the militia to restore order. Just across the Missouri line in Douglas County, two hundred men met in pitched battle. One hundred men were indicted for murder in the spring of 1861 as a result of this bloody fracas.[17]

The 1835 census revealed that Arkansas had enough voters to qualify for admission to the Union. Since Michigan was seeking entry at the same time, Southern leaders pushed Arkansas prematurely forward as a counter-balance. Thus, in 1836, a convention assembled in Little Rock to write a state constitution. Controversy developed as the yeomanry wanted white manhood suffrage and the planters wanted slaves counted under a "three fifths rule." Finally a compromise was worked out giving the yeoman control of the lower house, but tilting the balance in the upper in favor of the planters.[18]

In the eyes of many, Arkansas needed a bank to provide her with much needed capital. With Jackson's victory over the Bank of the United States and internal improvements, Arkansas could not count on any Federal assistance. Thus the first legislature chartered two banks. One was the Real Estate Bank, owned by private stockholders, who mortgaged 127,000 acres officially valued at $48 an acre. The state credit was pledged to this bank. The other institution, the State Bank, was capitalized at one million dollars and given the state cash surplus (i.e., the budgetary surplus returned to the states after Jackson paid off the national debt) and the state land donation. With just a few roll calls, the state obliged herself to a total of $3,500,000 when her income was about $40,000 a year. Entering into operation at the onset of the Depression of 1837, both banks, after short careers marked by bad luck, folly, and embezzlement, closed their doors in 1839.[19]

The bank, according to the *Gazette,* was ''a subject upon which there have been much clamor, ignorance, and delusion, and its affairs are shrouded and mystified.'' The yeoman farmer, who never asked for or received a loan, discovered to his dismay that his taxes were pledged to liquidate the planters' bad debts. Moreover the charter greatly limited state involvement. Those who broke the bank were subsequently installed as receivers to liquidate its resources. Within a brief time Arkansas bank notes fell from nearly par to thirty-five cents on the dollar. With the collapse of the banks the depression reached Arkansas. ''Distress, ruin, and embarrassment pervade every village, neighborhood, and family,'' the *Gazette* reported. Flush times were indeed a thing of the past.[20]

Now the state had to try to salvage her land donation, liquidate the banks, and redeem the state bonds. Much controversy insued, but little progress was made. Part of the bank debt was eventually repudiated by the state, leaving the state in gloomy financial condition.[21]

The failure of the state to grapple with the bank issue tarnished her reputation still further. The Helena *Southern Shield* offered this *post hoc* evaluation:

> If we had not established banks when we did, our state would now in all probability be in a condition such as would rank her among the first of this glorious Confederacy. But a false step has burdened her with a debt which she cannot discharge for a quarter of a century. Her destiny must remain darkened for many years to come, notwithstanding she has all the elements of greatness scattered in wild profusion around her.[22]

One result of the bank collapse was the further by-passing of Arkansas in favor of Texas. Some parts of the state lost population. Editor William Etter of the Washington *Telegraph* said of his town: ''A few years since nearly one-fourth of the town was tenantless, some having grown tired of the unprofitable monotony, and moved away, and others having caught the Texas fever.'' Indeed former inhabitants of Arkansas constituted the largest single source of Texas' population. Of those passing through Little Rock, it was estimated that ''not one out of twenty stops this side of Texas.'' The Mexican War, and the resultant prospect of Texas' statehood, increased Arkansans' fears. A Batesville man wrote: ''Texas annexed, and the fever up for California and Oregon, and we shall lose population for years.'' The State Auditor's report for 1844 showed a decline in state revenue of $4,000 and 538 less persons paying the poll tax. ''These,'' wrote a *Gazette* subscriber, ''are ticklish times.''[23]

Thus in 1850, a decade before the Civil War, Arkansas manifested little progress and bustle. "We have neither railroads, nor canals, nor turnpike roads, nor any other public works, either begun, or even contemplated," one editor wrote. Having failed with banks, the idea of a state program of internal improvements was launched. The first attempt at concerted action was the summoning of a convention to meet in Memphis in May, 1845. Little Rock responded by selecting a delegation. A report blaming the impoverished condition of the state on the failure of the Federal government to provide adequate roads was approved, but no positive action resulted.[24]

In the five years following this tentative step, Arkansas began to emerge from what editor Etter called her "Rip Van Winkle sleep." One correspondent to the *Telegraph* reasoned, "Our resources have remained undeveloped until now, for the reason that our state has been inaccessible." Adequate transportation was seen to be the *sine qua non* of economic development. Enthusiasm for tackling the problem spread. County improvement and agricultural societies were established. In 1852, Etter wrote:

> The past year was witnessed a Wonderful Change in the views and actions of our citizens. The public mind is engaged in eagerly discussing the various objects that immediately or prospectively affect the interests of the state.[25]

The new enthusiasm found an outlet in the desire for a railroad. One correspondent wrote, "I look upon it as a settled point that without a railroad Arkansas is a *gone coon.*" A convention was held in Little Rock. Albert Pike told the delegates that sectional feeling was the biggest obstacle: "The sectional feeling is here, it exists—it governs—it controls everything." Editor Etter warned:

> Once arouse sectional feeling on this subject and nothing will be accomplished. Each geographical division of the state and indeed every neighborhood, will be found advocating its immediate interests, and there is an end to the concentration of our means.

Batesville editor M. S. Kennard described the extent of sectionalism:

> There is a strange and unaccountable disposition in our population which prevents their being united in sentiment upon any subject. In some cases sectarianism and others political partizanship; in still others personal piques and jealousies distract and divide the people so that the accomplishment of any public enterprise in which the cooperation of a number of citizens is necessary is next to impossible.[26]

The problem was nearly insoluble, since there was no "universal good" in which all Arkansans shared. State Senator McClain of Johnson County confessed: "The north, and south, and east, and west seem wedded to peculiar interests which are impossible to reconcile so as to adopt any system or plan of general improvement." Residents of the northwest wanted closer ties with St. Louis *via* Springfield. A railroad from Little Rock to Memphis, or the alternate plan, from Cairo, Illinois, to

Fulton, offered them no advantages. Memphis (economically the largest town in Arkansas), Helena, and Napoleon all wanted to be the eastern terminus. The Helena *Southern Shield* asserted that Little Rock sought to make Arkansas "wholly tributary to our neighbors of the Chickasaw Bluffs," and urged moving the state capital in retaliation. In November, 1860, as the secession crisis mounted, Des Arc editor J. C. Morrill was in Little Rock lobbying to get his town made the capital. All this occurred because every little town or hamlet—Van Buren, Camden, Fulton, Washington, Pocahontas, Pine Bluff, *et al*—wanted to be on the line and begrudged any neighboring town the same advantage.[27]

The greatest obstacle to a state plan of internal improvements came from the leadership of the Democratic party. Throughout much of the South, the lowering or removal of property qualifications and the popular election of officials diminished the political control of the landed, slaveholding aristocracy. But in Arkansas, the same machine which governed the state in territorial days continued to be in power twenty years later. The Democratic leaders, the Conways, Seviers, Rectors, and the Johnsons, were bound together by complicated ties of kinship and friendship into a loose-knit "family." All were originally involved in land dealings, the Federal patronage, and eventually state politics. The Whigs, always a definite minority, were not bound by such ties, although possessed of men of genuine ability, such as David Walker, Jesse Turner, Albert Pike, and Robert Crittenden.[28]

Victory at the polls, the *raison d'etre* of politics, consisted for the Democrats of carrying the yeoman north with enough votes from the south to offset the Whig vote of the towns and large planters. This strategy worked. The trouble with the Whigs was that "sometimes the north has presented an unbroken front; and then again, the south; but never both at once." Only one Arkansas Whig ever held national office, and no Whig was ever elected governor. Democracy won the elections, but at a cost. No issue could be raised if north and south would differ on it. Since internal improvements was such an issue, it had to be sidetracked.[29]

The gubernatorial election of 1852 centered on internal improvements and a state railroad. Since the Memphis-Little Rock line was associated with the Whigs, some Democrats pushed for the Cairo-Fulton road. The Little Rock Democratic organ, the *Banner,* first warned the hardfisted yeomanry about the dangers of the railroad humbug and then endorsed building three roads, while candidate Elias N. Conway ran on a platform calling for good dirt roads. Whig editor William Etter vainly attacked the "family," to "whose despotic recklessness the best interests of the state have been so long sacrificed," and claimed this move "would now array the whole force of these prejudices against the construction of the Central Railroad." But the move was successful; "Dirt Road" Conway was elected governor in 1852 and again four years later.[30]

The defeat of internal improvements made the Arkansas picture dark indeed. C.C. Danley, editor of the *Gazette* after 1854, moaned that Arkansas was "without navigation, without railroads, deeply in debt, and dependent on her sister states for not only clothing her people, but for bread, bacon, and potatoes." Judge Brown of Camden confessed to his diary: "I feel that I am settled and my means invested and lying comparatively dead in the most hopeless portion of the United States." In Arkansas, he grumbled, there was a "want of everything like public spirit in the action of the people. Nothing is too erroneous for them to swallow if it is only called Democracy by the leaders."[31]

Arkansas's tardy development and Southern Gothic politics harmed the state in other ways. The half million acres of land given the state when she entered the Union was sold and proceeds given to the counties where it was squandered. Education suffered. "Education, as a system," wrote "Proteus," "is too much neglected in Arkansas." The school fund was used "to gladden the heart and replenish the till of some eastern booksellers. The good people of the state received a heterogeneous mass of obsolete school books—boxes of which are yet lying in the different clerk's offices throughout the state." In 1860, only three counties filed the reports specified by law, and two of these were totally devoid of the required information. There were only twenty-five common schools, only 652 schools of all kinds, and several counties had no schools at all. Until the founding of St. John's (Masonic) College in Little Rock and Arkansas College in Fayetteville, Arkansas had "no college—not even an academy to boast of. Schools here are taught in private houses, the rents of which are paid by the teachers." The state had been given seventy-two sections to support a seminary, but not until after the Civil War was a state university established. The money was "frittered away by arraying the poor against the rich—by the cry of aristocracy—by talking of rich men's sons and college education." Truly, as one editor remarked, "There is certainly a great amount of ignorance in many portions of the state, and many worthless teachers pretending to instruct the rising generation."[32]

Despite the omens, the period just before the war witnessed rapid economic growth. Taxable property increased from $42,900,080 in 1852, to $99,872,248 in 1858. Most of this increase came late in the decade. Between 1856 and 1858 taxable property increased by $29,115,203, or by almost half. Population alone, between 1858 and 1860, increased by one hundred thousand.[33]

The causes of this new prosperity were many. First, the state herself lured many people by means of liberal land policies. The Donation Law of 1840 gave tax-forfeited land to settlers on the promise of future tax payments. Second, the state sold, at low prices, her public lands given for school and internal improvements. Finally, the Federal government gave the state 7,686,335 acres of swamp land to be disposed of on generous terms. Half of this land was gone by 1859.[34]

The most important reason was that, as Texas filled up, Arkansas had the only supply of good cotton land left in the South. "Ere long," C.F.M. Noland wrote in 1857, "Arkansas will be the cotton state of the Union. If cotton will only hold present prices for five years, Arkansas planters will be as rich as cream a foot thick." And so it looked: One Pulaski County farm which sold for $600 in 1856, went for $1300 and again for $1500 and yet again for $2500 by 1861. Longtime booster William Etter rejoiced, "Arkansas has caught the grand note of progress that is sounding around here; she has received the glow of spirit that actuates the great works, and she has fallen into the ranks of those who are pressing onward and upward.''[35]

Immigrants brought with them money to capitalize local projects. By the outbreak of the Civil War, the Memphis-Little Rock railroad had made considerable progress over difficult terrain. The Mississippi, Ouachita, and Red River railroad had completed twenty-seven miles of track, and further building was an immediate prospect. Schools, churches, roads, newspapers, levees, and other signs of civilization increased greatly as Arkansas moved tentatively toward the American mainstream.

Increasing population created new economic patterns. One farmer feared that the country was filling up so thoroughly that men living in the hollows would have no place to run their hogs and would be ''compelled to steal or starve.'' The number of slaves increased more rapidly in the south than in the north. The number of slaveholders doubled, but those holding fifty slaves tripled. Thus, the yeoman slaveholder was losing out, holding only 30 percent of the slaves in 1860, as compared with 48 percent in 1840. ''Had slavery endured,'' its historian writes,

> within a short span of years Arkansas would have resembled in racial composition the state of Mississippi, where by 1850 there was an excess of slaves over whites in all the counties adjacent to the Mississippi, in most of the second tier of counties, and in others scattered over the state.[36]

But the changes were only beginning in 1860. Arkansas remained the home of ''small independent farmers who had a few slaves to help them in the arduous task of getting ahead.'' Her chief metropolis, Little Rock, only contained 3700 souls and presented a ''dingy appearance.''[37]

Thus, on the eve of the explosion of the sectional conflict, much of the state remained the home of crude, illiterate, violent, hard-fisted yeomanry, prospective planters, and men looking for the main chance. ''Our society here,'' one farmer wrote, ''is what I call good—no fighting, but little stealing, we use whiskey in moderation and have a jovial talk every time we meet, and as for revival, we have some here but just below they have it awful bad.'' Her political affairs remained the exclusive preserve of an entrenched oligarchy, and her thoughts and aspirations were focused more on getting ahead than on getting out of the Union. The conditions portrayed in the famous print ''the Arkansas Traveler,'' based on the experience of Sandford C. Faulkner, still were representative. The beau ideal was Elias Rector, planter and Indian agent, whose long blond hair and exotic attire was commemorated in verse by Albert Pike;

> Now all good fellows listen, and a story I will tell
> Of a mighty clever gentleman who lives extremely well
> In the western part of Arkansas, close to the Indian line;
> Where he gets drunk once a week on whiskey and immediately
>   sobers himself up completely on the very best of wine,
> A fine Arkansas gentleman
> Close to the Choctaw line!

This fine Arkansas gentleman has a mighty fine estate
Of five or six thousand acres or more of land, that will
   be worth a great deal some day or other, if he don't
   kill himself too soon, and will only consent to wait;
And four or five negroes that would rather work than not;
And such quantities of horses, and cattle, and pigs, and
   poultry that he never pretends to know how many he
   has got;
This fine Arkansas gentleman
Close to the Choctaw line![38]

2)
State Politics
on the Eve of
the Sectional
Crisis

"Them poor whites, they vote, but they don't elect nobody." —Harrisonburg (La.) *Advocate,* September 10, 1852, quoted in Roger W. Shugg, *Origins of the Class Struggle in Louisiana* (Baton Rouge, 1938), p. 121.

In the same way that Arkansas's history is a function of her geography, so was her role in the Confederacy largely determined by the politicians who managed her affairs. In 1860, the center of political gravity, the "family," found their well-oiled machine in serious difficulties. Paradoxically their present problems were in part the result of their past successes. By 1854 independent Democrats, including Senators Chester Ashley and Solon Borland, editor William E. Woodruff, and ex-State Auditor C. C. Danley, were either dead (Ashley), retired (Woodruff), or out of the party (Danley and Borland). Others (e.g., George W. Clarke) were bought off and made their peace. Many of their former supporters became Know-Nothings. In 1856 this nativist combination of ex-Democrats and ex-Whigs gave the "family" a brief scare, but Albert Pike, one of the national organizers, repudiated the party as unsound on the slavery question, and "Dirt Road" Conway beat their candidate James Yell by some 12,000 votes. The following year Arkansas was again a one-party state. The ex-Whig element, often called as elsewhere in the South, the "opposition," maintained only a shadowy existence. Thus the absence of any meaningful challenge to the Democratic monopoly deprived the "family" of their most useful weapon, the quadrennial exhortations to the faithful to maintain party (i.e., "family") regularity.

The rapidly increasing population brought in men who expected the state government to aid in establishing schools, railroads, levees, and roads. They were not interested in old bank scandals or old political obligations. They did not understand that "family" political control rested on a foundation of masterly inactivity. Thus a dangerous situation developed as an increasing percentage of the population owed less and less to the "family."

The first man to capitalize on these twin developments was Thomas C. Hindman, a native of Tennessee and a Mexican War veteran, who came to Arkansas from Mississippi, where he had made a small but noisy reputation by attacking Henry S. Foote. Finding the political pastures (and marital ones as well) greener on the western side of the Mississippi, he moved to Helena in 1854 at age thirty-six, taking up in name the practice of law, but in actuality that of politics. In the canvass of 1856 he battled fiercely against the Know-Nothings. The tremendous abuse that he heaped on that losing cause rankled his foes down to 1860, but it established his claim to "family" gratitude. In 1858 he was elected United States Representative from the northern district, which included both the "great northwest" and an appreciable amount of Arkansas and Mississippi River bottom land, stretching from Helena to Fayetteville. Once in office, Hindman turned on the "family," and sought to establish his own political empire.[1]

Hindman, with his long flowing hair greased back, seemed to one congressional colleague "perpetually anxious to have a duel." Whig leader David Walker decided that he had "good talent and much energy and industry," but was "unsound as a politician." Hindman's success was attributed to his use of the "most vehement and impassioned language." The Batesville *Democratic Sentinel* found him, ironically as it turned out, "fit to command a sortie but not a regiment."[2]

Hindman's eye was on the seat in the United States Senate held by William K. Sebastian. Sebastian, also of Helena, was the "milk and cider" Senator and a conservative in politics. He successfully avoided "the friction of antagonism," and his name rarely figured in the newspapers. Charles Fenton Mercer Noland noted, just before Hindman's onslaught, that "Wm. K. Sebastian, entered by no body in particular, has backers all over the state." Because the legislature was unlikely to select two senators from the same town, Hindman made every effort to destroy Sebastian. With exaggerated protestations of fealty to Democracy, he argued that Sebastian's renomination by the Democratic caucus was void because ex-Know-Nothings participated.[3]

Allies for Hindman came at an opportune moment. The state legislature passed an act cutting state taxes, which Governor Conway vetoed on the grounds that it amounted to repudiation of the state debt. When the legislature further insisted on taking *per diem* pay during a recess, against "family" wishes, a major revolt was underway. Allied with Ben T. Du Val of Sebastian County, the Speaker of the House, Hindman was enabled to build a state-wide power base.

In order to protect his interests, Hindman set up in Little Rock Thomas C. Peek, editor-for-hire from Virginia, who had just served as a Douglas editor in Illinois. His paper, the *Old Line Democrat,* began publication on September 15, 1859, in a blaze of glory, mentioning Hindman by name no less than thirty-eight times, with such effusions as would "sicken and disgust an Eastern Sultan." Hindman already possessed the Helena *State Rights Democrat* (among whose various editors was one A. J. Rodgers or Rogers, who was arrested in Augusta, Georgia, for kidnapping slaves).[4]

In times past, the "family" had faced some very dangerous insurrections, but had always been able to put them down. Against Hindman the "family" labored at a serious disadvantage. Hindman was the first Arkansas fire-eating Southern Rights demagogue. As one editor initially favorable to Hindman finally admitted, Hindman "inaugurated a new kind of political action—new to Arkansas, as the same kind of gurilla [*sic*] warefare [*sic*] — a wholesale denunciation of every one who does not truckle to his mandates and implicitly obey his behests."[5]

The "family," by contrast, operated on the older level of machine politics, political jobbery, and deference patterns. Issues were not carried to the people, but instead were decided in caucuses, conventions, and behind closed doors. The "family" might out-manipulate Hindman, but they had no one who could out-debate him.

When the year 1860 opened, Arkansas's "Harmonious Democracy" was badly split. Few, if any, substantial issues were involved. Hindman made devotion to extreme State Rights part of his platform; even so, much of his support came from the northwest, later the most Unionist part of Arkansas. In general, Hindman's popularity with the voters did not depend on his positions but on his talent for delivering exciting invective.

In response to taunts of cowardice Hindman announced that on November 24, 1859, he would come to Little Rock (which was outside his congressional district) and denounce the "family" to their faces. The great heralded day arrived. Senator Robert Ward Johnson made a special trip in order to be present. But Thomas C. Hindman never appeared, having gone home to Mississippi. Senator Johnson then issued a statement branding him "a bully and an imposter in the ranks of honor." While Hindman offered illness at home as an excuse for his absence, the Democracy of Arkansas more likely saw cowardice.[6]

At the same time, Elias C. Boudinot, editor of the Fayetteville *Arkansian,* claimed to have received a letter, the envelope of which proved to be made from a letter written by Hindman and published under the signature of "Viator" in the *State Rights Democrat*. These "Viator" letters had appeared in the press just after each of Hindman's public appearances, and had contained excessive laudations of Hindman's triumphs on the platform. Thus Hindman was also accused of having been the author of his own puffing. The *Old Line Democrat* denied the charge completely, refusing even to mention Boudinot by name. Then W. L. Martin of Helena submitted that he was the author. "Col. Hindman," said Martin, "had nothing whatever to do with their composition." Finally under pressure, Hindman admitted that parts of the letters were his own work, but he defended his conduct, saying that congressmen revised their speeches in the *Globe* before they were printed. Nevertheless, the result of Boudinot's expose was to make Hindmanites "vomit upon their heads his loathsome criminations."[7]

Hindman had reached his high water mark. Old influential "disorganizer" Democrat George W. Clarke called Hindman "a mercenary adventurer." Former supporter J. C. Morrill of the Des Arc *Citizen* abandoned him. The *Old Line Democrat* started to claim that Hindman was being persecuted, a sure sign that he was losing support. Efforts to find a candidate to run against him were intensified. Even a near duel between Hindman and Senator Johnson in Washington, D. C., did not redeem his reputation. Yet, notwithstanding the decline in Hindman's prestige, a ground swell of discontent against the "family" still remained. Other potential candidates sought to exploit the discontent. Among them was E. W. Gantt, "a facetious little disorganizer," who now launched a campaign to get himself elected congressman from the southern district.[8]

The start of the new year saw the "family" hard at work perpetuating their political control. The essence of their plan consisted in electing as governor R. H. Johnson, brother of R. W., and editor of the *True Democrat,* to replace retiring Governor Elias Conway. Thus the subject of who the new governor would be had been discussed in the press over the last year. The *Gazette,* either with amazing foresight or inside knowledge, had predicted, as early as February 19, 1859, that Johnson would run. Throughout the year various names were proposed: the *Arkansian* supported former governor John S. Roane; the Van Buren *Press* mentioned that Henry M. Rector, presently a Supreme Court judge, was available. The "family" bided their time, saw to it that no single candidate achieved any widespread support, and worked among their supporters to have Johnson's name put in nomination at the township and county conventions.[9]

"Family" plans came to fruition as the state convention met in Little Rock on April 2, 1860. Danley felt that Johnson was assured of success, "notwithstanding the fact that there are elements enough of opposition in the Democratic party to beat him, there is no Democrat who can unite those opposing elements."[10]

The past history of conventions in Arkansas and of their *modi operandi* demands a word of explanation. The use of a state convention in Arkansas was a victory won ten years earlier by the independent Democrats in order to break the "family's" hold on the caucuses. But the "family" managed to successfully organize the conventions. Conventions, the independents found out, were also subject to manipulation.

The process was as follows: Township meetings were held first, followed by county meetings. In these county meetings delegates were selected to the state convention, and resolutions on state and national affairs were passed. Frequently these meetings were marked by fights, fraud, intimidation, and charges and countercharges by opposing factions. The Madison County delegation to the 1860 Dover Congressional Convention was allegedly picked by "two men in the streets." Benton County was notorious for its meetings of "Harmonious Democracy." In 1860 two county conventions were held there, each claiming to be the authorized meeting, and issuing manifestos denouncing each other. In one, thirty-six men allegedly met around a whiskey barrel; the other was allegedly disrupted by Hindman supporters "shouting, hollowing [*sic*], stomping, and screaming like Pandemonium had been let loose." Finally after these spirited local forays, the county votes were frequently entrusted to proxies. In such circumstances the forces of political power, resting in the hands of trusted party men and local "squires," presented a Byzantine web of intrigue. The "family," with its numerous connections, money, and long experience, was in the best position to benefit by such an arrangement. The Camden *Eagle* was whistling in the dark when it pled: "Let there by no wire working, no *packing,* no limited expression, but a full attendance, a deliberate consultation, and a just and fair agreement."[11]

The convention which assembled on April 2, 1860, consisted of one group of delegates controlled by the "family" and a disorganized number of anti-"family" men desirous of defeating Johnson, but doubtful of success, and in any case, lacking a candidate. The initial step in the organization of the convention was to decide the matter of the two contesting delegations. One was the ubiquitous Benton County struggle; the other was from Phillips County. By a decisive vote, the convention decided to seat the Benton County delegation favoring the "family" (the thirty-six men), and to reject the Phillips County delegates led by Thomas B. Hanly. This seeming compromise was apparently all in the "family's" favor.[12]

When the convention rejected the Hindman delegation from Benton County, the election of R. H. Johnson seemed assured. With the votes of the counties allocated on the basis of the last gubernatorial election, Johnson received 10,783 on the first ballot, needing only 12, 394 to win. On the second ballot he received 13,459, and was proclaimed the nominee. His nearest opponent, Thomas Fletcher, got only 4,607 on the second ballot. Yet despite the seeming ease of Johnson's triumph, the Van Buren *Press* reported that "considerable feeling was manifested."[13]

Toward the end of the convention a number of Hindman delegates, led by Ben T. Du Val and P. R. Cleburne, signed a protest, claiming irregularities in the proceedings. Among the specifics was the assertion that the candidate should have been chosen by a two-thirds vote instead of a simple majority, that the adoption of the platform should have preceded the election of the candidate, that the 1856 distribution of county votes was incorrect, and that the proxies were miscast. This last charge was the most important, as it later came to light that the Van Buren County proxy cast for Johnson by R. S. Yerkes, Johnson's partner in the *True Democrat*, was a patent forgery, no county convention having been held in Van Buren County.[14]

Initial reaction to the results of the convention was mixed. Danley, still riding his convention hobbyhorse from 1852, contented himself with condemning conventions in general, and the rest of the "opposition" press was either silent or mildly critical, while J. C. Morrill, an independent Democrat, called Johnson's selection "unfortunate." The reaction of the Hindman press was predictable. In the name of party regularity, the *Old Line Democrat* raised Johnson's name on its masthead as the Democratic nominee for governor, but observed: "We believe his nomination was brought about by improper means and in opposition to the wishes of a large majority of the Democracy of Arkansas." The Pine Bluff *Jefferson Independent* charged that the convention "does not express the will of the people," who therefore were not bound by it, and called for a new convention to meet the first Monday in June at Pine Bluff. Many of the newspapers agreed with "Fairfax" writing in the *Citizen:* "His nomination will array more deep and inveterate opposition than any man in Arkansas and fix the fact beyond controversy that the 'family' govern the party."[15]

With some reluctance, other papers in the state endorsed Johnson. "We must do so," explained the Camden *Southern Star,* as it hoisted up Johnson's name. Among the papers the *True Democrat* found in support of Johnson were the Camden *Eagle,* the Pocahontas *Advertiser,* the Eldorado *Times,* and the Fort Smith *Times.* But beneath the surface, plans for another candidate were being formulated. The *True Democrat* blamed the bank party for initiating this scheme. According to the *True Democrat,* the bank debtors, whose mortgaged lands were security for the bank debt, wanted a governor who would make the state rather than the debtors pay off the debt. With the bank debts falling due in 1862, and with Governor Conway's policy being to make the debtors pay up, undoubtedly there was a grain of truth in the charge.[16]

Everything hinged on what the "opposition" did. So great was the discontent that William Quesenbury observed: "If no Whig runs, the nomination will not be worth a fingersnap." On April 30, 1860, a group met in Helena, calling itself the Opposition Convention. Although it elected to send to the Constitutional Union Convention at Baltimore C. C. Danley, Q. K. Underwood (editor of the *Southern Shield*), M. S. Kennard (editor of the *Independent Balance*), and George Grady of Desha County, it did not nominate anyone for governor. Despite an effort by the Washington *Telegraph* to get Judge Hubbard to run, no Whig candidate stood in opposition to R. H. Johnson.[17]

Meanwhile the *True Democrat* reported to the faithful some minor bits of encouraging news. One hundred guns were fired in Benton County in honor of Johnson's nomination, although it was discovered the next morning that some wag had hung Johnson in effigy on the county gallows during the night. In Arkansas County, a Democratic meeting, with Thomas Fletcher present, endorsed Johnson.[18]

Everyone seemed to be waiting for the results of the two congressional district conventions at Dover and Arkadelphia, to be held May 14. At Arkadelphia a tight race developed between C. B. Mitchel, an old swamp doctor, and the upstart E. W. Gantt. Gantt, a Hindman imitator, denounced the "family," and the *True Democrat* perforce supported Mitchel. Two county delegations were contested, but the division between the Gantt and Mitchel forces was so close that no selection was made, and the people were asked to decide. Diligent efforts were made to get the convention to repudiate Johnson. Some found this demand ridiculous. The Camden *Eagle* stated: "How can the district delegates *without instructions* render null and void the action of *instructed* delegates by the very same people? There is the lowest kind of demagogueism [*sic*]." The Hindman forces were defeated by a narrow margin, and the convention endorsed the state convention and its nominee.[19]

The Dover convention was an even more disordered affair. In Benton County an enormous petition allegedly containing the names of one thousand voters was circulated, protesting the exclusion of the Hindman Benton County delegation in the state convention. The Hindman forces at Dover took over immediately by the simple expedient of excluding all anti-Hindman delegates. A particularly bitter attack was made on Elias C. Boudinot, Chairman of the Arkansas State Democratic Central Executive Committee and quondam editor of the *Arkansian,* who was to take over the *True Democrat* editorship during the election. It was said that Boudinot, who was part Cherokee, was not a citizen, and hence no better than Dred Scott. Under such circumstances, Hindman was triumphantly returned. The convention went on to condemn the *True Democrat* and R. H. Johnson, and to endorse the *Old Line Democrat* as the correct expositor of Democratic views. The convention ended with an address by Hindman, calling for "the necessity of resolving to maintain our independence *out of the Union.*"[20]

Thus it came as no surprise when late in May another prominent Democrat announced his candidacy for the office. Henry M. Rector was no newcomer to Arkansas politics, having been "virtually" born in Arkansas through nativity in Missouri. Surveyor, bank teller, lawyer, and planter, Rector held claim to the Hot Springs. A cousin to Elias N. Conway, he was identified in 1853 by the *Telegraph* as "among the most reliable and devoted friends of the Governor." But Rector's ambitions were not satisfied with the seat the "family" gave him on the state supreme court. In fact his conduct as a judge was so mediocre that a writer in the Pocahontas *Advertiser and Herald* claimed that his resignation "was considered by all as a case of necessity on his part as the only way to save himself in a manner from public disgrace." The Fort Smith *Times,* while not endorsing Rector, took a different view: "He is independent, of fine talent, and a railroad man out and out, a ready debater, and fearless in expression of his opinions." William Quesenbury was closest to the mark: "Henry is a violent man and fights people."[21]

The Hindman press greeted Rector's announcement with cheers. Peek, unceremoniously substituting Rector's name for that of Johnson on his masthead, stated:

> Who is Henry M. Rector? A poor honest farmer of Saline county, who toils at the plow handles to provide bread, meat, and raiment for his wife and children. Do you not know him? There are many among the people who do—who have seen him laboring in the field, earning his bread with the sweat of his brow. But possessing the impress of manhood from nature, and from nature's God, at his country's greatest need, he arose like Cincinnatus of old and did his duty.

"Do you know him?" observed the *True Democrat*. "For ourself, we answer no sir. We know a gentleman of that name of Pulaski County, who owns quite a handsome property, is a lawyer by profession, and is entirely innocent of plowing." Professing no surprise, the *True Democrat* claimed that Rector's announcement had been arranged much earlier.[22]

Congressman Hindman was responsible for Rector's announcement. The strategy was the traditional "disorganizer" method: to bring out a good Democrat who could combine Whig and dissident support. In this case, however, the Whigs were entirely innocent. Hindman's object was the establishment of his own hegemony. Yet curiously, Hindman did not actively support Rector. His press was active in Rector's behalf, but Hindman himself, who supposedly had promised Rector that he would stump for him, was absent from the state most of the summer on the plea of his wife's sickness. Rector was left to go it alone.[23]

The announcement of Rector's candidacy brought a resounding thunderbolt from Congressman Albert Rust, "the friend and supporter par excellance" of the "family." In a stinging address, Rust declared that although the "family" had assured him of its support in his bid for the senate seat being vacated by R. W. Johnson, they were now quietly working behind his back to promote the interests of Governor Conway. Contending that the "subsidized interest" in the counties was being used against him, Rust said that the "family" had "exhibited an arrogant contempt of the popular sentiment of the people unparalleled by any of its former pretentions." Rust reiterated some of the old charges about "family" involvement in the banks and favoritism in government.[24]

This very eloquent address undoubtedly hurt the "family" at a most critical time. The *Old Line Democrat* seized upon it with glee, notwithstanding the Douglas and Unionist sentiments it contained. It is possible that Hindman was instrumental in

Rust's defection, since Hindman served to benefit, both by the bad publicity about the "family" and by the weakening of a potential political opponent's position.

The campaign opened with issuance by both candidates of circulars stating their positions on a variety of problems. Rector took the offensive. He claimed that the state convention had been a fraud, reiterated the Du Val protest, and revived the past charges against the "family" in the handling of the banks and in overcharging for public printing.[25]

Johnson returned the fire. He defended the state convention, charged that Hindman proxy Thomas C. Peek had miscast some of his proxies, and proved that the forged vote of Van Buren County was not essential to his success. He defended "Governor Conway's plan" as the only honest way to settle bank affairs, and denied his involvement in corruption.[26]

In accordance with time honored custom, the two candidates jointly took to the stump. The schedule, drawn up by Johnson, favored North Arkansas (where Johnson was weak), and avoided South Arkansas (where Rector, without the prior effect of Hindman's disorganizing, would be weak). The canvass, "one of the most exciting contests ever made in Arkansas," found Johnson at a disadvantage. The Batesville *Independent Balance* commented thus on one of his weaknesses: "He is about the poorest stump speaker we ever listened to. He would save votes by quitting the stump." On the other hand, a supporter from Burrowsville wrote:

> First arose Mr. Johnson, opening with a long argumentative address, massive and logical, under which his opponent flounced like a fish out of water. The address was like a solid wall of masony [sic] against which the light artillery of his opponent could have no effect whatever. His opponent's speech was like the flashing clouds of evening whose tints change as positions vary, and as soon as the sun sets are no more.[27]

An admirer said that Rector "was a natural born orator; his vocabulary was rich in words and richer in suggestive imagery; his natural logic was superb." Actually Rector's oratory was little more than an exercise in pompous verbiage. Fort Smith *Times* editor Wheeler commented that "the metaphysical jargan [sic] with which he secured the attention of his audience can be laid bare to the public mind, and his subtle arguments swept away with facts as potent as or as sweeping and unrelenting as the torch of Ormor." That Johnson was not the man to expose Rector may be seen from this description of a Rector-Johnson debate:

> Mr. Johnson's style is slow, dry, and prosy in a painful degree. To form a just appreciation of his oratorical powers, one should hear his style of saying "I . . . was . . . born . . . in Arkansas . . . and . . . if you don't elect me Governor . . . . . . I've no whar to go." Judge Rector is a very fair declaimer, his fault is that he is too wordy— his sentences are crowded with big six syllablers [sic] and that he dilutes his ideas until they are sometimes rather thin. He is an orator of the ka-larruping style, as shown in the following sentence: "I stand on my pedestal, shorn of the abominations and malpractices whereon they relied to cast the nomination upon the present nominee of the Democratic party."[28]

Most of the campaign was taken up with the debate over the legitimacy of Johnson's selection and over bank policy. Rector had the advantage on the first issue, since the Van Buren County proxy was an obvious forgery. The *True Democrat* and other Johnson papers suggested that perhaps the forgery was Hindman's work, and Johnson proved his selection was not dependent on that vote. But the cry of "family" had been heard for so many years that Rector's supposed high moral stand probably won him votes. In addition, with no Whig in the field, the "family" was deprived of their most effective past weapon, the cry of party loyalty.[29]

On the bank issue Rector ran into trouble. Under Rector's plan (a shifty thing at best), the state government would turn over the debt to the railroads, who, in turn, would be assisted by state aid. Few informed critics found anything feasible in this scheme. Danley, who preserved dignified silence throughout most of the campaign, came down from his perch to say "a more impractical or visionary scheme could not have been suggested," and that Rector's election on that basis would be "a public calamity." So many cogent arguments were advanced against Rector's plan that editor Peek (who married Rector's niece) finally admitted that it might be impracticable, but that it had "the virtue of opening the doorway." Rector, on the other hand, dismissed Peek's version of his plan as an "injurious misrepresentation," and disavowed Peek's handling of proxies.[30]

Rector also posed as a friend to education, and proposed that the budgetary surplus be distributed to the counties on a free white basis. Danley attacked this idea vigorously, as hostile to slaveholders, and Rector dropped the idea, substituting a tax cut instead.[31]

If the newly formed Constitutional Unionists had hoped for a battle royal to rebound to the benefit of Bell or shed any light on national issues, they were mistaken. The Batesville *Democratic Sentinel* reported that Rector "took the true Southern ground," but that Johnson "also took the true Southern ground." The *Old Line Democrat* claimed that Rector "was the more ultra," but in Benton County Rector told the voters that the election of a Black Republican was not sufficient cause for secession.[32]

Both candidates, in reality, needed the votes of the "opposition." The Johnson strategy involved trying to keep the Democrats in line, and in appealing to the "opposition" with a conservative financial policy. "The American party," noted Danley, "was alluded to in terms of gentle kindness with none of those tirades against the horrid oaths of midnight assassins which once formed the staple of Mr. Johnson's editorials in the *True Democrat*." Rector appealed to the Whigs with talk of railroads, internal improvements, and good government.[33]

According to the Rector press, much of the Johnson strategy revolved around the candidacy of Colonel Jesse Cypert for Congress against incumbent Hindman. Although he ran, and was consistently identified as an "old line Whig," the Whig press was slow to recognize him and a Union convention at Hot Springs failed to endorse him.[85] According to editor Peek, Cypert's candidacy was designed to draw off Whig votes for Johnson. Although the charge has some merit, Peek went on to say that the "family" wanted Bell to win in order that Cypert and Johnson could be elected. This was a dubious policy for an organization which allegedly existed on Federal patronage.[34]

In the press the campaign was marked by more heat than light. All the scurrilous newspaper tricks the experienced peek could command were used on Johnson. Black and Boudinot of the *True Democrat* retaliated in kind. The charges against Boudinot raised at Dover were revised, ending in a full blown editorial encounter, with Peek addressing the part-Cherokee Boudinot as the "colored editor." Boudinot retorted that such comments "have been the weapons with which other ignorant skulking poltroons have essayed to strike me down, and are well worthy of a man, who was purchased in Illinois, shipped to Arkansas, and bid by his owner to heap slander and abuse upon strangers and gentlemen." In the closing weeks, the main issue of debate was which candidate drank more temperately.[35]

The last episode of the campaign was the publishing of a statement in the *Old Line Democrat* by a gunsmith named Trumpler in which Johnson was alleged to have said he could buy the vote of every mechanic in Little Rock for a drink of whiskey. So shaky was the truth of the story, claimed the *True Democrat,* that the *Old Liner* held up its issue for eight hours until Johnson was out of town, before issuing the charge. The Johnson forces retaliated by holding a public meeting, but *Old Line* rowdies broke it up. On this dubious note the people of Arkansas went to the polls.[36]

The election of August 6, 1860, was a complete defeat for the "family." As expected, Hindman defeated Cypert, but Gantt defeated Mitchel, and worst of all, Rector won over Johnson, 31,948 to 28,847. "Is it not strange," wrote J. W. "Dummy" Woodward, the deaf and dumb editor-printer, "that now, when they were *right,* when they opposed stealing *per diem* pay and advocated an honest discharge of the bank debt, the people should turn against them?"[37]

The reasons for Rector's victory are not at all clear. Some found Rector's state policy the cause of his election. A distant cousin wrote, "The circular was the auspicious means of deciding your election." Others, no doubt, were influenced by Rector's apparent ability on the stump.[38]

But the big question of the campaign was: How did the "opposition" vote? No definite answer is possible. But the action of Judge Brown of Camden may have been typical. He reserved judgment until he heard the candidates speak. He then decided to vote for Rector, noting in his diary that Rector was "the right sort of man to use in breaking up" the "family." Those Whigs closer to the centers of power or more familiar with Rector did not agree. Woodward wrote that Whigs voting for Rector "laid aside their manhood." Woodward did claim, though, that former Know-Nothings (a group which included a number of ex-Democratic officeholders) "all went for Rector."[39]

In announcing the results of the election, the *True Democrat* asserted that the Know-Nothings were responsible; the *Old Line Democrat* retorted that the Know-Nothings had supported Johnson. Danley wrote some months later that the Union men voted for Johnson. John M. Harrell, sometime editor of the *Old Line Democrat,* wrote afterwards in *Confederate Military History* that Rector's election was due to a "combination of Democrats and old line Whigs." Confusion over the responsibility was evident in the election returns. Of the twenty-two traditional Whig counties, fourteen went for Johnson, and eight went for Rector. But since the Rector counties were more populous, the only difference in the total was an 888 vote plurality for Rector.[40]

The question of Arkansas's role in the Union played a silent if important role. The Johnsons' long association with the secession wing of national Democracy may have influenced some northwest yeomen to vote for Rector. One Unionist testified later that Rector "was elected in opposition to those who were known to be disunionists." In Bentonville, Rector supposedly said: "Though Seward *himself* were elected to the Presidency of the United States, it were no justifiable grounds for secession and nothing short of an overt act on the part of the North would justify such a step." Thus many Unionists, knowing the secession background of the Johnsons, may have been influenced by such statements from Rector into believing him the lesser of two evils. If so, they were mistaken.[41]

Perhaps the principal reason for Rector's success was his ability to appeal to the new voters. Unfamiliar with the older politicians, and vexed by the various unsolved state problems, the new voters had no ties to the "family," and no correct knowledge of the real meaning or issues of the campaign. Such men flocked to the Rector-Hindman-Gantt banners.[42]

Thus, quite inadvertently, Arkansas had elected the man destined to be known as the "War Governor." At the time, though, the thoughts of many were no doubt in accord with those of editor Wheeler: "Now as the state election is over with the excitement of the canvass, it may be profitable for our farmers to take a view of the farming interests of the county" and interest themselves in different varieties of corn, buckwheat, and turnips.[43]

3)
Arkansas in the Election of 1860

"You wanted to know how many secessionists we had here per acre. We have but one man now but what favors the doctrine and we intend to hang him."
—Bell Griffith to Ozias Holden, April 21, 1861. Department of Archives and Manuscripts, Louisiana State University.

The August election put state affairs to rest and allowed concentration on national issues. Foremost among the problems vexing Arkansas Democracy was the split in the national party. The tension which developed in the late 1850s between the Douglas and Buchanan wings had ramifications in Arkansas. While Arkansians had taken but little interest in the Kansas agitation and made only feeble attempts to aid the Southern cause there, Arkansas Democracy gave lip service to making Kansas a slave state. Thus when Senator Stephen A. Douglas refused to support the administration over the fraudulent pro-slavery Lecompton constitution, the *True Democrat,* which heretofore had looked with pleasure on Douglas, was reluctantly forced to abandon this national "disorganizer." A party machine fed on a diet of party regularity, greased with federal patronage, and faced with internal revolt could not afford the luxury of supporting a rebel.[1]

Despite the association of few Arkansas politicians with some of the Southern extremists, it was not the wary Democratic organs which first introduced Southern nationalism to Arkansas readers. Instead that honor belongs to the "opposition" press. The first persistent spokesman for Southern nationalism was Missouri-born *Gazette* editor C. C. Danley, who, in the 1850's began advocating direct trade with St. Louis, a Southern town in his estimation, rather than with abolition tinctured Cincinnati. Danley also counseled the reopening of the slave trade. To Arkansians, these were new issues. Concerned with getting ahead economically and with persons rather than issues politically, the great running debates of the last quarter century between Webster and Calhoun had not figured to any significant extent in Arkansas, nor had any Arkansas politician prior to 1860 contributed significantly to the national debate. It is indicative of Arkansas's remoteness from the Southern mainstream, that Danley felt compelled to write: "We were the first, and we believe, the only newspaper in the state to write a line or speak a word showing that the institution of African slavery was right." Economically there was much to commend the policy advocated by Danley. Arkansas lands needed development, but the high and rising price of slaves, keeping labor at a premium, slowed the state's growth. Nevertheless Danley's objectives were not economical. Danley and other "opposition" editors were frying other fish. As a writer in the Van Buren *Press* observed, the "opposition" was trying to "seize upon the extreme opinions of some democrats and denounce us as disunionists [or] we will be charged as truants to Southern rights."[2]

The truth of this contention was soon seen, for once the Democratic press took up these issues, the "opposition" press dropped them, and watched the Democrats disagree. Those papers which supported reopening the slave trade—the Des Arc *Citizen,* the Helena *State Rights Democrat,* and the Little Rock *Old Line Democrat*—were soon in the Hindman camp; those which rejected it tended to support the "family."

Thus within Democracy different positions were expressed. The Hindman supporters were the most vocal. Although masquerading as the "old line" or "simon pure" wing, these men, frequently transplants from the deep South and recent arrivals in Arkansas, took the ultra Southern ground. Following the demagogic appeals of Hindman, they stood for no compromise with the North, no election of Douglas, the reopening of the slave trade, new territorial acquisitions, and a congressional slave code for the territories. Before the arrival of Hindman and before the opening of the discussion by Danley, these topics were rarely discussed and seem to have been the cause for little concern among the masses.

Ironically Hindman's attack on the state level was directed against that "family" member, Senator Robert Ward Johnson, whose thinking on national politics most closely paralleled his own. The first stirrings of sectionalism in Arkansas had been made by young Congressman Johnson in 1850 when he opposed the Compromise of 1850 as injurious to the South. Johnson had fought for his political life in the election of that year over this issue. Although he came within one vote of being repudiated in the Democratic convention, and although the Whigs ran a strong candidate, Democracy united behind him enough to insure his reelection. Since that time his policy on national affairs had been shrouded in silence. His actions in Congress and in the Senate (to which he was elevated in 1853) showed him pursuing policies which would bring economic benefits to Arkansas, Indian Territory, and the Southwest. The "family" organ editor, brother Richard, was also inclined toward moderation. Only when the Hindman flank attack from the left hit the Johnsons did the need for clarity on national issues become important. The "family," most of all, were practicing politicians, not demagogues, orators, dialecticians, or statesmen. But the great unrest in the national party in the wake of the Douglas-Buchanan feud made them uncertain as to the safe ground. While privately Senator Johnson admitted that dissolution of the Union was imminent, he was unwilling to initiate a move toward that end. Accordingly, the "family" wandered in search of a policy until the rupture of the party left them little choice.[3]

Yet a different view was expressed by those Democrats, mostly "family" in orientation, who were nationalists. Among their number were such notables as Senator William K. Sebastian, Congressman Albert Rust, and reputed "family" hatchet man of "large size and blustering manners," Thompson P. Flournoy. The one characteristic they had in common was their conservative attitude on national affairs. They did not share the view of Senator Johnson that disunion was inevitable, nor did they agree with Congressman Hindman that it was desirable. Flournoy and

Rust were active supporters of Douglas; in fact Flournoy allegedly possessed "prurient desires" to be vice-president. They and their friends had long been associated with the "family," a clear indication that "family" politics prior to 1860 did not exclude nationalist sentiments. In general they agreed with ex-Governor Thomas S. Drew, believing in non-intervention with slavery, and fearing possible intervention as "positive old fashioned federalism" and "worse than Whiggery."[4]

The debate in the press over the issues facing the South, begun in part by the efforts of the "opposition," took an ominous turn in early 1860. Heretofore the issues had been largely abstract; few questions of office, patronage, or party loyalty were involved. But as National Democracy prepared for the showdown at the Charleston convention, men argued their positions with increasing urgency.

As might be expected, the Hindman press adopted an extreme stand. The *State Rights Democrat* demanded the breaking up of the convention rather than compromise the Southern position, the reopening of the slave trade, a Southern refusal to support Douglas, and "disunion upon the instant a Black Republican candidate is ever elected President of these United States." The editor added: "Those who say my views are not strictly Democratic, if any such there be, are themselves no Democrats." The *Old Line Democrat* was slightly less vehement, but from the first issue professed belief in the "absolute right of secession" and continually asked rhetorical questions such as "Shall the Southern Sampson wait till the Republican Delilah clips his locks?" Both editors seemed more anxious to accustom the public to thinking about secession than in trying to urge it at any certain time or under any particular set of circumstances.[5]

A more conservative position was taken by the "family" supporting the Fayetteville *Arkansian*. Speaking probably for the bulk of Arkansas Democracy, the *Arkansian* expressed unwillingness to give up the two-thirds rule at Charleston (which would result in the selection of Douglas), opposed reopening the slave trade, promised to support Douglas if he was nominated, and proposed to resort to "dissolution only in the last extremity." The Pine Bluff *Jefferson Independent* called the reopening of the slave trade a "doubtful policy and a dangerous experiment." Editor Johnson, while silent on most issues, declared: "The reopening of the slave trade is simply a question of dissolution of the Union—a question of revolution." The *True Democrat* varied its position as the editorship switched from Johnson to J. W. Woodward. It was undoubtedly Woodward who wrote in September, 1859, that secession was "subversive of the very end for which our government was created." Four months later Johnson stated that "the time may come."[6]

Indicative of majority sentiments among the Democrats were the resolutions passed at the county conventions preliminary to the state convention in Little Rock. Nearly all the county meetings endorsed the Buchanan administration and solicited the state convention to adopt resolutions protecting Southern rights. Radical expressions of the sort flaunted by the Hindman press were conspicuously absent. In Phillips County the platform was opposed as too radical and subsequently toned down. A Chicot County resolution, stating that the election of a Republican would be "sufficient cause" for secession, was unrepresentative even of South Arkansas.[7]

The press, however, was full of fire. The *Citizen* launched an extended attack on Albert Rust who, the editor claimed, "was engaged in a miserable intrigue to dragoon the South into the support of Mr. Douglas." Even more indicative of emerging trends was the response to congressional candidate Charles B. Mitchel's speech in Little Rock. Mitchel said that the courts would protect the South's rights in the territories and opposed congressional intervention. For this stand editor Peek blasted Mitchel as a traitor to Southern rights, bringing down on the head of the poor old swamp doctor the whole host of ailments to which the Southern politician was heir. The *True Democrat,* perforce Mitchel's supporter, was forced to "grease," by saying Mitchel really meant that the Northern majorities in Congress would not pass legislation. If the courts failed, Mitchel was represented to believe that secession was the remedy.[8]

The curbed tensions broke out when Democracy assembled for its quadrennial conclave in Little Rock on April 2, 1860. Besides the vexed question of the gubernatorial candidate, the convention would determine where Arkansas stood at the national gathering at Charleston. Thus formerly small matters like the platform, the electors, and the delegates to Charleston became matters of some import. Radicals, conservatives, and moderates early met in conflict. Napoleon Bonaparte Burrow, an Arkansas River valley planter and a Hindman Democrat, presented to the convention a set of resolutions which reaffirmed the Southern interpretation of the Cincinnati platform, and which concluded thus:

> Resolved . . . That the Representatives of the Democracy of Arkansas in the Charleston convention be instructed to insist upon the recognition by said convention of the principles heretofore declared, prior to ballotting [*sic*] for any candidate for the presidency, and if said convention refuse to recognize the rights of the South in the territories of the United States, the representatives of the Democracy of Arkansas be instructed to return from said convention, and refuse to aid in the selection of any candidate whomsoever by said convention.

In an effort to avoid controversy, these motions were referred to the platform committee, consisting of nine men: N. B. Burrow, chairman, G. W. Carroll, Thompson B. Flournoy, J. Gray, Daniel Griffin, W. W. Leake, Philander Littel, W. M. Randolph, and G. W. Taylor. With the exception of Burrow and Gray, these men represented the conservative and moderate elements of Arkansas Democracy.[9]

After the selection of Johnson as gubernatorial candidate was concluded, the platform committee made its report. First came the majority report, mostly routine. The first resolution expressed "confidence in the virtue and intelligence of the people." The third endorsed the two-thirds rule at Charleston. The fourth praised the Democratic party. The fifth condemned the Republicans, observing ominously that "the success of that party would be disastrous to the perpetuity of the union of these states." The sixth resolution extended "the right hand" to Northern Democrats. The seventh ordered abolitionists to stay home. The eighth said decisions of the Supreme Court "are conclusive and binding upon, and must be obeyed by every citizen of the

Union.'' The ninth resolution endorsed Buchanan's administration, and the last endorsed a thirty-fifth parallel railroad. The key resolution was the second:

> Resolved further, that we re-affirm the political principles enunciated in the Cincinnati platform by the Democracy of the United States, in June, 1856, and assert as illustrative thereof, that neither Congress nor a Territorial legislature whether by direct legislation or by legislation of indirect and unfriendly character, possesses power to annul or impair the constitutional rights of any citizen of the United States to take his slave property into the common territories and there hold and enjoy the same.

Apparently this was the limit of moderate and conservative common ground. On the one hand it refused to reaffirm the Cincinnati platform without comment—an action favorable to Douglas whose Freeport Doctrine was, after all, offered only as an interpretation of that platform. On the other hand the resolution did not call for congressional protection of slavery in the territories, the Yancey-Hindman position. Taken together with the eighth, this resolution implied that the Dred Scott case had been the final word on slavery and rejected both the Douglas and Yancey positions. It was not, as the *True Democrat* called it, "a Douglas platform."[10]

When the majority report came out of committee, W. M. Randolph moved that each resolution be considered separately, as he opposed part of the majority report. W. P. Grace of Jefferson County moved to strike out the word "constitutional" in the second resolution, though for what reason is not stated.

Chairman Burrow and J. Gray presented a minority report consisting of four resolutions. Two of these duplicated numbers one and three in the majority report. The second minority resolution stated:

> Resolved, that we affirm the political principles enunciated in the Cincinnati platform by the Democracy of the United States, in June, 1856, and assert as illustrative thereof, that neither Congress nor a territorial legislature, whether by direct legislation, or by legislation of an indirect and unfriendly character possess power to annul or impair the constitutional rights of any citizen of the United States to take his slave property into the common territories and there hold and enjoy the same, and that if experience should at any time prove that the Judiciary and Executive powers do possess the means to insure protection to constitutional rights in a territory—and if the territorial government should fail to provide the necessary remedies for that purpose, it will be the duty of Congress to supply the deficiency.

Burrow thus abandoned Calhoun's nonintervention doctrine and claimed instead that Congress had the power to legislate on slavery but only to protect and encourage it, not to retard it. "Popular sovereignty" was explicitly denied.[11]

But the real dissembling came in the third minority resolution. It stated:

> Resolved, that the representatives of the Democracy of Arkansas, in the Charleston convention, be instructed to insist upon the recognition, by said convention, of the principles hereinbefore declared, prior to balloting for any candidate for the Presidency.

What course the delegates should follow if the convention saw fit to repudiate such principles, or if it, like the state convention, chose to elect the candidate before the platform was adopted, was not stated. After a short struggle, unrecorded in the minutes except for the statement that W. P. Grace registered opposition, the minority report, on motion of Jilson P. Johnson, was adopted. The "family" had moved to the left.[12]

It might seem strange that little debate took place and that not one committeeman who helped draw up the majority report arose to defend it. The vote adopting the minority report was 22,598 to 766, with none of the majority members opposing its adoption. However the further proceedings suggest that a deal was made. Two of the committee men, Dr. Taylor and W. W. Leake, were selected state electors, on nomination of Douglas leader T. B. Flournoy. Besides the electors, T. B. Flournoy was himself selected as one of the eight delegates chosen to attend the Charleston convention. Apparently the Douglas men sold out the platform for political position.

The other delegates selected for the national convention were a mixture of party interests. N. B. Burrow was the only representative of the Hindman faction. Jilson P. Johnson, Dr. John A. Jordan, Senator Johnson's brother-in-law, and Colonel F. A. Terry, were of the "family," and the same was probably true of Van H. Manning and F. W. Hoadley. John I. Stirman, perhaps of "family" orientation, was conservative.

The divisions which were mostly covered up in Little Rock came to the surface in Charleston. Despite the heaven and earth patronage moving effort of the Buchanan administration, "the Little Giant" was clearly the favorite of the majority of the convention. Arkansas received formal recognition when T. B. Flournoy was called upon to preside as chairman pro tem. He was much applauded when, in stepping down, he urged "councils of moderation and harmony."[13]

The Southern radicals, inflamed by congenial surroundings and William Yancey, chose to make the platform the issue upon which to rest their case. They were determined to write a platform Douglas could not accept, and the Douglas forces were equally determined not to retreat from the line of the Cincinnati platform. "The irrepressible conflict had invaded the Democratic party, and its convention was a house divided against itself." On Monday, April 30, 1860, the Douglas platform was adopted 165 to 138; the Southern extremists walked out; and N. B. Burrow, Van Manning, and Dr. Jordan joined them. In justifying his conduct, Burrow had the temerity to say that their course was in accordance with the instructions of the state convention, and quoted his own unadopted resolution as proof. Jilson P. Johnson then arose and said that no consultation had taken place among the Arkansas delegates. The next day (during which the Georgia delegation withdrew) Johnson, Terry, and Hoadley followed the others, leaving only Stirman and Flournoy participating. Unable to function, the convention adjourned, to meet again in Baltimore on June 18, 1860, and issued a call to fill up the vacancies caused by the Southern walkout.[14]

Danley, who was in Charleston as an observer, blamed the breakup on "an excess of spoils fever" and astutely observed that "at present Democratic papers and leaders in Arkansas are on delicate ground.'' The *True Democrat,* following the lead of its delegation, came out unequivocally against Douglas. The Douglas platform, Johnson proclaimed, was ''thoroughly odious to the South'' and as for the crisis, ''Douglas and his odious squatter sovereignty doctrines have produced it, and until he is out of the way, there will be neither peace nor harmony in our ranks.'' Nevertheless Johnson refused to go all the way or rejoice in the outcome. ''We are unwilling to take the final step toward the dismemberment of that party until the last hope of obtaining justice to the South at its hands is destroyed and abandoned.'' Johnson urged that the original delegates attend the Baltimore meeting. Simultaneously a letter from Jilson P. Johnson appeared, announcing that he intended to go to Baltimore and that he had not surrendered his seat by participation in the Charleston walkout.[15]

Other delegates now hastened to make their positions known. Burrow, in a speech at Memphis, defended the seceders and said that they were the true Union men. Southerners, Burrow explained to those who asked why the convention had been broken up, were the descendants of the Cavaliers, and would never submit to dictation from the Northern Roundheads. Congressional protection of slavery, he added, was the ''ark of the covenant.'' John Stirman explained his position in a public letter and pointed out the falsehood of Burrow's claim that he was acting under instructions. Flournoy, in accordance with the tactic agreed upon at Charleston, issued a call for a new convention to meet in Little Rock on June 5, 1860, to select delegates for Baltimore. Defending the Douglas position, he asked why the South should now reject the same platform that had served in 1852 and 1856. Although Fournoy's proposed convention never assembled, the Madison *Journal* issued another call for a meeting on June 15 in Madison which did assemble.[16]

Political opinion, never sharply focused on national issues, tended to be critical of the two Douglas delegates. The *True Democrat* dishonestly accused them of disobeying instructions. Only the strong Douglas paper, the Van Buren *Press,* condemned the course of events and forthrightly criticized the seceding delegates. Burrow's home town paper denounced his conduct as ''highly reprehensible.'' More typical was the reaction of the Fayetteville *Arkansian,* which viewed the breakup with ''regret and alarm'' but avoided specifics.[17]

The convention in the congressional districts took the subject under advisement. The Arkadelphia convention appointed Senator Johnson, Josiah Gould, Dr. Hobson, and S. H. Hempstead, two conservatives and two radicals, as new delegates with authority to go to Baltimore or Richmond (where the Southern Democrats planned to meet).[18]

The Dover convention declared arbitrarily that Stirman and Flournoy had forfeited their appointments, and also held that their seceding associates were no longer delegates. The convention then chose a new slate, appointing N. B. Burrow and DeRosey Carroll, with Hindman and N. Bart Pearce as alternates. Finally the Douglas men meeting at Madison, selected Thomas H. Bradley, Dr. William Hooper, and David C. Cross. Thus Arkansas in effect had four overlapping delegations.[19]

Although few in number, the Douglas supporters were vocal. Albert Rust, whose bolt had provided aid and support for the Rector insurgent movement, had not hesitated to spare the "family" for their part in undoing Douglas.

> They are not disunionists, per se, but demand in violation of solemn compromise entered into by the National conservative men of both sections, as an ultimatum, what they know will not be, and do not desire to be granted.

In addition the Douglas cause in Arkansas was enhanced by the support of ex-Governor Drew, and three papers, the Van Buren *Press,* the Pine Bluff *Jefferson Independent,* and the Pocahontas *Advertiser and Herald.*[20]

One big unhappy family of unharmonious Democrats assembled in Baltimore on July 18, 1860. The strategy of the anti-Douglas moderates apparently was derived from *An Address to the National Democracy* which both Arkansas Senators signed. This letter urged a full attendance at Baltimore before any meeting at Richmond. It also repudiated both the newly elected Douglas delegates and the otherwise chosen anti-Douglas delegates. "The delegations already elected," the address stated, "are the only ones that can act and they must act on their own judgment in a conjuncture which does not allow opportunity for instructions by their constituents."[21]

But the convention refused to be so guided. The anti-Douglas Arkansas factions came together calling themselves the "Regular" delegation, and excluding the Madison group, whom they denounced in a public statement as bogus. Flournoy refused to sign it (Stirman was absent). When the convention decided to give representation to the newly elected Douglas delegates from Arkansas, Alabama, and Louisiana, anti-Douglas men seceded again, met in Richmond, and nominated Breckinridge and Lane. Only Flournoy and Stirman (although Stirman left before the election of Douglas) remained in convention of those originally chosen.[22]

Not until after the August state elections did the debate on the presidential candidates really get under way. Of the three parties in the field, the Douglas forces were the weakest. A Douglas convention was held in Little Rock on August 24, 1860, at which electors were chosen and a newspaper, the *National Democrat,* established. Doctor Meador, the *National Democrat* editor, was browbeaten by all. The Camden *Star* called him a "low contemptible, baseborn, heaven-despised, hell-deserving coward," who, for good measure, was also a "filthy, lousey, scavenger." Throughout most of the campaign, Rust and Flournoy, both able speakers, were absent in Virginia and Kentucky respectively. Before leaving for Virginia, Rust met Hindman in debate at Des Arc. Rust, the *Old Line Democrat* reported, "talked loud and long about the glorious Union; was exceedingly free in the use of such terms as disunionist, secessionist, Yanceyite, etc." As for Hindman, his speech was marked by the "vindication of the Democratic party from the charge of disunionism." Senator Johnson refused to debate Rust.[23]

Rust returned to Arkansas late in the canvass, and when Hindman refused to debate him again, set off on his own, making fourteen speeches in the closing weeks of the canvass. He met for his effort a determined attempt by local Breckinridge men to deny him a hearing. At Camden they refused to let him address their assemblage, and when Rust finally secured a place to speak, the Breckinridge men kept their following away, so as to deprive Rust of his audience.[24]

The Douglas effort was pitifully weak. The *National Democrat* failed to achieve prominence and soon ceased publication. Few speakers of note, except for Flournoy and Rust, canvassed the state. The expected round of barbecues, gatherings, parades, polls, and liquid refreshments seems to have been in short supply. The voters were accustomed to such festivities, and probably thought the less of the Douglas cause for its failure to provide them.

The Constitutional Union party arose from the ashes of the old "opposition." Although in 1860 the Arkansas "opposition" was nearly dead, the breakup of the Charleston convention galvanized it back into life. Danley, for one, would have preferred a national candidate of Democratic antecedents with less vulnerability, such as Sam Houston, but withal Bell did not seem too much of an embarrassment, especially at the South. By entering no candidates in the state election (save for the legislature), the Constitutional Union party saved their strength for the main encounter.

The Bell forces reached the voters more effectively than the Douglas men. The old Whig and Know-Nothing press became Constitutional Union organs. Although there were only five pro-Bell papers, these were influential and long established organs, such as the Little Rock *Gazette,* the Camden *Ouachita Herald,* the Helena *Southern Shield,* the Batesville *Independent Balance,* and the Washington *Telegraph.* At least one other paper, the Des Arc *Constitutional Union,* was subsequently established. Besides newspapers, the Bell forces were able to stage large rallies. One at Washington attracted about a thousand persons. A typical rally was one held at Camden on October 23:

> The Bell Mass meeting. Beautiful day. The longest, grandest and most imposing meeting ever seen in Camden. Our own and Washington Brass Bands, Barbecue, Dinner, Marches, Procession, Horseback and Carriages at night. The light procession five hundred transparencies—March through the whole length of our beautiful young city.[25]

Breckinridge inherited the Johnson and Hindman elements of Arkansas Democracy. Although less was heard of their feud after Charleston, the divisions over state issues, signalized by Rector's insurgency, persisted. Inevitably these differences had ramifications which related to national issues. Peek, it will be recalled, tried to show that Rector was the sounder on national issues, that the "family" wanted Bell to win in order that R. H. Johnson might also be elected, and, after Rector's election, that the results supported Breckinridge. The *True Democrat,* on the other hand, wondered how a Douglas editor in Illinois could be an honest Breckinridge man in Arkansas, asked why the *Old Line Democrat* hoisted Breckinridge's name without comment, and predicted (correctly) that once the gubernatorial canvass was concluded, Peek would leave Arkansas and let someone else edit the paper for the national canvass.[26]

In view of these differences, it is no wonder the Breckinridge campaign got off to a rickety start. Two of the electors, Dr. Taylor and W. W. Leake, ran into trouble. In late August, Taylor, who was apparently being worsted by Bell elector H. F. Thomason, tried to draw a gun on him and subsequently quit the canvass. Leake had to be hushed up after he honestly admitted at Camden that Breckinridge could not win, but was the Southern candidate and ought to be supported as such.[27]

The strategy of the Breckinridge forces was to claim that their man was the real Democratic candidate, that the convention in Richmond represented National Democracy, and that Douglas was simply a national "disorganizer," to be dealt with as the "family" did state disorganizers. In essence, the Breckinridge Democrats sought to fight this campaign just like any other. The Bell men, they said, were really Whigs; the Douglas men a troublesome rabble. Future secession in the event of Lincoln's election, the reopening of the slave trade, and other alarmist positions were ignored or soft-pedalled. Because of this ostrich-like attitude, it cannot be said that a fair debate on the meaning of the Breckinridge candidacy ever took place.

Running true to form, the Breckinridge men made big protestations about dangers to Southern rights. Nothing would do but the complete acceptance of the South's position. *Old Line* editor Harrell declared that "compromises which only avert danger weaken the defense." Albert Pike, a former leading Whig, supported this view in a pamphlet which the *True Democrat* called "the great paper of the campaign." According to the Breckinridge press, the election of either Bell or Douglas would be as bad as that of Lincoln. Douglas was engaged in a "war against property," and popular sovereignty was but "a shortcut to abolition." As for the Constitutional Unionists, "their own party is very little better than the Black Republicans."[28]

The Bell and Douglas forces returned the fire. Flournoy and Rust defended Douglas's record and accused the Breckinridge men of perfidy. Danley attacked Breckinridge's past utterances on slavery as less sound than those of Bell. Solon Borland came to Little Rock to aid the Bell cause. "Madam Osorio" defended Vice-Presidential candidate Edward Everett because he was favorable to women and had helped with the Washington Monument Fund.[29]

The Douglas-Bell rhetoric played up the accusation that Southern extremists were bent on disunion. Illustrative was Danley's charge:

> They did not dare to nominate their leader Yancey, to effect their treasonable ends. They continue to support Mr. Breckinridge in full view of the foregone conclusion of his defeat, with no other end or object than the hope that, by dividing and distracting the South, they may be instrumental in electing Lincoln, the Black Republican candidate, when they intend making another desperate effort to dissolve the Union.

Similar charges were made by Rust, Flournoy, and the Bell electors.[30]

Perhaps a typical confrontation was the debate between Hindman and Thomason at Des Arc. Hindman attacked Bell's record, supported State Rights, said it was the principle of Democracy, and called the Bell men Federalists. Thomason attacked State Rights, praised Douglas (*vis-a-vis* Breckinridge), and defended the Union. According to a Democratic editor, Thomason "was driven to the wall repeatedly."

But Danley thought otherwise, and criticized Hindman for defending secession, observing that Hindman had "great elasticity and tact both as a debater and a dodger."[31]

The Breckinridge press contrived various ingenious answers to the charge of disunion. "The constitution and government of the United States," wrote Harrell, "combines such wisdom and beauty of construction as to possess a strength sufficient to withstand all these disturbing influences." Congressman-elect Gantt told a Little Rock audience that "the Union was to be saved by the contrast of these conflicting elements." Such arguments were persuasive. The voters had heard disunion cried before and nothing had happened. Harrell wrote:

> We believe that the monster absolutism may be strangled without the aid of the sword or revolution, or the brand of intestine strife—that the equality of the States, while that equality is boldly maintained by themselves, cannot be invaded.[32]

On this note the voters went to the polls. Although John Brown thought election day "the most important day to these United States and perhaps to mankind since the Fourth of July, 1776," many Arkansans did not share these sentiments. Over seven thousand fewer votes were cast in November than in August.[33]

Lincoln won the election, but Breckinridge carried Arkansas. The vote was 28,732 for Breckinridge; 20,094 for Bell; and 5,277 for Douglas. "I never had any hope of the State," moaned William Quesenbury from Fayetteville. Judge Brown, who found Breckinridge sentiment strongest among "people who do not read," blamed Democratic prejudices for the outcome. "The people of the county have been sadly blinded by falsehood and appeals to their Democratic prejudices so as to lose sight of the basic issue in the contest and most of the Democrats voted accordingly." Similar sentiments were expressed by Danley, who claimed that Houston, because of his Democratic background, would have made a far stronger candidate than Bell with his Whig associations. The Democrats had educated the masses to vote instinctively against any Whig; that defeated Bell, not the merits of the Breckinridge canvass.[34]

The election figures reveal much about Arkansas's political alignment. No county went for Douglas, although Crawford gave him 357 votes, over 100 more than Breckinridge received there, though 17 less than Bell. Jefferson gave him 442, the highest number he received, though less by 222 and 158 than what Breckinridge and Bell respectively polled in that county. Both counties, significantly, were served by Douglas newspapers. The Jefferson County vote was exceptional, since that planting county was the home of Robert Ward Johnson. In Pulaski County the weak *National Democrat* was unable to make much headway, as Douglas polled only 172 votes, compared to 819 for Breckinridge and 899 for Bell. Nevertheless the total Bell-Douglas vote nearly equalled that of the Breckinridge faction. Had the Bell forces controlled more papers, or if the Douglas forces had worked at maximum potential, the result might have been different.

Throughout the state the vote followed the old Democrat-Whig alignments, though with some interesting variations. Generally the northwest, stronghold of the hard-fisted yeomanry, was solid for Breckinridge. By contrast the rich planter counties went for Bell. Both Bell and Douglas did far better in the towns than in the country. One reason the Bell-Douglas campaign failed in the northwest was that few residents there read newspapers. In the former centers of Whig strength on the Arkansas River, only Crawford County went for Bell; on the upper White River, only Independence County. In what was to be the heart of Union country during the war, only five counties (Crawford, Independence, Searcy, Washington, and White) returned anti-Breckinridge majorities.[35]

In the Mississippi River counties, however, the Bell forces combined the traditional Whig vote of Mississippi, Crittenden, and Phillips Counties, with that of normally Democratic Desha and Chicot. The second tier of counties back from the Mississippi—Jefferson, Monroe, Jackson, and St. Francis—returned anti-Breckinridge majorities; St. Francis went for Bell outright. Thus it would appear that the Bell-Douglas efforts were more successful in convincing the conservative large planters that Breckinridge posed a danger.

It was in the South and Southwest, however, that the Bell-Douglas forces took their greatest beating. Only in Hempstead County did the Bell-Douglas vote combined exceed Breckinridge's. Six former Whig counties (Lafayette, Hempstead, Ouachita, Union, Dallas, and Saline) were lost. Thus among the smaller planters the greatest Breckinridge strength was to be found.

Obviously the election was no mandate for secession. On national affairs at least, Arkansas returned to the two-party system. How this alignment would stand up when the question of session arose remained to be seen.

4)

Arkansas and The Union, November, 1860– March, 1861

"My opinion is if the Southern States was a Bull Arkansaw would be its tail end. She is allways [sic] behind feeling for the current."—[Andrew?] Chester, to "Dear Brother," February 3, 1861. Arkansas History Commission.

The news of Lincoln's election, while slow in reaching Arkansas, came as no surprise. Even before the news arrived, Danley tried to head off agitation for secession: "Let us act calmly, coolly, and as becomes wise and patriotic men." In most of the press, moderation was the order of the day. "Give him a trial," urged the *Arkansian,* and if he fails, "impeach him, damn him, and damn him forever." The newly established Des Arc *Constitutional Union,* opposing the call for secession issued by the *Citizen,* found Lincoln "not so bad a man as the disunionists would have us believe." The Helena *Shield* reported finding "not five in favor of immediate and unconditional secession." Speaking for the "family," the *True Democrat* announced: "The best course, perhaps, is to do nothing. We are opposed to premature agitation or hasty legislation." "Family" leader, retiring Governor Conway, went further and asserted that the whole sectional agitation was the result of a well developed British plot financed with British gold. Albert Rust reassured the voters that Lindoln's election was "no justification for a thought of revolution." As for the yeoman masses, "the old frontiersman, sitting musingly in his chimney corner, on the slope of a mountain spur, could not see wherein the election of Abraham Lincoln had injured him." Nevertheless Judge Brown noted, "It is true that those who have voted with the Democrats are not all for what is called secession, but the tendency is that way."[1]

Thus it was in the face of generally adverse public opinion that Henry M. Rector, in his inaugural address on November 15, 1860, became the first public official to call positively for secession. According to Rector, the North in electing a sectional candidate had "revolutionized the government." All the states were now independent and, as "sooner or later dissolution must come," it ought to come now. Arkansas should prepare for the inevitable and irrepressible conflict. In taking this stand Rector sought to rally disunionist forces in the legislature.[2]

There was little evidence that Rector's speech reflected widespread public opinion. One Unionist asked, "Suppose we had elected Mr. Breckinridge President, and the Northern states in consequence had seceded, would we have thought they were doing right?'' In Camden Judge Brown found secessionism limited to ''a few reckless spirits;'' the ''older men'' were all for the Union. On November 17, 1860, when a secession meeting was called in Camden, only four persons showed up.[3]

Public attention centered on the legislature and how it would react to Rector's requests. Although certain Little Rock ladies began to distribute blue cockades among the secessionist members, one observer found ''strong Union sentiment pervading the halls of legislature.'' Another correspondent reported: ''There is no probability of the legislature taking any rash steps. A large majority of the members seem disposed to be conservative in their views.'' Nevertheless a few secessionist members openly avowed their positions. A ''family'' spokesman, F. A. Terry, in late November presented to the Senate a series of resolutions which exemplified secessionist views and objectives in Arkansas:

> 1. We view with sorrow and regret the results of the last presidential election.
> 2. We do not regard the election of Abraham Lincoln alone as a breach of our federal rights, but the spirit which prompted it is cause for great alarm.
> 3. We will defer to our older Southern sisters; but if they choose to submit we will abide their decision, but if they, or any of them, deem it wise and prudent to withdraw, we will regard it as our duty to follow.[4]

Coming nearly a month before South Carolina's secession, these resolutions sought to align Arkansas with the states of the lower South. Conservative sentiment was manifested in counter resolutions introduced by A. H. Carrigan:

> 1. That the state of Arkansas, being sovereign and capable of judging of her rights and wrongs, and this general assembly being chosen for the purpose of perpetuating and not destroying or dissolving the government, will impress upon the people a due forbearance.
> 2. Arkansas claims to be competent to judge and act for herself independent of rash or ill-advised action. If she defers to any it would be more manly to follow the lead of the frontier slave states.[5]

Proponents of secession, sensing that their cause was lagging, sought to increase pressure on the legislature. Congressman Hindman and Congressman-elect Gantt addressed the legislature on November 23 and 24. Danley reported that their efforts were ''bold and unequivocal and unmistakable in their meaning. They had a good effect, but a contrary one to that for which they were intended.'' Others were not so certain. One observer stated that Hindman's speeches would ''do more harm than [*those of*] any other man in this state.'' Senator Johnson, in a public letter of December 1 to his constituents, stated that Arkansas ''should rejoice in the course taken by South Carolina'' and support the action of her sister state. Albert Rust was alleged to have declared that the Union cause was hopeless and that it was ''as futile as to attempt to arrest the course of the Mississippi by throwing straws into its current.'' Danley responded by printing Jackson's Proclamation of 1832 against South Carolina on the front page of his paper.[6]

Meanwhile the legislature continued in the even tenor of its ways. John I. Stirman, former Douglas supporter and conservative Democrat, was elected secretary of state. Items of local business, land issues, railroads, and other normal business continued to be the main concern of most legislators. Only two bills, one making Negro-stealing a capital offense, and another encouraging home manufactures, indicated that the times were not normal. Furthermore the legislature planned to elect a new United States Senator to replace the retiring Robert Ward Johnson. Secessionists urged that as Arkansas would soon leave the Union the selection of a Senator was both unnecessary and undesirable.

The idea of electing a senator was vigorously opposed by Governor Rector, who, with few friends in the legislature, would be unable to secure the position for one of his kin. Thus Rector sought to head off the senatorial election by steering the legislature back to secession. Accordingly on December 12, he issued a special message asking that a convention be summoned to determine the will of the people. In addition he requested the legislature to refrain from choosing a senator and to pass an act forbidding the importation of slaves into Arkansas unless accompanied by masters who intended to settle. This measure, he said, will "compel the border states to take care and protect their own slave property."[7]

Simultaneous with Rector's message, Dr. J. J. Gaines, Rector's private secretary, founded in Little Rock the *Southern States* to advocate secession. The *Old Line Democrat* also sounded the call to arms: "Our destiny is irrevocably linked with that of the other cotton growing states; and we should not falter for one moment to seek that destiny, or pause to deliberate the consequences which may follow." At the same time Ben T. DuVal presented a bill calling for a convention. The secession campaign was now fully under way.[8]

After a protracted struggle the legislature decided to select a senator. Each of the candidates was invited to address the legislature on the affairs of the day. Editor Danley preserved a summary of each speaker's position. George C. Watkins believed Texas ought to be divided up into five states, opposed hasty action by South Carolina, advocated home manufactures, and had no objection to Lincoln appointing Southern men to serve as postmasters at the South. General S. H. Hempstead, a conservative "family" member, said that to date the South had suffered no actual harm, urged a "wait and see" attitude, and stated that the acquisition of Mexico and Cuba would end sectional strife. Hempstead said he would not vote an appropriation to force a seceding state back into the Union. C. B. Mitchel, who had been so bitterly assaulted in April for being unsound on slavery in the territories, said he was an "out and out, flat-footed States Rights Democrat," that the "South should prepare to meet dangers," but that there was no present cause for Arkansas's secession. N. B. Burrow, the Rector candidate, advised Arkansas "to trust to the Lord and keep our powder dry," and added, "A state has the same right to secede from the Union that a citizen has to emigrate — secession and emigration are analogous doctrines." Ben T. DuVal, who said he was not a candidate but spoke nevertheless, told the legislators that "existing circumstances justify secession." Thus some diversity of opinion was present, most of it moderate. But the division of moderate votes resulted in the election of Mitchel on the ninth ballot. Mitchel, however, had stated that Lincoln's election was not a valid cause for secession.[9]

Ascertaining that the legislature was not going to be cooperative, the secessionists changed their rhetoric and loudly called for the "sovereign people" to decide. The withdrawal of South Carolina cheered the secessionists. Guns were fired in her honor in Little Rock, and W. P. Grace and James Yell went over to the secessionist side. Yell late in December at Little Rock publicly called for "out and out secession." When Dr. Lorenzo Gibson answered him by taking the ground Jackson took in 1832, he was booed by the secessionists in the crowd. Clearly secessionism was gaining.[10]

The legislature felt the effects of the heightened campaign as resolutions and petitions from the southeastern counties began to pour in. By this means the secessionists hoped to convince the legislature that the people were for secession. While the content of these resolutions and petitions varied, all were in favor of summoning a state convention. Desperately the conservative members sought some counter-balance. In an address to his Washington County constituents, John Crawford said he opposed calling a convention unless he "was satisfied that it was the wish of the people," and asked for instructions from the voters.[11]

The greatest acquisition for the secession cause was the long-anticipated resolution of differences between Hindman and the "family." Such a reconciliation had been predicted by the Unionists for some time, and, as Rector apparently sought to establish his own machine without Hindman's help, there was no longer any cause for outstanding differences between Hindman and Johnson. Hindman wanted the *Old Line Democrat,* the visible but money-losing sign of his independence, to be merged with the *True Democrat,* and the combined operation to be given the public printing. In return he was willing to concede to the "family" a seat in the Senate and the state auditorship. The Johnsons rejected Hindman's proposal because they were already certain of getting the public printing, and they thought that they had a good chance of picking up the other plums. Mitchel was elected to the Senate, the *True Democrat* got the public printing, and in early January the *Old Line Democrat* ceased publication. But Johnson and Hindman were cooperating.[12]

The first of several of their joint messages reached Little Rock on December 21, the day after Mitchel's election to the Senate and the secession of South Carolina. In these communications, Johnson and Hindman pressed for the summoning of a convention to take Arkansas out of the Union. The first joint message, coinciding as it did with secession speeches by Yell and Albert Pike, and with increased petition activity in the southern counties, added another pressure to the already harassed legislature. Another joint message, dated January 8, 1861, not only called for a convention, but also explicitly urged immediate secession: "If the South remains in the Confederacy, she surrenders to Black Republicanism."[13]

Late December and early January witnessed intensified efforts in the propaganda campaign. Although Henry C. Lay, Missionary Bishop (Episcopal) of the Southwest, issued a pastoral letter urging moderation, the general trend among preachers (especially Baptists) in South Arkansas, was in the other direction. Unorganized, the Unionists were assaulted at every level.[14]

Unionists claimed that Arkansas, as part of the Louisiana Purchase, had been bought with Federal funds, making secession dishonorable and ungrateful. Legislators were reminded they had taken an oath to preserve the constitution, not destroy it. And dire consequences, economic, military and political, were predicted if secession took place. Danley celebrated the New Year by informing his readers that secession seemed inevitable. The Gulf states had "precipitate (d) a revolution in which the border slave states must join or be ruined. We think the dissolution of the Union can be averted only by the miraculous interposition of Providence." He blamed the politicians, "the buzzards that roost around the carcass," for the nation's plight and vented his wrath by hurling maledictions at them. On January 12, 1861, in a semi-capitulation, he cited Arkansas's exposed position with respect to the Indian Territory and the Mississippi River, and urged the state to prepare the proper defense. Such an attitude by the leading Unionist editor was hardly calculated to cheer conservative men.[15]

Meanwhile the exertions of secessionists in the cotton counties were paying off. A glorious future, secure and serene, was held out if Arkansas would leave the Union. Moreover delay in joining the Confederacy not only endangered the state but cast the stigma of cowardice on Arkansians. In Ouachita County Judge Brown noted, "The Demon of secession is daily becoming more powerful." A week later he noted, "A great effort is making to bully the people of this state into revolution." County resolutions from Clark, Arkansas, Desha, Jefferson, Chicot, Pike, Dallas, and Calhoun all favored a convention and secession. The tone of these resolutions varied from mild to strong. The Dallas-Calhoun resolution illustrated the latter:

> If Congress of the United States now in session, does not by the Fourth day of March next, give us a sufficient guarantee for slave protection in the Union, we hereby pledge ourselves to take our chances with such of the slaveholding states as may secede from the Union, and risk the consequences.

More equivocal were the Pike County resolves, generally Unionist in tone, but yet favoring a convention. The South should issue an ultimatum to the North for the protection of Southern rights, the Pike resolutions stated, but if protection was not assured, then all the Southern states should go out *en masse*. In Clark County two sets of resolutions were submitted, one mildly secessionist, the other mildly Unionist.[16]

Under such pressure, the disheartened and disarrayed Unionists finally yielded. The lower house passed a convention bill on December 22, 1860. Danley, who heretofore had argued that any steps taken toward secession constituted a violation of the oath the legislators had taken, now reluctantly acquiesced. The plea of letting the people decide was hard to oppose, and the more conservative senate on January 16, 1861, passed the convention act. By the terms of the law, the people could vote for or against holding a convention, and simultaneously, select delegates to serve in the body in the event it was approved. Such phrasing naturally favored the secessionists, in that a potential Unionist candidate carried the double burden of opposing a convention and advocating his own election to it. Furthermore critics objected that the law did not provide that any action of the convention be voted on by the people.

"This," wrote David Walker, "is a gross outrage."[17]

Nevertheless the secession issue was now before the people. Many yeoman farmers agreed with an old resident who declared, "I do not go much on conventions no way." While some trusted to the innate common sense of the masses, others were not so certain. "As to the People being better than the common demagogues," William Quesenbury wrote D. C. Williams, "I am sure you are mistaken. The People generally are a great set of rascals." A. W. Dinsmore, a Bentonville Unionist candidate, reported that all conditions favored the secessionists. The wording of the proclamation announcing the election, he claimed, would discourage the Union vote by implying that the issue to be decided was whether or not to hold an election. "The secessionists," he added, "are posted and instructed how to proceed. [*They*] are *great Union men also* when they are talking to the people." From Fayetteville, the heart of Union country, David Walker wrote: "The *Southern heart* is now too fired to reason. I expect to run for the convention, but with little hope of doing much good." Bishop Lay went so far as to instruct his clergy in the event of secession to substitute the Governor of Arkansas for the President of the United States in their prayers. The tide was plainly running in the secessionists' favor.[18]

But the Union cause was by no means dead, and the thing that kept it alive was the silent loyalty of the common man. D. C. Williams of Van Buren, "a man of sugar and coffee, cold water, theology, and idiosyncracies," whose highest political office was that of city alderman, issued a broadside which received wide circulation and had "considerable effect" in northwestern Arkansas. While not a fancy political theorizer like Albert Pike, Williams undertook with sincerity and determination to inform the voters as to just what was involved in summoning a convention. A convention, he wrote, "is presumed in law to be the People themselves, and that consequently the decision of a convention is the supreme law of the land." He cautioned the voters not to be "deceived in the views of your candidates." Most important, he added, every candidate should be made to pledge that the convention's action on secession should be referred back to the people for final decision. Issued on January 29, 1861, Williams' broadside initiated a resurgence of Unionism.[19]

The Unionists faced many different problems. Voters in the hills and out of the way places had to be informed that an election was going to take place. Candidates had to be selected, and tickets made available. With the whole power of officeholding Democracy committed to secession, Unionists were hard put to keep partisan prejudices out. The selection of the Crawford County representatives illustrated some of the problems involved in balancing a ticket. Initially the Unionists were supporting Jesse Turner, an old line Whig, and a Mr. Wilcox, a Democrat, "to keep party feeling down." But Wilcox went over to secession, and the Unionists were forced to draft H. F. Thomason, another member of the old "opposition," even though by this they excluded the Democrats. "It has been threatened by some," Thomason wrote, "that old party lines shall be drawn in this election, and I doubt not such an attempt will be made."[20]

In general, the Unionist position was stated by Danley: "Select no *office seekers,* no excitable and inconsiderate men, no one but in whose judgment and disinterested motives and feelings you have the most implicit confidence.'' In Benton County the Unionists went so far as to draw up a platform first, and then invite candidates to run on it.[21]

To show to the state that not everyone agreed with the cotton counties, strong Unionist resolutions began to pour in from the northwest. Expressions of loyalty came from Sebastian, Marion, Carroll, Newton, and Searcy Counties. The last named blamed current problems on the ''continuous agitation of the slavery question by partisan demagogues, both North and South, as a means of self-aggrandizement,'' and promised that Searcy County would ''support the President in the discharge of all constitutional duties.'' Van Buren County was blunter: ''We follow no secessionist, Yancey, Seward, Greeley, Tom Hindman, nor any set of disunionists who have nothing in view but their own selfish and hellish designs.'' One of the strongest statements came from Sebastian County, Ben T. Du Val's home ground. It declared that Lincoln's election was no cause for secession; that no right of secession existed; and that the idea of a Southern Confederacy was a ''chimera, wholly impractical, if desirable, and wholly undesirable, if practicable, existing only in the imagination of disappointed aspirants to political office.'' It concluded, ''The people are for the Union as it is!'' Sevier County, closer to the cotton counties, urged moderation and implored the South to ''make at least one more effort.'' These expressions of Unionism were not without their effect, though most Arkansans must have agreed with the Des Arc *Constitutional Union,* that they simply came ''too late.''[22]

Just as the campaign was getting under way, a potentially explosive situation developed in Little Rock over the status of the United States Arsenal. In November, 1860, Captain James Totten and sixty-five men of the Second United States Artillery had been sent to Little Rock to garrison the previously unoccupied arsenal. Their arrival had aroused no excitement or comment until late in January. When at that time a telegraph line finally reached Little Rock, a rumor was sent out to Memphis that additional reinforcements were to arrive from Fort Gibson, Indian Territory. A public meeting was held in Helena where it was resolved that Governor Rector should seize the arsenal and five hundred troops were volunteered for that purpose. When this offer reached Little Rock, Adjutant General Edmund Burgevin apparently informed the Helena citizens that he could not accept volunteer troops, but ''should the people assemble in their defense, the governor will interpose his official position in their behalf.'' Burgevin's message gave the Helena troops and others all over South Arkansas the impression that the governor wanted them to seize the arsenal.[23]

Meanwhile, on January 28, Governor Rector informed Captain Totten that reinforcements, or the destruction or removal of the supplies, would not be permitted. Totten's reply of the next day stated that he knew of no plans for reinforcements, but that he took his orders from the Federal government and not from the state governor. Totten also wrote to Washington asking for instructions ''by a reliable agent, and not by mails, as they are not entirely trustworthy at present.'' Meanwhile the first volunteers began to arrive.[24]

Rector, who said he expected the Secretary of War to inform him of the future status of the arsenal, continued to show impatience. Then, in early February, the rumor reached Rector that Federal troops were on their way up the river to Little Rock aboard the *S. H. Tucker*. Rector gathered his volunteers and planted guns on the wharf, but no troops arrived. The guns were taken down and the volunteers temporarily disbanded. On February 4, large bodies of men began to arrive by foot and boat from Phillips, Jefferson, Prairie, White, Monroe, Hot Spring, Saline, Montgomery, and St. Francis Counties, all firmly believing that the governor had requested them to take the arsenal. "The excitement," Rector testified later, "became intense."[25]

The governor was now caught in a cross fire. When the city council called on him for an explanation, he publicly stated that he had not called the volunteers. On February 5, the city council, Unionist merchants almost to a man, drew up a resolution opposing unauthorized seizure of the arsenal and demanded that the governor "interpose his authority to check any such movements if unauthorized by him." Rector either had to send the volunteers home (and risk their discontent) or take the arsenal and bear the onus of making an unprovoked assault on the Federal government prior to the state's secession. Complicating his position was the advice received from Washington. Senators Johnson and Sebastian telegraphed: "The motives which impelled capture of forts in other states do not exist in ours. It is all premature. We implore you prevent attack on arsenal if Totten resists." Johnson was even more emphatic to his brothers: "If Totten resists, for God's sake deliberate and go stop the assault." Similar advice was sent to John Pope in a joint telegram of Pike and Johnson.[26]

Faced with considerable pressure from the more moderate secessionists, Rector sought a way out. A mass meeting, presided over by R. H. Johnson, asked Rector to assume command and to order the surrender of the arsenal to the state authorities. Thus on February 6, Rector wrote Totten that though he had not authorized the volunteers, it "has assumed such an aspect that it becomes my duty, as executive of this state, to interpose my official authority to prevent a collision." Thus Rector asked for Totten's surrender. The city council addressed a resolution to the governor and the commander, pointing out the damage that would result to the city if any attack took place, and urged a settlement "if it can possibly be done consistently with a proper sense of duty and honor."[27]

Captain Totten, not having received any instructions from Washington, and with only sixty-five against possibly five thousand, yielded to the seemingly inevitable. He agreed to turn the supplies over to Rector as custodian, marched out with his troops, boarded a boat amid great ceremony, and proceeded to St. Louis. The ladies of Little Rock showed their appreciation by presenting Totten a sword. Totten's report praised the "honorable, high-toned, loyal, and law-abiding" citizens and blamed the governor for creating the crisis. As for the worried Senator Johnson, Burgevin telegraphed him, "Spoke too late, like Irishman who swallowed egg. Arsenal in hands of Governor."[28]

Had Totten chosen to resist, the results might have been civil war. As it was, the Unionists believed Governor Rector had engineered the crisis in order to obtain a majority for secession in the upcoming elections. Before the arsenal affair, it was generally known that Rector was an avid secessionist; after the confrontation, it was believed that he would stop at nothing to obtain his ends. As for the secessionists, Senator Johnson expressed their sentiments in a telegram to his brother: "Arsenal yours. Thank God! Hold it."[29]

The scarcity of available evidence makes it impossible to ascertain the degree of Rector's complicity. Rector at the time and John Harrell later ascribed events to a series of accidents. Yet the wording of Burgevin's telegram, as Harrell remembered it, hardly seems innocent in the light of later events. The volunteers, who assembled not merely from Helena but all of South Arkansas, believed to a man they were summoned by the Governor's orders. As previously noted Totten blamed Rector, and most Unionists shared his view. Albert Rust, on the other hand, thought Hindman might have instigated the crisis. No one, however, implicated the "family," and this canny group emerged from the event with enhanced luster.[30]

Public reaction to the capture of the arsenal was hardly the enthusiastic ovation that its planners had anticipated. The Van Buren *Press* denounced the seizure as "untimely and uncalled for," and an act designed "to excite the people into the belief that the Federal government was their enemy." The editor warned secessionists that Sebastian and Crawford Counties would defend, not seize, their arsenal at Fort Smith. Albert Rust wrote from Washington that the seizure was "greatly to be deplored." The now mildly secessionist editor of the *Constitutional Union* stated:

> [The capture] savors of the actions of lunatics. We deem the whole affair to be one gotten up for political effect in order to bring the state into a rash and exalted secession attitude, because there exists some fears that the moving of Arkansas out of the Union might not be done precipitately enough.

William F. Holtzman, Danley's partner in the *Gazette* and a witness to the events, reached the same conclusion: "The excitement which has been gotten up in our city was to affect the election—nothing else—but we think it has had a contrary effect."[31]

Broadly conceived, the capture of the arsenal was but a part of the highly charged atmosphere in which the secessionists were operating. The seizure of Northern steamboats, the crating and shipping of an abolitionist to Lincoln at Grand Glaize, and other acts of mob violence enforced conformity in the planting counties. But, if the secessionists thought the taking of the arsenal would produce a ground swell of favorable sentiment in the yeoman counties they were mistaken. Instead, the Union cause, weak and lethargic two weeks earlier, now sprang conspicuously to life. Besides the local effect of the Williams broadside and the arsenal seizure, the Unionists were encouraged by the assembling of the Peace Convention in Washington. The latter offered visible evidence that adjustment was possible and "dispelled in a great measure the gloomy anticipation by which the country was beset." When the meeting ended in failure, the politicians were accused of sabotaging it, but hope was expressed that the common sense of the masses could still save the Union.[32]

The Unionists began to formulate a response to the secessionist position. Seeking to avoid the label "submissionists" which Senator Johnson and others sought to place on them, they frequently chose to call themselves "cooperationists." By this they meant that Arkansas ought not to secede on her own, or in conjunction with the Gulf states, but only together with the border states, especially Tennessee, the native state of many Arkansans. The distinction between submissionists and cooperationists was expressed by the Van Buren *Press:* "We want conservative men, not submissionists."[33]

The positions of the Union men were expressed in their platforms. J. H. Stirman, brother of the secretary of state, and a Unionist candidate from Washington County, espoused cooperation with the border states, advocated the resubmission of any act of secession to the people, and opposed coercion. Jesse Turner of Crawford took a stronger line, denying any right of secession. Typical of the cooperationist line outside the mountain counties was that set forth in the address of Joseph Stillwell, candidate from Pulaski County. Stillwell opposed immediate secession, proposed that Arkansas act in accord with the border states, and favored the Crittenden Compromise or some similar solution. His views were endorsed by fellow Pulaski County candidate A. H. Garland, and with reservations by M. S. Kennard, editor and candidate from Batesville.[34]

Given the time of year, the backwardness of much of the country, and the shortness of time preceding the election, the Unionists worked wonders. Although one secessionist croaked that the Unionist orators "to me sounds like some good old hard-shell Baptist divine singing psalms to a dead horse," the yeoman masses thought otherwise. In Pope County secession was voted down four to one in a straw ballot, and thirty-three guns fired to honor the occasion. Decidedly favorable to the Union cause was the result of the Tennessee election of February 11, in which the summoning of a convention was rejected by almost 12,000 votes and secession itself by 67,000 votes.[35]

Together with positive declarations in favor of the Union, economic, political, social, and military reasons were advanced against secession. In the northwest voters were informed that if Arkansas seceded and joined the Confederacy, they would be disfranchised by a slaveholder voting qualification. "Do you know that in that Confederacy your rights will be respected?" asked one circular, "that you will be *allowed a vote* unless you are the *owner of a negro?*"[36]

In addition the leading secessionists were accused of having unpatriotic motives. Gantt, Hindman, and Rector already stood accused of lying to the voters to gain election, but now the attack was extended to local figures. Ouachita County candidate and editor A. W. Hobson asked of his opponent:

> Did they dare say even, that the election of Mr. Lincoln would be sufficient cause for dissolution, when they were asked the question! If they have thus so easily changed their *principles* in so very short a time, how can we trust such fickle men with our interests and our whole fortunes in this trying hour?

Finally the Unionists were urged to beware of secessionist tricks. One broadside urged voters to "stand firmly by their principles, and in no event to be influenced by rumors and telegraphic dispatches manufactured for the occasion to influence your vote.''[37]

Secessionists were by no means inactive. Senator Johnson's address to the voters, coming out the day after the arsenal surrendered, urged immediate secession. The proposed compromises, he asserted, "will not protect us five years." Furthermore united action by the entire South would be accomplished without bloodshed. In Pulaski County B. F. Danley, brother of C. C. Danley, and John F. Pope, announced their candidacy in a circular. Justifying secession on the ground that the alternative was to support abolitionists, they also stated that evidence of Lincoln's hostility to the South could be found in the repeal of the tariff on sugar. Congressman-elect Gantt was simply ludicrous:

> Rapidly expanding monarchical elements exist at the North as to render fraternal Union impossible. In the Union there is neither safety, peace, nor equality, nor could there be under any possible state of future circumstances.[38]

On February 18, 1861, the voters of Arkansas who cared enough to brave near-freezing weather went to the polls and voted down secession. According to the computations of the *Gazette,* the count was 23,626 for the Union and 17,927 for secession, based on the candidate vote. The summoning of a convention was approved 27,412 to 15,826. The secessionists were dismayed. "Contrary to all my expectations," wrote Ben T. Du Val to Governor Rector. Union men, he reported, were arming, and the governor needed to be especially cautious in distributing the arms in the arsenal.[39]

The Unionists triumphed not from lack of strong opposition but because they *"worked and worked hard."* Nevertheless on election day there was "great indifference." Over twenty thousand voters stayed home. The secessionist *Constitutional Union* believed that two-thirds of these voters were Unionists, and other estimates ranged as high as four-fifths. In some yeoman counties (e.g., Johnson, Clark, and Perry) no Unionists ran. In others the voters could not be certain of where their candidates really stood. According to the *Gazette* "a variety of sentiment" existed before the election: "Some are for immediate and 'precipitate' secession, some are for 'cooperative' action by the border states, while others cling to the last hope of the Union." In Prairie County the *Constitutional Union* endorsed Judge B. C. Totten, believing him a Unionist, over R. S. Gantt, a radical, and continued to support Totten even after Totten became a "mild" secessionist. J. H. Quisenberry, the other candidate, was handicapped both by his unequivocal Unionist stand in secessionist-inclined cotton-producing Prairie County, and because he had lost his last five election bids.[40]

Some people did not even know an election was being held. Alfred E. Mathews, who fled from Texas through Arkansas during May and June, was told outside Arkadelphia (in Clark County, where no Unionist ran) that the election "was conducted secretly or else Arkansas would have been for the Union stronger than ever." Near Batesville, where heavy Unionist majorities were received, the story was repeated. Obviously many did not know that momentous issues were at stake.[41]

Some potential Union voters were afraid to go the polls. Judge Brown recorded that "threats and intimidations have been practiced to alarm the timid and ignorant, by innuendoes that they might be driven from the country when the state goes out. Many did not vote." At Pine Bluff Bishop Lay observed that the disunionists wanted "to hang every man who says a word against Immediate Secession."[42]

Yet, wherever the hard-fisted yeomanry were in the majority, and a real choice of candidates was presented, the Union cause was generally triumphant. In Ouachita County, although Judge Brown despaired of the result and the Union candidate was late in announcing, the people repudiated secession. With a Unionist mandate from the masses, it now remained to be seen what the convention would actually do.[43]

5)
Arkansas Leaves the Union

"The secessionists look very blue."
—W. F. Holtzman to D.C.
Williams, February 10, 1861. D. C.
Williams Papers, Arkansas History
Commission.

On March 4, 1861, America anxiously waited to see what the new president would promise in his inaugural address, for his policy would determine the course of action of the border slave states. Nowhere was the recognition of this reality as patent as in Arkansas, as the delegates assembled for the opening session that same day.

Delegates gathered under two banners, Unionist and Secessionist. The conservative group was the more experienced. David Walker and Jesse Turner represented the older generation, Walker being the only delegate who had also served in the 1836 convention. He had also served on the state supreme court, besides being a Whig candidate during the life of that party. Turner, another influential Whig, was now greatly interested in the construction of a Little Rock to Fort Smith railroad. Indeed all five merchants in the convention were Union men. Many of the Union men had legislative experience. John Campbell, Isaiah Dodson, Frank W. Desha, Samuel Kelley, R. K. Garland, and J. Stillwell had served in the lower house, while Isaac Murphy, W. W. Watkins, and A. H. Carrigan had been members of the state senate. Carrigan and Watkins, in fact, were members of the present body. Two Unionists, A. W. Hobson and M. S. Kennard, were editors. Those prominent in recent state affairs included Jesse Cypert, Hugh Thomason, W. W. Mansfield, and William Fishback. Furthermore the Unionists were a younger group than the secessionists.[1]

The secession side was the less impressive. Their best talent was legal. Charles W. Adams ("Pike the second"), Josiah Gould, Felix Batson ("a regular Red River raft"), Thomas B. Hanly, and W. W. Floyd had served as circuit judges. Hanly and Batson had served on the state supreme court. The two Tottens, B. C. and James, had served as circuit judges in Tennessee and Mississippi, respectively. Josiah Gould was the author of Gould's *Digest*. Those with service in the state senate included Hanly, Gould, Floyd, B. C. Totten, and B. F. Hawkins, while H. Flanagin and Jilson P. Johnson had served in the lower house, as had all the members of the senate except Hawkins. Four members, Hanly, Johnson, Adams, and B. C. Totten, had important "family" connections. Hanly was rated by one Unionist "the ablest and most prominent man on that side," while Jils was a cousin and Adams was Senator Sebastian's law partner. Two delegates, G. W. Laughinghouse and W. W. Floyd, had the reputation of being "fire-eaters." James Yell, "a very strong man without much cultivation" had been the Know-Nothing candidate for governor in 1856 and a Bell elector in 1860. His Jefferson County colleague, W. P. Grace who was "rather vehement in style", had been a Douglas elector. Among the ex-Whigs who had gone over to Democracy in the 1850s, Adams, Batson, and Harris Flanagin were prominent.[2]

Nevertheless by comparison with the conventions of the other Southern states, the Arkansas delegates were lacking in experience. No past governors, U.S. senators, or congressmen sat in the body. Most were men whose antecedents were difficult to trace, and whose involvement in politics was directed toward only one issue: secession.[3]

An analysis of the 77 members of the convention reveals that only four were native Arkansians. Twenty-five were born in Tennessee, and fourteen in Kentucky. Twelve were natives of North Carolina, four of Georgia, Alabama, and South Carolina; two were from Pennsylvania and Massachusetts, while one each came from New York, New Jersey, Ohio, Illinois, Virginia, Maryland, and the District of Columbia. Thus in nativity of delegates, the convention did not have a deep-South orientation.[4]

The typical delegate did have an economic interest in Negro slavery. Ralph Wooster in his study, found that 61.1 percent of the delegates held slaves, though the average holding was 11.5 slaves per member and the median was one. Since Wooster failed to identify two of the largest slaveholders in the convention, these figures are probably far too low. Typically, secessionists held more slaves than non-secessionists, and they had greater wealth.[5]

"Our city is a B hive," reported one resident as the delegates assembled. According to delegate A. H. Carrigan, "Little Rock was filled with politicians of excitable natures who were anxious for secession at any cost; adventurers and would-be soldiers." The convention, an out-of-town reporter discovered, had "a considerable amount of excitable material in it." Many expected trouble to develop. The *Gazette* warned that "every outside pressure will be brought to bear upon and if possible to influence its actions." Yet surprisingly, there were "no disturbances of any kind."[6]

As the delegates arrived in town, they were claimed by one side or the other. Invariably some side shifting took place. Unionist H. F. Thomason complained that some three or four delegates who "were understood at home to be very conservative are acting so far with the secessionists." L. D. Hill of Perry County, for example, described his politics as "conditional secessionist." Apparently the conditions were satisfied, for Hill, a representative elected unopposed from a yeoman county, voted with the secessionists. Similarly, Milton D. Baber of Lawrence County, a borderline county, claimed to be "anti-immediate secessionist" and voted with the secessionists. On the other side of the fence, Thomas H. Bradley, a Crittenden County planter with ninety-five slaves, was nominated for the convention in January on a platform calling for secession in the event southern demands were not fulfilled. Nevertheless Bradley was a leading Unionist in the convention.[7]

The convention began its labors on March 5 with the selection of a chairman. With conservative Jesse Turner temporarily presiding, this became, in delegate Thomason's words, a "test vote" on the relative strength of the two sides. Thomas H. Bradley, the East Arkansas Unionist, nominated David Walker. The other anomaly, L. D. Hill, nominated Prairie County's Judge B. C. Totten. Walker was elected, forty to thirty-five. Elias C. Boudinot, a Unionist despite his "family" orientation, was chosen permanent secretary on nomination by H. F. Thomason. The forty to thirty-five margin, which stayed nearly constant, reflected the permanent division between secessionists and Unionists, and, with some minor exceptions, represented the geographic divisions between the yeomanry and the planters. It paralleled divisions present in the constitutional convention of 1836.[8]

The first matter of concern for the Unionist delegates was what the new president promised in his inaugural address delivered on March 4. There was a great rush to obtain a copy of the address, and Union members, fearful of secessionist tampering, paid seventy-eight dollars to have the message telegraphed from Washington.[9]

No one in Arkansas was jubilant over the speech. The conservative Van Buren *Press* reassured its readers that "nothing in it should cause alarm." Editor Danley was less sanguine. Finding the message "very objectionable," he abused the Democrats for creating the situation that put a Republican in the White House.[22] On the other hand the convention Unionists received a telegram from Memphis from David C. Cross, W. H. Carroll, and J. H. McMahon affirming that the inaugural was satisfactory. Senators Crittenden and Douglas also telegraphed the Unionists: "There is a hope of a satisfactory settlement if you stand firm."[10]

Among the "fire-eating" papers, abuse was the order of the day. The *Arkansian* called it an "insulting message," and characterized those who defended it as "political bigots" and "hardened political fossils" who endorsed "His Satanic Majesty." Although the secession papers were less than fair to Lincoln, their misrepresentations undoubtedly hurt the Union cause.[11]

The issuance of Lincoln's inaugural gave the secessionists at home the occasion to set off a new round of petitions calling for secession. Conservatives replied that these petitions were frequently based on "false representations of the meaning of Lincoln's message." At Ozark, N. B. Burrow organized a meeting and presented a resolution calling for the reconvening of the legislature and the submission of secession to the voters. When the resolutions failed of adoption, Burrow turned them into a petition which a minority of the assemblage signed. Burrow's performance reminded one observer "very much of some camp meeting scene."[12]

As the delegates pondered the meaning of the inaugural, the secessionists launched their attack. Initially the secessionists were optimistic; the *True Democrat* predicted that Arkansas would be out of the Union in twenty days. As the Memphis *Avalanche* correspondent explained: "There are many among the Union men who it is well known can and will be brought to vote for an ordinance of secession whenever it can be demonstrated that there is no longer a hope of getting a recognition and enforcement of our rights." The question was how best to convince these conditional Unionists. Lack of harmony hurt the secessionists. Caucus chairman James Yell later stated, "The only way that I had to keep our own men together was that I would decide the subject of the Arsnal [*sic*] out of order.'' Some secessionists, e.g., Patterson of Jackson County, seemed to want a full debate and no haste, believing this would unite the state. Others, including some Unionists, wanted to vote immediately and adjourn. The initiative rested with the secessionists, for the Union men ''were on the defensive and simply attempted to keep wrong from being done.'' Apparently the secession causes decided to try to pressure the convention into passing an ordinance of secession immediately and unconditionally. One leader in this scheme, W. W. Floyd, ''was very belligerent in the beginning.'' Therefore on the first day W. P. Grace presented a resolution calling for the creation of a committee to draft an ordinance of secession. Hot debate followed, and Grace was induced to withdraw his resolution.[13]

On Wednesday, March 6, A. C. Spain and D. P. Hill, representing South Carolina, were seated within the bar of the convention. Spain, in addressing the delegates, claimed that since South Carolina was responsible for the admission of Arkansas into the Union, Arkansas should now follow her out.[14]

Thursday, March 7, witnessed the oratorical flight of James L. Totten. ''Totten of Arkansas,'' Jesse Turner wrote his wife, ''is on the floor making a long speech on Southern wrongs and Northern aggression—out of order but he's got to make the speech and might as well make it now as at any other time.'' In condemning Lincoln's inaugural and calling for the ''instant dissolution of those ties that bind her,'' Totten:

> Went back to the time of Cromwell and traced the genealogy of the Roundheads and Puritans down to the present time. The speaker showed an intimate acquaintance with the people of the North—their past history, customs, institutions, and conditions. His statements concerning childhood training, the education and religious notions of Northern people were as edifying as they were original.

The Unionists were not lacking in eloquence either. Jesse Turner told the assemblage:

> Dissolve the Union and the earth will send up a moan from the graves of our Revolutionary fathers for the toil, the blood, and the treasure vainly expended in establishing our government; and from the far off lands across the waters we may listen for a wail, when there it is known that this is no longer the home and the refuge for the poor and the oppressed; and if we could remove the veil, and look into the presence of the Most High, we would see angels bedew with their tears the graves which contain the last hopes of those who held that man was capable of self-government.

At first this clash of oratory was exciting. A. H. Carrigan recalled the scene:

> The pressure was intense. The Union men were taunted as submissionists, and all kinds of raillery came from the lobbies. The galleries and lobbies were always crowded and it was constantly feared that violence might occur, and at times it looked as if it were inevitable.

At times the secessionists had their problems. General Yell's speech on the sixth day—a speech delivered "with a bland winning eloquence, loftier and nobler far than anything we have yet heard in Little Rock"—was interrupted by "an eternal chitter chatter kept up in the galleries," so that part of "the venerable old man's mild, classic and elevated discourse" was lost.[15]

But as the debate dragged on and the Union men remained unswayed, it became tedious. The *True Democrat* complained: "We are tired of heavy gentlemen giving us their biographies, where the fathers of gentlemen are buried, these and kindred subjects; apostrophies to the stars and stripes, to the American eagle and g-e-lorius Union, might be very properly dispensed with just now." At length delegate M. S. Kennard sought to curb rhetorical effusions by moving:

> that every delegate in this convention be authorized and requested to write out in full his views upon every conceivable question connected with the present condition of affairs, and have them spread upon the record of the convention, or published in the newspapers, *ad libitum,* at his own expense.

Jesse Cypert wrote later that Kennard's resolution "was indefinitely postponed," but that "it had the desired effect."[16]

Meanwhile the Unionist majority held firm. Two leading secessionists wanted Vice-President A. H. Stephens to appear, but that worthy declined. Probably he could not have accomplished much, but the desire for his appearance evidenced the strong Whig orientation of the Union members of the convention. By Friday, March 8, many of the fire-eaters had lost all patience. As the Union members voted down every effort to draw up a secession ordinance, Jilson P. Johnson complained, "We have yet to get the first intimation of what the gentlemen of the other side want or are willing to do." The Unionists, however, had made it perfectly clear they would vote down secession, as A. H. Garland announced, "with a light heart and clear conscience." Moreover some of them made it clear they believed that allegiance to the national government took precedence over state loyalty. The Achilles heel in the Unionist position, however, was their opposition to coercion. It was a Unionist, the devious Fishback, who introduced the resolution "that any attempt, on the part of the federal government, to coerce a seceding state, by an armed force, will be resisted by Arkansas to the last extremity."[17]

An address by Governor Rector on Friday reiterating points made in earlier speeches left the convention unconvinced. Instead the governor's intervention merely served to intensify the hostility of the Union members toward the governor. One of the problems in the organization of the convention was that the election in Fulton County had resulted in a tie vote. The convention ordered the governor to instruct the sheriff of the county to call a new election. Rector refused, and in an indiscreet message, lectured the convention on the limitations of its powers. A committee headed by M. S. Kennard made a sarcastic retort and the convention reordered the election. The Unionists also pursued Rector over the arsenal seizure, demanding first an explanation for its seizure and later a statement furnishing the costs of holding it. The Unionist feeling against Rector was intense: "Thousands of them," wrote General Yell, "would have killed him freely if only they could."[18]

Monday, March 11, found the Unionists in a good mood. Senator Mitchel telegraphed the convention the news that President Lincoln planned to evacuate the Charleston forts. And it was decided to have each session opened with a prayer from some local minister. The secessionists, on the other hand, were utterly exasperated. The *True Democrat,* which had already provoked the ire of several Unionists, likened the recalcitrant majority to the despised *per diemists* who sat in Little Rock, spending the taxpayers' money with nothing to show for it. "Let us have action," thundered editor Johnson. "In a few weeks the Union party will not contain a corporal's guard. Cooperation at this late date is an unmitigated humbug that means nothing."[19]

Thus prodded by the press and by secessionist orators, and sure of their strength, the Unionists took the initiative. On Monday H. F. Thomason presented a set of proposed constitutional amendments designed to end sectional strife. Actually these proposals offered nothing new: the line of 36^030^1 would divide the remaining territories; Congress could legislate only to protect slavery; an indemnity would be paid for unrecoverable fugitive slaves; states would enforce the fugitive slave laws; transit of slaves through free states would be allowed; Negroes would be disfranchised at the North; and all states would have to agree before changing any of these amendments. Apparently the Unionist majority agreed with Washington *Telegraph* editor Jno. R. Eakin that Arkansas could play peacemaker for the nation. "Commencing with a huge preamble and getting smaller by degrees and beautifully less to the close," the *True Democrat* responded.[20]

Monday's debate turned to the question of whether to recognize the Confederacy. Although the *True Democrat* called the move "eminently conservative and proper," the Unionists disagreed. William Fishback and H. F. Thomason said that the proposed action would violate the constitution and hinder later reconciliation. Jesse Turner went further by denying that any state had the right to secede. Stillwell supported Turner: "He wound up in an eloquent appeal to 'wrap him up in the stars and stripes and bury him with the American eagle.' " W. W. Floyd replied that "he despised the American flag: it was the flag of a Black Republican tyrant."[21]

Debate continued on Tuesday. Jilson P. Johnson pictured for the delegates an immense slave empire extending over the Antilles, Mexico, Central America, and South America. At the conclusion of his speech, a lady in the gallery threw him a bouquet. Charles W. Adams, noted for his "long orations," also spoke. At one point in his speech the reporter for the *True Democrat* noted, "Here feelings which had been gathering and swelling in the breasts of his hearers, and which they had endeavored to suppress at least until he finished, became wholly incapable of longer control, and broke forth in a strong deep burst of heartfelt applause, during which it was a relief to ourselves to stop writing, that the tumult in our own breast might also subside."[22]

The secessionist failure to weaken the Unionist majority caused P. H. Echols on Wednesday to move "that the remarkable strong Union sentiment which prevails in this convention leaves us no hope of the secession of the state. The convention is a nuisance and should be adjourned *sine die* immediately." Talk of dividing the state had been in the air since February, but with Echols' resolution it came closer to reality. According to rumor, the secessionists would call a new convention or recall the legislature, adopt an ordinance of secession, and submit it to the people. Nevertheless the majority of the secessionists were unwilling to go so far until thoroughly convinced they could not shake the few votes they needed; the debate continued. On Tuesday ex-Senator R. W. Johnson and Senator William K. Sebastian arrived from Washington. Johnson, a known Southern nationalist since 1850, spoke for two hours on Wednesday evening. He argued that

> there is no hope for a reconciliation, or compromise—the North will make no concessions—secession is our only resort, and in it, our only safety. The Bible, he said, commands us when we are hit on one side to turn the other and be hit on that—we, the South, had been kicked all over. His address produced a profound impression, and was received throughout with great applause and enthusiasm.[23]

On Thursday the debate continued. The first principal secession speaker, Josiah Gould, was answered by Jesse Cypert, who, a hostile reporter asserted, "exercised his lungs and arms violently for over an hour." Cypert claimed that slavery was not the root of the present trouble, but that it was being used for that purpose by the Yanceyites. His denial that there were any Southern emancipationists prompted J. H. Patterson to ask Cypert what he thought of Cassius M. Clay. Cypert, the reporter assured his readers, "wilted." Following Cypert, William Mayo of Monroe County spoke for two hours on Thursday and continued throughout Friday morning. Among his reasons for justifying secession was the splitting apart of the churches, attributable to "the overbearing and fanatical spirit of their northern brethren."[24]

In the Friday afternoon session, the *True Democrat* figured prominently. First H. F. Thomason complained of the charge that the Unionists were procrastinating. He said that they were ready to vote now and hoped everyone was satisfied. J. H. Patterson "retorted in a bold, defiant, and excited manner," disclaiming for the secessionists any responsibility for the editorials, and suggesting Thomason take it up with the reporters. Thomason, now also heated, alluded to the personal insults which the press had heaped on certain of the Union leaders (e.g., that morning's paper spoke of Turner as "a Southern Lincolnite" and disparaged the "mad ravings of this *eccentric* old man."), and claimed the Unionists "would not submit to them [*any*] longer." Patterson in turn again denied any responsibility on the secession side for the editorials, pointed out that there was no remedy short of breaking up the convention (which might have been editor Johnson's purpose), claimed that the convention had higher purposes "than to wrangle with newspaper reporters," and that he was perfectly willing to relinquish his share of the *per diem* money if the others agreed. On this note "the matter dropped, the utmost urbanity prevailing between the parties."[25]

Jesse Turner now took the floor and offered a thorough-going statement of his Unionism. He described the glories of the Union and the madness and folly of secession. Then he attacked the theory of secession, quoting Jackson, Cass, King, Toucey, etc., and claimed that rebellion had taken place. "When you speak of the *right* of secession, he knew of no such right. Call it revolution and he understood it.'' Turner denied that he favored coercion, or that the Unionists were abolitionists. He defended slavery, but pointed out that Arkansas had lost only a few runaway slaves, while the Gulf states had lost hardly any. ''Dissolve the Union and twenty slaves would run away where one does now.'' Turner endorsed the Crittenden proposals, suggested that the Northern people would repudiate their leaders and repeal their obnoxious laws, and disunion would be a patricidal deed staining the memory of the Founding Fathers and the American Revolution.

Replying for the secessionists, G. P. Smoote asserted that whatever happened, South Carolina deserved the credit. ''And when we are all united in a great Southern Confederacy, as he trusted in God we soon should be, he wanted a monument or triumphant column, whose summit should pierce the very heavens, erected in a central spot, and engraved upon every stone, 'Honor to South Carolina, the advance guard of southern independence.' '' At this point, ''loud stamping and clapping in the galleries'' occurred. The last speaker of the day was Arkansas native Samuel Kelley. ''He is slightly bald,'' the *Appeal* reporter noted, ''wears specs, has a square phiz, and looks and speaks like a Baptist preacher.'' Parson Kelley, for such indeed was he, spoke ''in regular camp meeting fashion,'' claiming that not one hundred men in all Arkansas had ever heard anything about these personal liberty laws upon which the secessionists had been dwelling. He even uncharitably attacked the ladies in the gallery who kept throwing ''boketts'' at the secession orators.[26]

On Saturday Williamson S. Oldham, representing the Confederacy, presented his credentials. Oldham, now from Texas, had once been an important anti-''family'' politician in Arkansas, but his defeats caused him to ''*grease* and back out.'' At the afternoon session only fifty-seven delegates, less than a quorum showed up, and a brief delay insued. On Monday Oldham addressed the convention. His speech, apparently reproduced *in toto* by the press, began by recounting the Southern grievances, which, curiously, he limited to the slavery issue:

> It has been the cause of all the prejudice and hostility of the North against us. It is impossible to settle it in the old Union—it cannot be compromised. It is as impossible as it would be to stop the tide of the Mississippi with a dam made of sand. Where is the man in the North that has yielded to compromise on this question, that has not been overwhelmed by the popular condemnation?
>
> Five millions of southern freemen have raised their standard of independence and have pledged themselves to maintain their institution of African slavery, and they will do it, or they will immolate themselves beneath its folds.
> [*Applause*]

Unless slavery was allowed to expand, he argued, it was doomed. The slaves would be freed, and northerners would rule the South. The national government, he claimed, was ''a mere machine for phlebotomizing and depleting the Southern States.'' Southern cities were depressed, northerners collected twelve dollars and fifty cents on every Southern bale of cotton, and while the North, in turn, was pampered and enriched by friendly legislation.[27]

Yet all this would be changed by independence. The free labor of the North was really dependent on the slave labor of the South. When this lesson was properly taught, northerners would repudiate their present leaders. "When we shall be separated from these very fastidious, virtuous and conscientious people, they will no longer feel responsible for the supposed sin of slavery." Accordingly "the great vital interests of the country will then claim the attention, long withheld, which they demand."

Oldham then turned his attention toward Arkansas. He was blunt. If Arkansas remained in the Union, then the Confederacy would have to discriminate against her as against Massachusetts. Oldham then concluded by offering the new constitution to anyone who cared to examine it. On this note his speech ended, a rather peculiar performance, especially from a former resident of Northwest Arkansas.[28]

The afternoon session witnessed the great climax. At half past three the ordinance of secession finally came up for a vote. The roll was called. Alexander Adams of Izard voted no. Charles W. Adams of Phillips "arose at his seat and in a firm, clear voice said:"

> Mr. President, I have the honor of representing on this floor a county that has always been true to the South. They imposed no instructions upon me, except to aid in taking the State of Arkansas out of the Union as soon as possible, and I feel it an honor to record my vote aye. [*Tremendous cheering followed this announcement.*]

Milton Baber told the convention that "he was from a Union county, but under no instructions. The gentlemen with whom he acted already understood his position. He felt it his solemn duty to his country to record his vote aye. Another enthusiastic uproar of applause followed this gratifying and unexpected announcement." Directly Thomas H. Bradley cast his vote, saying, "in his peculiarly dignified manner": "I represent the only Union county on the Mississippi River; the county opposite Memphis, and I am *proud* to cast my vote *NO!*" A few Union cheers were heard and a lady threw him a bouquet. Several secession votes followed with a flourish, including that of Samuel Robinson, the other Lawrence County delegate, who said: "I represent one of the northern counties; my heart has always beat responsive to the sentiments of the South. I glory in voting aye. (Loud cheers followed the vote of this venerable delegate.)" Other secession votes were reported as received with "loud and deafening applause," "tremendous cheering and hurrahing," and "enthusiastic applause." Secession papers failed to record that as Jesse Turner announced his negative, a woman in the gallery threw him a bouquet. All the shouting failed to conceal that the convention had rejected secession by a vote of thirty-nine to thirty-five. The rest of the day was spent in wrangling. Yell submitted another ordinance, which, together with Thomason's resolutions, would be submitted to the people. This and other efforts to pry the Unionists loose were beaten down as several delegates spoke. No record of their speeches was preserved, for as the *Appeal* reporter observed, "my back will become tired sometimes."[29]

The defeat of the secession ordinance was celebrated in the northwest. In Van Buren thirty-nine guns were fired to honor the thirty-nine men who rejected disunion. Many secessionists however now advocated extra-legal tactics to achieve their ends. One traveler returning from Napoleon reported: "The disunionists have, I believe, given Arkansas up as a hard case and are going home to secede from northern Arkansas." In Drew County a public meeting recommended that the local delegate work for "a speedy and peaceable division of the state." While the *True Democrat* reported and magnified such rumors as one more reason why secession should be referred to the people, the *Gazette* objected to such talk and took the secessionists to task: "No one of the least political information will pretend to say that counties occupy the same relation to a state which states do to the federal government." Instead Danley analyzed this as just another insidious form of pressure: "Appeals are now made to men to vote for secession in order to avert the calamity of civil war—that certain men, in certain portions of the state, will not submit to anything but the secession of the state from the Union."

Meanwhile the convention continued its sitting. Tuesday, March 19, began with further debate, but the determination of the secessionists to proceed to extra-legal steps unless accommodations were reached led the convention to adjourn in the afternoon and go into conference. During the next two days the details of a compromise agreement were worked out. There were four main points, each side claiming two. On the secession side, the convention agreed to let the people vote for either "secession" or "cooperation" in August. If secession was their choice, the convention would reassemble and pass the necessary ordinance. If cooperation won, the convention would work with the other border slave states to get a satisfactory settlement. Second, the convention adopted the report of the committee on federal affairs, pledging Arkansas to resist any coercion. The Union side could claim two victories. First, five delegates, Albert Rust, S. H. Hempstead, T. H. Bradley, E. A. Warren, and J. P. Spring, were to represent Arkansas at any border state convention. "This," delegate H. F. Thomason wrote, "has been violently opposed by the Secessionists, but they have agreed to offer no factious opposition to it." Second, the convention adopted a series of resolutions on national affairs similar to the Thomason proposals. This was obviously repugnant to many fire-eaters, as William Mayo offered instead of the amendments a resolution calling for immediate secession. This move, however, was defeated, and the convention went on to adopt the proposals forty to twenty-four. Some secessionists probably agreed with Harris Flanagin, who explained his vote thus: "I assent to the abstract declarations in the above resolutions, but hold that we cannot get sufficient guarantees to remedy the present evils, and if we could, they would not be observed." Against secessionist wishes the convention had gone on record as favoring a peaceful settlement within the Union.[31]

Nevertheless for a second time pressure tactics had wrung from a Unionist majority a partial victory. In each case the argument that the people should decide was hard to resist, even though the secessionists only believed in consulting the masses in cases where it suited their purposes.[32]

Following adjournment of the convention agitation for secession was intensified, even though the election was not scheduled until August. Obviously the secessionists hoped that developments on the national level supported by a well-conducted propaganda campaign would bring them victory. The *True Democrat* made arrangements to supply a special campaign rate of the paper through August for only fifty cents, and predicted that it would then announce "the large majority of votes cast in favor of the secession of the state from its unholy union with Black Republicanism, Tariffites, Infidels, Abolitionists, and Enemies." The blatant propaganda of this paper was not appreciated by the Unionists, one of whom called it "the most outrageous dirty little sheet that ever poisoned the atmosphere." While the daily which Johnson published during the convention suspended after that body's adjournment, his acrid editorials and slanted news did not. "The Literary Leviathan of the *True Democrat*," one irritated Unionist wrote, "has during this excitement made a perfect ass of himself." Nevertheless it was feared that Johnson was "too successful in misleading the people."[33]

In response to the *True Democrat's* secession sallies, the *Gazette* made a special offer. "Danley's paper we intend shall have a full circulation," reported Little Rock merchant S. H. Tucker. "We can raise the money here to do it. And by the by you must pay our paper at Van Buren. Men can't work without pay, never mind, my friends, a few hundred dollars." Plans were made to provide free papers to the poor just prior to the election. But as the national scene offered little encouragement to the Unionists, the rejoinders grew less effective.[34]

An indication of the strategy the Unionists hoped to employ was given by William Fishback, who declared that the Van Buren *Press,* the leading Unionist organ in the northwest, must shift its emphasis from news, and, taking a leaf from the *True Democrat,* function *"as a campaign paper until the election."* He further advocated emphasis on two points which he deemed most effective with the voters, "viz., to show a settled design to break up the government on the part of the secessionists and to prove their hostility to compromise."[35]

In addition the Unionists distributed one thousand copies of Washington's Farewell Address in each of three northern counties and varying quantities elsewhere. "It will always command a hearing," explained one Unionist. Loyalists were encouraged to establish Union clubs and "make at least as great a show of zeal as possible, it encourages the people." Nor were the South Arkansas Unionists inactive. Editor-delegate A. W. Hobson reported, "I will continue to give them as good as they send."[36]

Secessionists backed up their newspaper efforts by sending their leaders to stump North Arkansas. The secession speakers—Robert W. Johnson, John F. Pope, Congressman Hindman, and Congressman-elect E. W. Gantt, among others, initially announced that they would not debate Unionist opponents. But this policy was not systematically followed. The far-seeing R. W. Johnson was conciliatory. William Quesenbury, no political friend, reported that Johnson's address in Fayetteville "was not the delivery of pre-studied, pre-arranged invectives and shameless and false assertions," but rather a statesmanlike appeal.[37]

In the south, where the force of public opinion was already molding external conformity to secessionism, the prospect of intrastate separation if secession should fail was revived. Delegate I. H. Hilliard, in an open letter to his Chicot County constituents, suggested an irrepressible conflict: "Unfortunately our state is divided into two sections whose pursuits are totally dissimilar— the grain and stock-raising portion looks with no friendly eye on the cotton planter.'' That secession was justified even if rejected at the polls was indicated by the Lake Village *Chicot Press* in explaining that it was ''hard to convince the bigoted or enlighten the ignorant.'' The *Gazette* responded to these assaults on the hard-fisted yeomanry by asserting that the big planters would disfranchise the poor if given a chance. Probably the burden of this debate was more to intimidate the wavering than really to cleave the state.[38]

There were, however, plenty of hotheads impatient with elections. When the citizens of Cincinnati refused to complete the shipping to Arkansas of part of the arms for which state commissioners C. C. Danley and T. J. Churchill had contracted in February, a vigilance group at Napoleon forcibly seized the *Ohio Belle* in retaliation. A cannon shot fired on this occasion has been characterized by some as the first shot of the war.[39]

Most of the violence was verbal. Secessionist papers had already unleashed most of their choicest vocabulary during the sitting of the convention. Still several leading Unionists were violently criticized in the press. The *Sage of Monticello* claimed William Fishback had signed a petition asking for pardon for John Brown, while one of the Fort Smith papers accused him of being ''to all intense [*sic*] a Black Republican in favor of Brown raids and in favor of force to compel Southern states back into the Union.''[40]

Perhaps the outstanding clash of the attenuated campaign centered around President Lincoln's tendering of the superintendency of Indian affairs to Sebastian County delegate S. L. Griffith. Judge Wheeler of the *Times and Herald* charged that Griffith's Unionism was based on his desire for patronage. Griffith, who had been a friend of Wheeler's for twenty-two years, met him on the street and shook his hand, ''but it was to bid him *farewell forever*. Never in my life had my feelings [*been*] so hurt.'' To combat the ''poisonous influences of the lying secessionist papers,'' Griffith's friends held a meeting to endorse his conduct. They also arranged for the distribution of one hundred copies of a defense of him which appeared in the Van Buren *Press*. In addition he was serenaded by The Brass Band. The crisis passed, but it showed the immense hostility which could be aroused even by an innocent act of the president.[41]

Another blow to the Union cause was the publication of *State or Province? Bond or Free?* by Albert Pike. Unionists said that it was but ''a reproduction of the political heresies, that thirty years ago called down on John C. Calhoun, the anathema maranatha of Andrew Jackson,'' and regretted that Pike, rumored dead in 1859, had lived to pen such a piece.[42]

The campaign also had its lighter side. ''Dixie'' became popular in Arkansas, and while Albert Pike's lofty lyrics were the most widely sung, others appeared. This version issued from the *Gazette*:

> Away down here in this Southern nation
> People have got up a great sensation.
> Look away, &c.

> They want to break this great communion
> With dissention and disunion
> (chorus) But there is no word like Union
> Hurrah, Hurrah,
> With colors true red white and blue
> Oh Boys, don't ask for something new.

To which the *True Democrat's* poet replied:

> In the Southern part of this great nation
> We feed on nothing but sensation.
> Get away, &c.
> We want to save this great communion
> By discussion and disunion.
> Get away, &c.
> (chorus) There's nothing like disunion
> Hurrah, Hurrah!
> With colors blue for they are true
> Oh girls do ask for something new
> Hurrah, Hurrah, Hurrah for disunion.

Another song modified for secessionist proclivities was "Wait for the Wagon," which when rendered into "The Southern Wagon," asked:

> Missouri, North Carolina, and Arkansas are slow—
> They must hurry or we'll leave them.
> Then where would they go?[43]

It is difficult to gauge how the voters were responding to the campaign. The *True Democrat* predictably told in glowing tones of the great upsurge of disunion sentiment; but the *Gazette* countered with reports that the people were awakening to the insidious secessionist design. Many Unionists no doubt felt as did S. H. Tucker, who wrote, "My whole Heart, mind, body, and Soul have been wrapped up in the Union question." Perhaps, however, the secessionists were gaining the upper hand in the weeks preceding the firing on Fort Sumter. William Mansfield reported many voters "indifferent" and goaded Union men to work harder. The Union cause was hurt by the reported defection of Albert Rust and E. A. Warren, both of whom had been among those chosen as delegates to a border state convention.[44]

Meanwhile the campaign continued, although the leaders of both sides must have known that the issues were really past debate, and that Arkansas's course of action depended mainly on Lincoln's policy toward the Confederacy. South Arkansas was already determined on what her policy would be in the event of war; the question was whether secession agitation had brought about the acquiescence of the northwest yeoman sitting unconcernedly on his mountain spur.

On April 12, 1861, Confederate guns fired on the beleaguered Union garrison in Fort Sumter. For the North the Confederates were the aggressors; but for the South the attempt to reinforce the garrison was the *casus belli*. Robert Ward Johnson, speaking at Bentonville at that time, "was hissed and hooted down" until the news arrived; then "all was changed in a moment."[45]

The Unionists were confused and downhearted. Many were "overwhelmed by the popular excitement." S. G. Stallings, delegate from Conway County, recalled that the convention had pledged Arkansas to resist any attack on the South. But Stallings opposed recalling the convention, was averse to secession, and wanted to wait, as planned, until the August election. Yet he admitted: "If the worst comes to the worst, we ought to be united." Perhaps most representative was the view of William Stout, delegate from Pope County:

> I believe it is the President's duty to put down rebellion. I have always thought So. I have always thought that General Jackson was right in 33 if he was right then Lincoln is right now but it Seems that there is going to be war between the north & the South—for me to take the Side of the north against my brethren of the South that would brand me forever with valainy [sic] that would be too bad and roll up my Sleeves and go to kiling off men that never did me any harm and never intends to do me any . . . The Secessionists here are rejoicing best pleased in the world a thousand times better pleased when they heard that Fort Sumpter was taken than they would have been to have heard that a plan was devised to put at rest forever all political differences and raised the Strips and Stars again over a free contented happy and prosperous people— these are hard things to say but I believe in my soul it is so and can I ever cooperate with a people whose heart is so decidedly in the wrong place I think no I see no way to do that—

In fact Stout was certain only that "our intentions were good." Many former Unionists who agreed that the South had been subjected to an overt attack and that war was necessary still could not bring themselves to endorse secession as a constitutional answer. Instead they called for a declaration of independence, asserting the right of revolution in place of the alleged right of secession. While some favored neutrality, most were now committed: "We fought manfully for the Union," S. H. Tucker wrote D. C. Williams, "let us now fight manfully for the South."[46]

Legally the decision on what was to be done rested with David Walker in Fayetteville, for he alone had the power to summon the convention prior to the scheduled August meeting. Uncertain what to do, Walker wrote Governor Jackson of Missouri asking what course that state would take. Jackson's reply was not calculated to prolong Walker's Unionist sentiments: "Missouri will be ready for secession in less than thirty days; *and will secede,* if Arkansas will only get out of the way and give her a free passage." Arkansas secessionists put pressure on Walker. Thomas B. Hanly informed him that there would be no stopping South Arkansas now; the convention must be reconvened to speak for the state; and in recalling the convention Walker could take his proper place among the great leaders of the state. Furthermore the *Gazette,* the leading Unionist paper, gave up the ghost: "The Work of Coercion Commenced" ran the headline. "Let the People of Arkansas Resist It as One Man." To Secretary of War Simon Cameron's call for Arkansas to furnish 780 men "to suppress combinations," Governor Rector, with popular support on his side, replied:

> In answer to your requisition for troops from Arkansas to subjugate the Southern States, I have to say that none will be furnished. The demand is only adding insult to injury. The people of this commonwealth are freemen, not slaves, and will defend to the last extremity their honor, lives, and property against Northern mendacity and usurpation.[47]

In the weeks following the bombardment of Fort Sumter the majority of the Unionist leaders came to favor some action. S. H. Tucker, C. P. Bertrand, S. H. Hempstead, Albert Rust, and Hot Spring County delegate Joseph Jester signed a public letter attacking Lincoln for "duplicity and treachery," and urging Walker to recall the convention. On April 27, 1861, the Pulaski County delegates, Joseph Stillwell and A.H. Garland, endorsed the demand for reassembling the convention. Ouachita County delegate A. W. Hobson, without waiting for Walker's call, issued a summons for the convention to meet on April 29. Editor-delegate M. S. Kennard of the *Independent Balance* summed up the sentiments of many conservatives when he observed that rebellion *(not secession)* was now "a mournful necessity, and those who shall be responsible for it will receive as they deserve, the execration of posterity." Thus while still denying the constitutional legitimacy of the secession, these conservatives advocated revolution—another road to the same end.[48]

Walker, keenly aware that public opinion throughout most of Arkansas strongly favored secession, and fearful that the secessionists would usurp control if he did not act, ordered the convention back into session on May 6, 1861, in Little Rock. It is noteworthy, however, that Walker's course was repudiated by some of his mountain constituents, who, when he asked them for instructions, replied that they opposed secession, wanted the people to vote before any action was taken, and preferred cooperating with the border states to joining the Confederacy.[49]

Before the convention could reassemble, the rumor reached Governor Rector that Union reinforcements were headed for Fort Smith from Indian Territory. Rector ordered militia Colonel Solon Borland with four companies of volunteers and a four-gun battery to seize the fort. With editors Johnson in the ranks as a private, and Danley as an observer, the expedition headed up river for Fort Smith. Although reinforcements were picked up in Van Buren, when the force arrived at the fort on April 23, they "were very much mortified (a private who was there said 'gratified') to find that the enemy had fled in the night." Leaving General N. B. Burrow in command, the force returned to Little Rock. Historian D. Y. Thomas states that on the trip back "the members of the company were so hilarious that, according to the owner, they damaged the boat transporting them to the extent of $500.00."[50]

The occupation of Fort Smith, although militarily unnecessary since secessionists at Pine Bluff had already rendered the fort untenable by seizing supplies destined for the federal garrison, accomplished results opposite to those obtained earlier by capture of the Little Rock arsenal. Among secessionists a wave of patriotic rejoicing took place. Only the persistent Unionists were not elated. The Fort Smith seizure,

Jesse Turner wrote, was "a foolish and unnecessary adventure but in keeping with these times which are so sadly out of joint."[51]

Even before the secessionist steamboats arrived at Fort Smith, the conservative leaders were laying their plans. Danley wrote David Walker that the convention must be summoned, that a declaration of independence rather than an ordinance of secession should be passed, and that the conservative men, majority intact, must take over the government. In a similar vein Danley wrote W. W. Mansfield, "I think the conservative men of the convention should take charge of the affairs of the state and prevent the wild secessionists from sending us to the Devil." The chief of these "wild secessionists" was, of course, the governor. In the weeks that followed other conservatives echoed Danley's thoughts.[52]

Meanwhile public attention was focused on the convention, which, by Walker's proclamation, was to reconvene on Monday, May 6. A. W. Bishop recalled:

> The Saturday previous delegates and citizens began to swarm promiscuously into Little Rock. There was but one subject of interest, one topic of conversation, and on Monday morning the steps of all were bent in the same direction.

Whatever hopes the conservatives had of delaying secession was effectively quashed by the reported secession of Virginia and Tennessee. News of border state secession produced "astonishing changes," Turner reported, and as one delegate wrote, "the sentiment had change [sic]." The belief carefully cultivated by the *True Democrat*, that all the border states would secede, although doubted by some farseeing Unionists, effectively ended Unionist resistance in Arkansas.[53]

At ten o'clock Judge Walker called the convention to order. "Every nook and corner was occupied. The aisles were full—the galleries crowded—men jostled ladies, and ladies each other. Boys perched upon window sills, and nestled by the chairs of members." After routine opening business, the convention adjourned until the afternoon. At the start of the afternoon session W. P. Grace proposed an ordinance of secession. No speeches were made; "the intensely excited throng could not brook the ordeal of discussion." A. W. Dinsmore then moved that the proposed ordinance be amended to provide for its referral to the people. By a fifty-five to fifteen vote, this amendment was tabled. The vote was then taken on the ordinance itself. Only five delegates cast negative votes: Isaac Murphy and H. H. Bolinger of Madison County, John Campbell of Searcy County, T. M. Gunter of Washington County, and Samuel "Parson" Kelley of Pike County. Except for explanatory remarks by a few Unionists, there was complete silence during the roll call.[54]

David Walker was the last man to vote. As he arose he pleaded with the five holdouts to change their votes: "Now, since we must go, let us all go together; let the wires carry the news to all the world that Arkansas stands as a unit against coercion." All the dissenters then changed their votes, except Isaac Murphy. For a moment there was a "death-like stillness. 'Murphy,' 'Murphy,' was now shouted from the lobby, the gallery, and at last from the floor of the convention." Senator Sebastian and Judge English were seen in conference with him. At last Murphy arose: "I have cast my vote after mature reflection, and have duly considered the consequences, and I cannot conscientiously change it. I therefore vote 'no.' " "Storms of hisses instantly burst forth. 'Traitor!' 'Traitor!' 'shoot him!' 'Hang him!' madly resounded through the hall, but no personal violence was attempted" then or later. Instead Mrs. Frederick Trapnall, widow of a long-time Little Rock merchant, threw him a bouquet. At ten minutes past four o'clock, May 6, 1861, Arkansas left the Union amid "general acclamation that shook the building to its very foundations."[55]

Despite a persistent and deep-rooted attachment to the Union on the part of a large percentage of the population, the aversion to making war on the other Southern states proved stronger, at least with the Unionist leadership. The firing on Fort Sumter "instantly drove—it did not convert—all conservative into radical sentiment." Secession, Jesse Turner wrote D. C. Williams, "was a sad and deplorable necessity, but was unavoidable under the circumstances of the case." To his wife he confided:

> Perhaps you will think I done [sic] wrong in voting for this act of revolution. Would to God that it could have been otherwise. But a stern and inexorable destiny seemed to demand it—The people of the State demanded it, and I could not escape it without abandoning my post, which I could not do—God knows what is to become of our unhappy country. All is darkness and gloom ahead. Our people are thoroughly inbued with the revolutionary spirit. Madness and folly rules the land and I fear that the end of free government approaches. The conservative men who were for the Union cannot stay the rushing tide of revolution. I fear it can only be quenched in oases of blood.

It is doubtful, as one Unionist later claimed, that "Arkansas never seceded by the will of the people. If they had been consulted fairly and justly and left free to exercise their deliberate judgment, the honor and escutcheon of the state would not have been disgraced by rebellion." Jesse Turner was nearer the mark when he told his wife that a referendum would have been futile.[56]

The hard rock Unionists went into retirement. "We shall have a rough time of it, I know," wrote one old settler. And Judge Brown inscribed in his diary, "I quietly labor in my office, and am mentally training my mind to bear up with fortitude under adversity."[57]

Throughout South Arkansas there was "a perfect blaze of excitement." In Camden, according to Judge Brown, "the war spirit is decidedly in ascendant, many are rejoicing." Des Arc celebrated secession with "a general jollification," marked by a torch-light parade with a banner emblazoned "Arkansas slow but sure." "Henceforth," wrote William Quesenbury, "guns, sabres, bayonets, and all the paraphernalia of war should engage the energies of our people, and not letter writing and street argumentation." But such was not to be the case.[58]

As Arkansians adjusted themselves to the state's changed condition, the convention continued its labors by rewriting the state constitution. Whig objectives were fulfilled, including legalized banking, moving state elections from August to October, and creating equal senate districts to be reapportioned with every census. Other changes included changes in required county size, appointment of judges by governor with advice and consent of the senate (rather than election by general assembly), and popular election of prosecuting attorneys (rather than their election by the general assembly). It was with regard to Negroes that the most changes were made. Whereas the old constitution spoke of "all free men," the new document said "all free white men and Indians." Whereas the old document guaranteed slaves accused of crimes impartial trials with juries and counsel, the new constitution allowed the general assembly to pass whatever laws needed. And, whereas the old constitution forbade emancipation without consent of the owners, the new constitution forbade it altogether. Thus despite minor changes, the form of govenment remained the same. Other actions included the enactment of a stay law, a prohibition of paying debts due Northerners, the confiscation of alien property, the creation of four congressional districts for the new Confederate government, and the issuance of state war bonds to finance the war effort.[59]

The second session also continued the running battle with the governor. Since the firing on Fort Sumter Rector had behaved "as though the state had already seceded." Despite subsequent events, the Unionists still doubted his integrity and distrusted his motives. The fundamental and longstanding differences between the two sides nearly came to a head in the second session. The basic issue, the extent of the convention's powers, was not new, having first appeared in the confrontation over the Fulton County election. Rector's narrow view received some support in April from the *True Democrat*. Prior to the reconvening of the convention, editor Johnson suggested the reassembling of the legislature "so that the conflicting laws may be modified, harmonized, or repealed to suit the new conditions of the state." Probably there were political motives as well, as the legislature had shown itself more friendly to the "family" than the convention was liable to. Furthermore, Johnson caught Rector between the Charybdis of a "family" controlled legislature and the conservative Scylla of the convention.[60]

Pursuing divisive tactics still further, Johnson the next week gave verbal support to Rector's position. "We dissent," he wrote, "from the notion and opinion of papers and persons who advocate the power of the convention to do everything that could devolve on the legislature." The convention did not have the power to appropriate money. The *Gazette* jumped for the bait, and in following the lines put forth by D. C. Williams, claimed that the convention "can do anything which the legislature can do, and many things which the legislature can not do."[61]

There matters stood. Rector did not recall the legislature but neither did the conservatives relent. The idea of Rector as war governor with his powers *in statu quo* caused conservatives to shudder. At best they had "no confidence in the men who have destroyed our Union;" at worst they sought to promote their own partisan interests.[62]

When the convention reassembled it was first rumored that they would remove Rector from the governorship. Since the majority disliked and mistrusted him, and the minority of the secessionists were of "family" persuasion, it was possible. Rector had few friends in the convention, and his leader there, the blundering James Yell, was only a recent convert. Rector himself, in a hastily scribbled note, revealed his fears: "Col. Webb says that when the convention meets they will try to declare my office vacant. Oh Hell." But when the convention actually assembled, "it was the friends of the editor of this paper [Johnson of the *True Democrat*] who stood between him and them, who pleaded for him and stayed their hands.'' If so, small gratitude Johnson received.[63]

The biggest conflict was over military affairs. Danley pointed out that the militia officers had been elected during peacetime largely for the honor when there was no prospect of their actually leading troops into battle. Accordingly they should resign, and the military should be reorganized, with professional direction provided. That Danley also disliked some of the leading officers, including Major General James Yell, helps account for his position. In particular Danley singled out General N. B. Burrow, left in charge at Fort Smith. According to Danley's report, ''Things have been carried on in a manner at once so extravagant and so pompously unmilitary as to render the pronunciamentos and home wars of Mexico almost respectable.'' Reorganization was ''imperative.''[64]

But instead of the thorough reorganization many desired only piecemeal changes were instituted. First the convention, following the precedent of several other Southern states, established a military board. Thomas C. Hindman has been generally credited with the authorship of the measure, but James Yell in a letter to President Davis stated that he wrote them ''to save the state from civil war,'' but that ''they were greatly injured by amendments.'' The purpose of this ''most miserable military board bill'' was ''to divert their minds.'' As finally approved, the board had three members, the governor, who served as chairman, B. C. Totten, ''a moderate minded man and under the desperate influences of the Johnson family,'' and C. C. Danley, conservative editor and wounded Mexican War veteran. According to the convention's plan, all forces were to be turned over to the Confederacy, and no troops would be called into service unless the state was invaded. Thus the board would be mostly administrative in nature.[65]

Second, the convention decided that for the time being, trusted officers must be appointed to superintend the gathering troops. Accordingly delegate and former United State army major Thomas H. Bradley was assigned to command as brigadier general in charge of the eastern section. And N. Bart Pearce, West Point graduate, was to command in the west. By no coincidence, both men were ''very strong Union men.'' As for Pearce, ''no more unpopular appointment could have been made by the convention,'' for he had ''heaped abuse'' on Rector and ''every prominent man in the state who favored secession.'' James Yell remained major general, but only in name. As agent for the board, Danley left for Richmond to tender the troops then in arms to the Confederacy.[66]

If the convention thought that these arrangements would work, they were mistaken. On May 11 Pearce, pursuant to taking up his new duties, submitted his resignation as a colonel in the militia to Rector. The governor refused to accept it, and asked Pearce to ''define your authority.'' Pearce replied that the convention was his authority. The next day, Rector wrote the convention that by the constitution he was the commander-in-chief, sworn to uphold the laws, and that no one was his military superior. Although he deemed the convention's actions unconstitutional, Rector curiously promised to ''cooperate cheerfully and zealously with the convention in all things.'' If the governor hoped to win over the convention by charging in opposite directions simultaneously, he failed. Pearce assumed command in Northwest Arkansas, although the secessionists continued to harass him. Bradley fared even worse as his men refused to fight under him.

Despite Rector's defeat over the Pearce appointment, the governor did not give up the battle. His next plan called for the reconvening of the general assembly on May 23, 1861, while the convention was still in session. This time the *True Democrat* did not support Rector. Fearing ''collision'' between the two bodies, Johnson cautioned that reconvening ''can do no good'' and asserted Rector's impending confrontation with the convention would be ''the most unfortunate step of his life.'' But the order was never issued. The convention on hearing of the call demanded he withhold it. Rector, fearful of the consequences, backed down again.[67]

Disgust and dismay at Rector's conduct prompted the last move against the governor. By ''artful design, silently and ingeniously executed, without attracting at the time the slightest attention or suspicion, the political guillotine was prepared for him.'' Jesse Cypert moved that ''the next general election for officers of this state, under this constitution, not otherwise herein provided for, shall be held on the first Monday in October, 1862, in the manner now prescribed by law.'' This motion, passed by the convention, meant that Rector came up for reelection in 1862 rather than at the expiration of his normal term in 1864. It was later charged that this move was a ''family'' plot. But by May both the conservatives and the ''family'' were equally anxious to rid the state of Rector, and both undoubtedly worked to that end.[68]

While the governor and convention quarreled, business went on. Robert Ward Johnson, A. H. Garland, Albert Rust, H. F. Thomason, and W. W. Watkins, all conservatives except Johnson, were elected delegates to the Provisional Congress. Garland, Thomason, and Watkins were delegates of the convention. Hindman and Gantt were the favorite secessionist candidates. Johnson was chosen with Unionist support because of his ''high standing and integrity.'' The ''fire-eating'' Des Arc *Citizen* complained that ''the convention will be long remembered for rewarding submissionists.'' Many, tired of tricking and trading, agreed with the Washington *Courier* that the convention has succeeded ''after four weeks zealous labor in doing what might have been done in four days.'' Conservatives, on the other hand, were pleased. Judge Brown concluded that the ''body were a step in advance of any we have had in the state heretofore.''[69]

Apparently the members still serving shared Brown's views, for they showed no inclination to quit their labors. When A. H. Garland resigned to go to Congress, his place was filled by election with George C. Watkins, ''possibly the ablest man that Arkansas has produced.'' Down to fifty-six members, the convention rejected a motion to adjourn on June 1. To force the issue, Grace, Patterson, Robinson, Adams of Izard, both Tottens, and chairman Walker offered their resignations. Thus when the convention reassembled on Monday with George C. Watkins presiding, no quorum could be had. The convention finally adjourned, though with the provision that the chairman, the governor, or the military board could call them back.[70]

Thus secession did not spell an end to politics, and the passing of an ordinance of secession was not the only important act of the convention. Caught in the middle, and lacking the support of both the people and the politicians, Governor Rector "sincerely believed he had the ability to govern the world, to lead armies, and manage an empire." Thus the scene was set for continued internal conflict in the months ahead.[71]

6)
The First
Year of
the War

"We are now all to be tried—as it were by Fire." —Mrs. M. B. Eskridge to Wm. E. Woodruff, June 4, 1861, Worley, *At Home*, p. 25.

Arkansas from the beginning played only a minor role in the strategic thinking of the Confederate leaders. Partly because they were better bureaucrats than revolutionaries, Jefferson Davis and his advisors did not adequately appreciate either the needs or the opportunities arising from the war on the border. Owing to excessive concentration on the eastern, and to a lesser degree, the central theatres, the infant Confederacy failed to initiate actions which might at an early date have secured the vast resources of Missouri and given Lincoln three major fronts to think about rather than merely two. Yet in the Southern mentality broad concerns gave way to considerations of local nature. Though Arkansans ultimately realized that their safety was inextricably linked to that of Missouri, at first even they thought only in terms of self defense.[1]

During the early months of 1861, Arkansas was in a state of turmoil. The secessionists had seized the Little Rock arsenal in February, forced the evacuation of Fort Smith in April, and seized enemy shipping on the Arkansas and Mississippi Rivers. Governor Rector cooperated with the Confederate authorities by permitting the erection of a battery at Helena to guard the Mississippi, and tacitly assisted in the arming of companies preparing for war.[2]

Many Arkansans were worried about their western border. Over the years Arkansas newspaper readers were kept well posted on Indian affairs. The Indian superintendency was the choicest patronage plum in the state, and every prominent Indian official owed his appointment to the efforts of Senator Johnson. Yet the Indians were as divided in their sentiments as the whites. For ten years Arkansans had been warned that Northern Baptist missionaries were winning converts to Christianity and abolitionism, and this group was regarded as a source of great danger. On the other hand, the Chickasaws, Creeks, and Choctaws, living south of the Arkansas River, were considered to be Southern in their leanings.[3]

From Kansas, that hotbed of abolition, it was popularly believed that the notorious Colonel Montgomery or Senator Jim Lane was preparing to descend on Arkansas. In late May it was rumored and widely believed that their forces, numbering 8,000 invaders, had entered the state, captured Pocahontas (or Fort Smith), ravished the country, and moved on Little Rock. The Military Board assembled 4,000 men to protect the capital against the imagined invasion, while a large volunteer force embarked on steamboats from Jacksonport bound to rescue Pocahontas. The ease (in the virtual absence of telegraphic communications) with which this ridiculous rumor gained credence, indicated the pervasive sense of insecurity, and forcefully demonstrated the need for some means of defense.[4]

The attack on Fort Sumter, while not producing unanimity for war, did arouse the martial spirit of nearly every young male south of the Arkansas River. "Man after man unresistingly succumbed to its influence," Henry M. Stanley recalled. "Even women and children cried for war. If every man did not hasten to the battle, they vowed they would themselves rush out and meet the Yankee vandals. In a land where women are worshipped by the men, such language made them war-mad." Although it took the anonymous present of a "chemise and petticoat, such as a negro lady's maid might wear," to convince the English-born Stanley to enlist, others were not so hesitant. "I had always like to read history of war," one veteran remembered, "and always determined to go to a war should the opportunity turn up." And another recollected: "So impatient did I become for starting that I felt like ten thousand pins were pricking me in every part of the body, and started off a week in advance of my brothers." For many former Unionists, "it was then Fight or play traitor to my country."[5]

War was not yet a grim reality of death and carnage. As conjured up through the misty visions of the Romantic writers like Sir Walter Scott, it was the triumph of youth and manhood over evil and cowardice. On the score of Northern cowardice, Southerners need have no fear. Colonel Decius McCrory, late of the state legislature, told White Countians that one Southerner could whip two Yankees in a fair fight, and it would take two more Yankees to make the first two fight. "Of course at that time I believed every word of it," one grizzled volunteer later recalled. Even the women could handle the Yankees, and it was probably Colonel McCrory who asserted that Mr. Travis's school girls could defend Searcy.[6]

A major problem was how to convert this enthusiasm into an organized army capable of making a useful contribution to the war effort. When Arkansas was enveloped with fear of abolitionist raids, the idea of state self defense naturally came to the fore. The historic chief means of defense was the militia, but this body was in a lamentable condition. Throughout the ante bellum period there was in Arkansas little of the elitist military spirit which it has been claimed was typical of the deep South. If the plantation system engendered the habit of command, the Arkansas frontier encouraged the rejection of all authority and an every man for himself attitude. Arkansas had only a few military academies (one combined with a female institute) and few native trained soldiers. Militia duty, in the palmy days before the war, had either been a social frolic much as pictured in Longstreet's *Georgia Scenes* or else simply avoided. In some counties the militia was virtually nonexistent. "The milata [sic] is in bad condition in these parts," wrote a correspondent from Scott County, "Ther is not any officers. I have bin a trying to organize the malita [sic] here but I cannot do anything with them." Election to a militia office was mainly a matter of social prestige. Danley, a Mexican War veteran observed: "A few of them, and very few, have a small smattering of the rudiments of common *militia mustering*. Some of them do not even know that much.''[7]

The plan of the convention was that the Military Board would oversee the raising and arming of volunteers. These men were to be turned over to the Confederacy at the earliest moment, while the militia would remain a source of manpower and a last ditch defense. However the militia officers proved unwilling to agree to play dead and proceeded to call out their companies, so that the recruiting, organizing, and arming of volunteers paralleled and competed with the efforts to raise the militia. Naturally Governor Rector, anxious to conduct the war himself, encouraged every effort to create a state army.[8]

Conflict between the various forces developed early. In the belief that the war would be of short duration, enlistments in the state forces were made for twelve months. Rector's mouthpiece, the *Daily State Journal,* observed later: "It would have been 'death in the pot' had the authorities while we had plenty of men and equipments, refused to take men for twelve months and demanded their services for three years.'' Actually, as experience would show, it would have been easier to get men then for three years than after they had once had a taste of fighting. The Confederacy, meanwhile, accepted twelve month men only if they were armed. As local supplies of arms soon vanished, volunteers without arms were taken in for the three year term.[9]

The process of raising and equipping a regiment, battalion, or company was not simple. Although at first there were plenty of volunteers, outfitting them was frequently a difficult problem. Uniforms were often homemade since few towns had adequate facilities for manufacturing them. In Camden a ladies' sewing circle was organized two weeks before the secession of the state. In Little Rock, Theatre Hall was converted into a manufactory, turning out seventy-five pairs of pants and two hundred jackets a day. The first Camden companies were much better equipped than the average. The Camden City Guards wore:

> Gray satinnet pants and roundabout, trimmed with red flannel stripe down the pants, coats stripped shoulder cuffs with the same, leather belts, Camden Knights uniform is gray coat, roundabout, black cap, black pants, and leather belts. The Ouachita Grays have gray kersey, trimmed with green flannel and belts. All the men wear caps.

But elsewhere in Arkansas a company marched off in homespun to the tune of a homemade drum and cane fife, and instead of such fancy names as Camden Knights or Calhoun Escopets, there were also the Arkansas Canebreakers and Muddy Bayou Heroes.[10]

Some of the elitist groups at first operated more like social clubs than military commands. Drunks were expelled by majority vote, "as we were determined not to have any drunkards in our company if we *know* it." Attempts were made to discourage card playing and Sabbath defamation. One Arkansas boy wrote early in the war:

> Last Sunday night I saw some young men playing. Frank and I told them that it was

Sunday, but they did not heed. The most of men seem to become reckless by being out in camp. If this war lasts a few years our country will have retrograded fifty years. A war is very demoralizing to any people.

For many the temptations of getting away from home were too great to be resisted. The diary of one Des Arc soldier recorded that on Sunday, June 9, 1861, in Fort Smith "drinking, gambling, fighting, &c. went on much as usual." The next Sunday the private himself wrote: "This morning I feel like—well if you was ever good drunk I need not waste time in telling." And on other occasions he reported himself to be "over gayful," "spun in the head," and "bust scull." When Arkansas soldiers marched north to Missouri, tippling wagons and professional gentlemen followed in their wake.[11]

An important initial step in the organization of a company or regiment was the election of officers. In most instances the men instrumental in recruiting and equipping the soldiers were rewarded, but not always. Prewar political influence sometimes was the overriding consideration, as in the instance of Thompson P. Flournoy and James B. Johnson. Governor Rector had authorized Flournoy and Johnson to raise the first regiment requested of Arkansas by the Confederate government. But when they stood for election as colonel and lieutenant colonel they were defeated. According to the *True Democrat,* "they had *prematurely* loved the South more than they loved the Union," while Danley defended the right of the men to elect whomsoever they thought best, even if in so doing they disregarded "family" wishes.[12]

Once clothed and officered, the men still had to learn the rudiments of war. In Camden, Judge Brown's son, a graduate of Kentucky military school, fated to die of consumption within a year, arose from his death bed to drill the local companies. Elsewhere it was harder. "We have no tactics in this state," reported state Brigadier General N. Bart Pearce, a West Point man, to the Secretary of War. "Can you send us five hundred copies of Hardee's *Tactics?*" Since many officers were only country lawyers, training and discipline naturally got off to a poor start.[13]

Arming the troops presented the greatest problem. At the fall of the arsenal in Little Rock, the state acquired a quantity of arms. But in the months that followed, these weapons were dispensed to groups manifesting secessionist proclivities, with the result that few remained to supply the enormous need created by the beginning of war. Some of the regiments heading east for the "seat of war" were equipped at state expense even though destined for Confederate service. T. C. Hindman, who raised a regiment for state service at his own expense and was then refused state arms, went to Richmond, where he got his unit accepted and equipped by Confederate authorities. Many less influentially placed officers had to rely initially on home supplied muskets, shotguns, pikes, lances, and "very long disemboweling tools."[14]

Once mustered, sworn in, and armed, the soldiers were theoretically ready for war. Invariably there was a flag presentation at which some esteemed young lady addressed the soldiers in glowing language (supplied for her in one instance by a local preacher). Miss Whitney at Des Arc told the volunteers:

The liberties of all future generations stand suspended in doubtful poise, and you must go forth and contend for the prize. 'Tis true many of you have ties at home which it is almost death to sever. 'Tis true that the tears and sobs of an aged mother, and decrepid [*sic*] father, the trembling accents of a loving wife and darling sisters, are enough to wring drops of blood from the heart that is not steel, but, gentlemen, no wailings, no cries are equal to those of expiring liberty as she lies prostrate, bleeding at every pore. Then, in behalf of the ladies of West Point, I present to you this banner wrought by their own hands. When marshalled before the booming cannon and exposed to the solid sheets of liquid death, may it inspire your souls and nerve your arms and lend new courage to your drooping spirits.

To which the commanding officer responded:

While contending for our cherished rights we will plant this flag triumphantly on our soil or find a grave beneath its verdant sod. And while battling for our rights under this banner, we will call to mind the donors of this beautiful flag, who are far away from us, like angels of mercy, sending up their war prayers for our success. Again ladies, we bid you a farewell, hoping God will protect you at home while we defend you abroad.

Thus inspired these and other "brave Southrons" departed for the war, urged on by the waving of flags and the kisses and prayers of their loved ones. At Searcy the girls presented the Yellow Jacket company with a flag inscribed "No Backing Out." The first two companies to leave Camden had a more substantial boon in the form of two thousand dollars in spending money. Along the way the soldiers were cheered on by admiring throngs. A member of one unit reported:

The ladies would come out at every house and crossroads to give us their smiles, and they brought bouquets and flowers of the sweetest fragrance, fruit of the rarest and richest quality to distribute and also buckets of cool fresh water. We received nice vegetables, fruit, melons, and cakes that were adorned with roses and evergreens.[15]

In South Arkansas so intense was the enthusiasm that not thirty-five Union men were left. In the northwest, however, it was different. When the Union leadership there went over to secession in May, it was naturally assumed that the masses would follow, but such was not the case. Although an anonymous "Western Arkansian" warned that the people were three to one in favor of the Union, the degree of hostility to the Confederacy and the war was from the start underestimated. But even the ex-Unionists believed it. David Walker's assertion in 1862 that "the mountain counties as well as this [Washington County] have turned out nearly every man for duty, and without conscripting," was not true. A common saying was "the South commence it and the South may fight it out." And some asked, "Why don't the sons of the merchants volunteer?" At Greasy Cove in Montgomery County the farmers "don't intend to go fite till they are drafted and if they gete tuck prisoners they will tell north they would note of faught agante them they was compelde to do so."[16]

Attitudes toward the war were reflected in the number of volunteers sent from the various counties. As of February 20, 1862, prior to conscription, Calhoun County had sent 316 to war out of a voting population of 625. Arkansas County, another planting county, sent 455 out of 862. By contrast urban Pulaski sent 585 out of 1,574; Independence County 700 out of 2,163; and Sebastian County 475 out of 1,700. In the mountain areas, volunteering was virtually non-existent. In Madison County only 210 out of 1,300 went; in Franklin only 300 out of 1,048. Moreover those who attempted to raise companies among the yeomen had "all kinds of opposition thrown in the way." Few persons in the summer of 1861 realized the degree of alienation or the possibilities for mischief.[17]

The coming of the war also brought a train of economic and social problems for the homefolks. *"Times* are so *distracting,"* wrote Mrs. Mary Eskridge. "I have never had such difficulties in simple transactions." As secession agitation began, "improvements almost ceased and property lowered near one-half already for cash." By early March there was "a great deal of suing." Men with money at interest found considerable difficulty in collecting. One agent reported that he sought out a debtor and "dunned him hard" without success. When the convention passed a stay law, collection of debts almost stopped. John S. Hornor wrote that a debtor of his acquaintance

> seems absorbed in the Military movements of the country and appears to have lost sight of his personal liabilities and promises, resting perfectly easy, no doubt, in consequence of the disposition on the part of our Civil Authorities not to press the collection of any debt.

By December, 1861, Judge Brown reported himself unable to collect on anything. James Touchstone complained, "I have not got one cent to pay my taxes and do not know when I will git it." Another observed, "This is the first time in my life that I was ever brought to a dead lock in money matters. I fear that it will continue until we can sell cotton." Speaking for the planting interests, the *True Democrat* declared: "The merchant alone of all the citizens of the South has made money in the last six months."[18]

Compounding the money situation was the shortage of currency. "Arkansas," the *Daily State Journal* commented, "being without banks, feels the pressure of the times more severely than any other state in the Confederacy." The alarms of spring and summer resulted in the hoarding of gold. In addition, expenditures for arms, uniforms, and other essentials, and the inability to sell cotton, contributed to the disappearance of specie. The state bonds, one million dollars of which were soon in circulation, were not designed to be a currency, but in the absence of any other, soon drove out what specie remained. When the Military Board used bonds to pay the soldiers, the makeshift currency glutted the market. By October the bonds were down to seventy cents on the dollar. In November the *Daily State Journal* reported "Our war bonds have become so depreciated through the machinations of money-sharks and usurers that they have become near worthless." And as they continued to fall, holders needing specie were forced to sell them at a ruinous discount.[19]

In North Arkansas, many, fearing "the state government might bust," preferred hides, pelts, or barter for their transactions. Some simply refused any currency

—state or Confederate—associated with the odious rebellion. This unpatriotic attitude, together with the less obnoxious but more universal practice of "shaving" the bonds, contributed to popular discontent and distrust.[20]

The beginning of the war also witnessed a general disruption of civil government. In Saline County it was reported: "There will be no sheriff, no lawyers, and Shoppach [J. W. Shoppach, County Clerk, 1852–1962] says he has a mind to resign and let the whole business come down." Governor Rector, who admonished elected officials to return to their duties or resign, stated in a newspaper announcement: "In many counties there are neither sheriffs, judges, coroners, nor Justices of the Peace to administer the laws or enforce justice."[21]

In the absence of local law enforcement, much of Arkansas reverted to *ad hoc* justice. In part, the use of vigilance groups was motivated by a widespread fear of slave insurrection. "We anticipated trouble upon the part of the negroes, growing out of an abolitionist triumph in the North," recalled one Chicot Countian, but the fears ultimately proved to be "without foundation." Many Arkansans feared "bad white men" more than the slaves and took steps to warn these men away. At Walnut Hills in Lafayette County, one Josiah Brunson was expelled from the county for "being unfriendly to the South and advocating anti-slavery doctrine." Such vigilance activity seems to have peaked in late May, coinciding with the fear of Montgomery and Lane. At Hickory Plain, twenty miles east of Des Arc, an alleged insurrection was broken up and one of the slaves received one hundred and four lashes. At Jacksonport two men were arrested for giving whiskey to two Negro boys under dubious conditions. A Methodist preacher from Oil Trough was hung at Searcy for plotting insurrection. In St. Francis County an old farmer denounced a local vigilance group; a mob attacked his house, and he died in the fight. Three Negroes and a white man were hung at Pigeon Roost in Prairie County, and the action was endorsed by a public meeting presided over by R. S. Gantt. Such actions were supported in the press. Editor J. C. Morrill stated that an abolitionist "deserves instant death and it costs something to keep him a long time in jail or under surveillance." But conservative men like Judge Brown feared the "danger of great abuse" in such proceedings and hoped that "sober minded men" would join "to prevent rash action." As a precaution the watches were strengthened, and at Camden the older men organized themselves into the Bradley Guards. A resident of Arkansas County reported in late July that the slaves were still "pretty closely watched," but that "the fear of insurrection is nothing like as great here now as it was three months ago." In fact, he added, the slaves "have been more dutiful and have given their owners less trouble this season than usual in this section of the country."[22]

The same fears which prompted harsh actions against suspected insurrectionists also contributed to a stifling of political opinion. G. H. Kyle of Dallas County, a defeated conservative candidate for the convention, took to the press to deny charges that he was "an advocate for the Union too long." Refugee Alfred E. Mathews reported the instance of a man in Batesville who publicly declared he was still for the Union and was nearly hung. Joseph Harlinson of Brownsville had his head shaved for unspecified incendiary language. Nevertheless William Holtzman, during

Danley's absence, made an oblique attack on slavery in an editorial of the *Gazette* by suggesting that Southern unity could be best obtained if every free white man could be given one slave, and hence an economic interest in slavery.[23]

What pressure did not accomplish, propaganda did. Reports of the atrocities of Sigel's "lopeared Dutch" were invaluable for convincing the doubting that Union armies would not protect their rights. By mid-June it was reported that Union sentiment was "fast dying out." One newspaper correspondent observed, "Naught save peace and fraternity prevails in our section now. All former differences of opinion of politics and parties have entirely buried."[24]

Whatever harmony did exist soon disappeared. At the center of controversy was the Military Board. The convention-appointed generals, Bradley and Pearce, were soon in hot water. Bradley was never able to effectively exercise command. According to one account he ordered the abandonment of a scouting party and supplies. His troops, mostly original secessionists led by Colonel Patrick Cleburne, declared him deposed. Bradley appealed to the convention, but that body declined to interfere. Meanwhile the secessionist papers were highly critical. Des Arc editor J. C. Morrill said Bradley was "a drunkard, a coward, and incompetent in every respect." A court-martial was called in Little Rock to investigate the charges, but finally on the request of both parties, disbanded without taking action on the charges or restoring Bradley to command. Instead the Military Board called General James Yell into service and sent him to assume command at Pocahontas.[25]

Pearce, mustering his forces in northwest Arkansas, encountered similar hostility. It was claimed that his father-in-law owned the campsite and expected to collect $20,000 for its use. Pearce was held personally responsible for lack of tents and other supplies. When he rejected a company of mounted men allegedly because he had no arms for them, members of the company protested to the governor that the real reason for the rejection was their identity as original secessionists. In defense of Pearce it was claimed the men had "a personal feeling" against him, and a general meeting of officers cleared him of any blame. Nevertheless the assaults continued. Even as late as September prominent Democrat W. D. Reagan ran a card claiming Pearce was "without capacity or nerve enough to make a respectable third corporal."[26]

These manifestations of a lack of faith in the state commanders should have brought prompt corrective action from Confederate authorities. A. H. Garland, James Yell, and the visiting Indian commissioner, David Hubbard, all suggested that one or two Confederate commanders were needed, but until late June nothing was done. Brigadier General Ben McCulloch, ex-Texas ranger and Indian fighter, was the first Confederate general officer in Arkansas, but he had no authority beyond providing for the defense of Indian Territory. When McCulloch was in Little Rock in May, he was, according to General Yell, in "family" captivity the entire time, and Yell was unable to see him. McCulloch's report reflected the company he had been keeping. Without naming Governor Rector he asserted that state military supplies were "scattered over the state in every direction, without any method or accountability, and it is impossible to tell what has become of them."[27]

As Pearce and McCulloch mustered their forces in the northwest, C. C. Danley, the conservative board member, resigned on June 5, alleging the press of business, and headed for Richmond to tender the state army to the Confederacy. However upon his return the board refused to agree to the conditions and the troops remained in state service while Danley returned "to the den of his editorial malignancy to welter like a venomous toad in the loathsome slime of old political ulcers." Another conservative, Sam W. Williams, succeeded Danley on the board.[28]

The board, with Rector firmly in the saddle, was now devoted to the idea of a permanent state army. By contrast, both the *Gazette* and the *True Democrat* took the national position. In pointing out that the Military Board was violating the mandates of the convention by not turning over the troops, Johnson wrote: "It was never intended that we should have and maintain a separate state military organization." This was interfering with the Confederacy. "Is this foresight? Is it wisdom?" he asked. Yet Rector, in writing Secretary of War Walker made it clear that the board would turn the troops over to the Confederacy only if the troops personally approved the transfer and if the arms were to be used to defend Arkansas. When Walker promised only the "watchful care of the Government," Rector refused the transfer.[29]

Meanwhile the Confederacy, on June 25, belatedly ordered Brigadier General William J. Hardee to command all of Arkansas. His initial force, however, consisted only of Hindman's regiment. Hardee dallied and did not assume command until July 22. Meanwhile the unstable conditions in Missouri deteriorated further.[30]

Brigadier General Nathaniel Lyon in assuming command of the Union forces began vigorously pushing the Missouri State Guard southward. McCulloch, who had been considering offensive operations in Kansas, now joined forces with General Pearce, and, on June 29, issued a call for "every man" in Arkansas for three years or the war along with a new request to Richmond for arms. The Military Board met this affront by also issuing a call, for 10,000 troops, for only twelve months service, to rally at different points all over the state. The press, with Danley and Johnson leading the way, severely condemned Rector for this call. Danley reminded Rector that the board was intended to be merely "a subordinate auxiliary." Moreover the troops would be of no use scattered all over the state. The Van Buren *Press* claimed that the volunteers in that region would prefer going to McCulloch, but since the state was offering the lesser term, McCulloch received few recruits.[31]

While Governor C. F. Jackson and General Sterling Price were attempting to save Missouri with unarmed men against the determined advance of General Lyon, McCulloch, united with Pearce in northwest Arkansas, was also trying to get arms. Through formal and informal sources Richmond was warned that McCulloch was "in a very bad fix as regards arms," and "in great want of ammunition." McCulloch himself complained on July 9 that since his arrival he had received "neither arms nor ammunition."[32]

While the danger of a major battle in southwest Missouri mounted, part of the Arkansas troops continued to collect at Pocahontas and Pitman's Ferry in northeast Arkansas. According to Confederate military thinkers, this force would be strategi-

cally placed to operate either in defense of the Mississippi River to the east or to aid
McCulloch in the west. However, practically speaking, the location was flanked by
swamps on one side and mountains on the other, and northeast Arkansas proved to be
of no strategic importance throughout the war. When Hardee finally assumed
command on July 25, his command was "much in want of clothing of every
description, shoes, shirts, socks, pantaloons, and coats and hats." One battery had
no harness and no horses, and there was not enough transportation for field service.
Hence Hardee, good West Point officer that he was, settled down to perfect his
organization and informed Price that he could not aid in saving Missouri.[33]

Hardee's position was complicated by the agreement he entered into with the
Military Board on July 15, providing for the transfer of certain specified Arkansas
regiments, not including those raised under the call of June 30. Under the terms of
the agreement, the men had to approve or reject their transfer, and in the event a
majority of a company decided to reject transfer, the entire company disbanded.
Furthermore officers were not transferred with the men. The state commander at
Pocahontas, General Yell, "used every argument he was capable of using to prevent
them from entering the service of the Confederate States," as did General Burgevin.
After nearly half of the first regiment went home, members of the other four were
retained by the expedient of mustering them into the Confederate service before
Adjutant General Burgevin could reach them. As a result, Hardee's force was
depleted. Thus the first part of the transfer was something less than a success, and
Hardee, "badly equipped, and without discipline, without instruction, and without
transportation," remained idle throughout the summer.[34]

Before the transfer of the northwestern troops could take place, the battle of
Wilson's Creek (or Oak Hills) was fought. Price, Pearce, and McCulloch, the last
acting with reluctance and believing himself to be exceeding his instructions, moved
to meet Lyon at Springfield, but were attacked by Lyon instead. One of the bloodiest
battles of the entire Civil War resulted, ending in Lyon's death and the rout of his
army. However instead of following up the advantage, McCulloch and Pearce
withdrew into Arkansas. McCulloch did not consider Missouri his area of responsibility, distrusted Price and the discipline of his state forces, and lacked supplies.
Pearce's army was faced with expiring terms and the transfer problem. Thus Price
alone was left without adequate supplies to attempt the recapture of Missouri.[35]

The transfer of Pearce's troops after the battle created even more trouble than the
Pocahontas affair. According to Rector Pearce was to blame. Pearce on June 21
refused to let Inspector General Dandridge McRae swear in the troops and drove him
from camp. Had the swearing in taken place, Rector asserted, the troops could have
been transferred. Later, after the transfer agreement with Hardee had been reached,
N. B. Burrow was dispatched, accompanying the army into Missouri. However as
Hardee had no agent to receive the men and Pearce refused to let Burrow transfer
them, nothing was done. Pearce then marched the army back into Arkansas and
dismissed them. "The army had been turned loose, not discharged," Rector
claimed, "for not a solitary paper of the kind was given, within my knowledge."
Thus by September the victory army numbered eighteen men.[36]

Pearce's story, corroborated at various points by Hindman, McCulloch, and others, placed the blame for the disbanding solely on the Military Board. Pearce's position was that the men could be transferred without their approval, for the duration of their terms. Apparently that caused him to drive McRae from camp in June, although Rector's claim that swearing in the men would have made possible their transfer ran opposite to the board's official position at that time. After Hindman, Hardee's agent, arrived, Pearce appealed to the board to void the voting requirement, but the board remained adamant. Patriotic speeches by Hindman being of no avail, the troops refused transfer, ''like so much livestock,'' and disbanded, save for one company. A threat to lynch paymaster Ben T. Du Val was blocked by the timely arrival of board member B. C..Totten with the necessary funds to pay the troops. Totten's arrival also saved some arms, though many muskets had been carried home by disgusted soldiers. When word of the dissolution of the army reached Little Rock, the board decision was reversed on September 10, but by then the army was gone.[37]

Thus three months extensive preparations were annihilated in two weeks. Besides the eighteen men left in the northwest, Hardee had only 805 transferred out of the northeastern force. This unfortunate situation was attributable to various circumstances. First, the plan to move all the troops of Pearce's former command away from their homes, leaving northwest Arkansas unprotected, was highly unpopular. Second, the men had received no pay from the Military Board, and were in want of clothing of all kinds, an important consideration especially with winter approaching. Finally many naively believed the enemy beaten and the war over.[38]

While the air was hot with criminations and recriminations over the responsibility for the situation, the Federals secured hold of Missouri and insured victory in the war on the border. During this valuable time, efforts were made to get transferred the rest of the state army, the eight regiments (of the ten called) raised under the call of June 28. When Hardee tried to get Rector to include these men under the July 15 transfer agreement, Rector refused, saying that they were needed ''as a valuable body of reserve.'' Eventually the board changed its mind, and Colonel Jilson P. Johnson, an authorized agent for the Confederacy, received the men into Confederate service, though over the objections of Hardee who held that unarmed twelve month men could not be accepted.[39]

For the moment, though, the returning soldiers represented not a strategic disaster of the greatest magnitude, but the bronzed veterans of one of history's great campaigns. At Van Buren a huge barbecue was held. Over a trench fifty feet long, all kinds of meats were prepared to serve the hungry seated at tables three hundred feet long. The food was ''utterly routed with great slaughter.'' At Neosho Professors Adams' and Joblin's brass and string ensemble played for the military ball, featuring the Grand Overture—Totten's Lament—the Fancy Dances—Seigel's [sic] Quickstep and Soloman's Retreat—and ending with the Battle of Oak Hill Set-too.[40]

The men came home breathing fire toward the ''universally obnoxious military board'' and ''majors and colonels of mushroom growth.'' Furthermore they had little love for the Missourians. General Pearce had supplied Price with six hundred muskets before the battle, and not all of these were returned. In addition, many unarmed Missouri soldiers accompanying the march to Springfield fled at the start of the firing. Others had taken arms off the dead and wounded, to the disgust of the Arkansas soldiers. McCulloch had not concealed his dislike for Price or his distrust of the discipline of the Missouri forces; the Missourians for their part having received almost no aid or supplies from the South were left alone following McCulloch and Pearce's retreat into Arkansas. There was "but little cordiality of feeling between the two armies."[41]

The dissolution of the army left the Confederate and state authorities in a predicament. Arkansas, as of August, had only two regiments enrolled for the war. In great alarm various pleas were issued. McCulloch, with authorization from the Secretary of War, called for five regiments for three years or the war, three of whom were required to arm themselves, the other two to be armed by the Confederacy (from Pearce's former weapons). At the same time Secretary Walker requested Rector to assemble some ten or twelve regiments for McCulloch, but did not inform the governor of the authorization given McCulloch or specify that the men must be enrolled for three years or the war. Accordingly the Military Board issued a call for five regiments for one year, and, on August 9, Rector called for 3,000 men for General Hardee. Hardee, on his own authority, also directed Colonel Hindman to raise a brigade, either for twelve months or three years, out of the disbanded soldiers in the northwest. Finally late in October, when the Federal drive into Tennessee threatened, Governor Rector called for 10,000 men for General Albert Sidney Johnston.[42]

Meanwhile in September, Hardee was ordered by General Leonidas Polk, whom the Secretary of War had put in command of Arkansas without informing anyone, to march his force across the Mississippi. By the first of October Hardee was gone, leaving only a small command under Colonel Solon Borland at Pocahontas.[43]

The welter of calls brought little response. McCulloch was forced to change his call from three years to twelve months, and to meet even this request, Hindman offered to have the men he had raised counted as part of McCulloch's call if McCulloch would arm them with the old state weapons.[44]

The two calls of McCulloch did result in a serious conflict with Rector over state rights. Rector protested to McCulloch that all troop calls ought to be channeled through the governor. McCulloch's reply did nothing to smooth the governor's easily ruffled feathers, and Rector protested to the Secretary of War:

> My idea of the rights relatively belonging to the States and to the Confederate government is that those pertaining to the former were by no means abridged by the withdrawal from the old Confederacy and a union with the new government. This history of the United States, I believe, furnishes no precedent for the raising of men by proclamation emanating from generals commanding nor from the President. No example by authority ought to mar the text sheet of Confederate history.

Rector admitted he had not taken exception to McCulloch's earlier call in June, but claimed the precedent encouraged "illy-advised calls, discordant effort, confusion, contrariety of opinion, unsatisfactory results, and great waste and improvidence.''[45]

The various calls also resulted in a conflict over arms and terms of service. Rector made repeated efforts to get arms from his one year men, but the Confederate government remained adamant. Even in November, when Rector reported a Union invasion of Arkansas, the Secretary of War replied: ''I cannot give a single arm to any but troops mustered into the Confederate service for the war.'' General Albert Sidney Johnston, although desperately in need of men, finally ordered some of the men disbanded over protests from Rector and the Arkansas legislature.[46]

In justice to Rector it should be noted that a three year army could not be recruited. ''A mysterious lethargy has seized upon the minds of our people,'' the Van Buren *Press* reported. General Burgevin, though hardly a disinterested party, reported ''great apathy and want of spirit'' and ''a widespread disinclination to enter the service and particularly for a longer period than twelve months.'' Success, one correspondent reported, has ''lulled the masses into comparative indifference.''[47]

But Rector hoped to use this state of affairs to further his own pet scheme of having officers appointed by him go around recruiting, rather than having the men elect their leaders. Foremost on the list of those Rector hoped to thus reward was Edmund Burgevin. The ''family'' was more successful in securing positions, however. James B., and Jilson P. Johnson were colonels; Flournoy, Rust, Churchill, Reynolds, Pike, Cleburne, and Hindman benefited from ''family'' assistance.[48]

Autumn of 1861 witnessed expiration of the last round of volunteering. McCulloch's and Rector's calls continued to work at cross purposes, and McCulloch found it ''next to impossible to raise men for a longer time than twelve months.'' The disbanded soldiers proved poor recruits. Even Rector finally admitted: ''A man once in camp rarely takes service again.'' The *Daily State Journal* observed: ''Some half a dozen gentlemen have been trying for several weeks to organize companies, but it's no go.'' Arkansas remained virtually defenseless throughout the fall, causing Rector's paper to complain: ''The Confederate government has abandoned Arkansas to her fate.''[49]

Thus by winter Arkansas had actually lost ground. The immense outpouring of enthusiasm which greeted the war was neither properly caught nor efficiently channeled. In part this was true throughout the Confederacy, but Arkansas stands as an extreme example of official incompetence. The Secretary of War provided no general officer until much of the damage had been done, ignored the realities of geography by assigning Hardee to Pocahontas and then superseding Hardee with Polk across the Mississippi, and by his confusing orders caused needless conflict between national and state authorities. Intelligent and coordinated control was needed on the western front; the lesson of the first six months of war was that this control could not be issued piecemeal from Richmond. In the absence of an overall commander, each petty squabble had to be referred to the harried and inept Secretary Walker, whose sometimes unthinking responses, in turn, caused new problems. Finally the low priority in sending arms and munitions to aid the Missourians allowed the Federal government to take the necessary steps to counteract the results of the battle of Wilson's Creek while Confederate forces sat in idleness. Most authorities agree that if the South could have won her independence, she had to do it in that first year. Events in the west provide an indication of why such victory was not achieved, even though the opportunity was present.[50]

The summer and fall of 1861 witnessed a revival of the scramble for political office. Three ill-defined factions, the "family," the Rector men, and the former Unionists were active, but neither party lines nor public vehemence were as much in evidence as in past struggles. The months following the adjournment of the convention saw a subdued effort on the part of the "family" to regain control of the state. One *True Democrat* correspondent promised that "no man shall be elected who was not true to the state in March." Pointed barbs were exchanged between the *Gazette* and the *True Democrat* until their mutual animosity toward Governor Rector drew them together. But by fall the ex-Unionists and the old machine Democrats were again united against Rector. The state electoral slate, for instance, was the joint work of Jno. R. Eakin, R. H. Johnson, and C. C. Danley. Of the six electors, Edward Cross, W. W. Mansfield, and David Walker were conservatives; John A. Jordan, W. C. Bevins, and H. L Grinsted were "family." Governor Rector had no part in the selection.[51]

In November when the three conservatives either resigned or were unable to be in Little Rock, Rector made overtures to their constituents by appointing three more conservatives—Charles Bertrand, S. H. Tucker, and S. H. Hempstead—to fill the vacancies, a move which, according to the *True Democrat,* "created much surprise and no little comment here." Rector's paper, the recently established *Daily State Journal,* edited by Thomas C. Peek, attempted to construe the *True Democrat's* remarks into "the beginning of that bitter and endless persecution," and urged conservatives to support Rector. But it was for naught, and Rector continued in political isolation save for the company of those benefiting from his patronage.[52]

Under the new Confederate constitution, Arkansas was to elect in November four congressmen who were to replace the delegates selected by the convention. Each of the four districts was the scene of some political conflict. In the wake of the early successes which had attended the Confederate cause, original secessionists were generally victorious at the polls. In the first district, comprising northwest Arkansas, Felix Batson, a moderate secessionist, defeated former delegate H. F. Thomason. Curiously, ex-Unionist Thomason lost heavily in the extreme northwest counties where Union sentiment lingered the longest. In the second district, located in southwest Arkansas, secessionist Grandison D. Royston, with the endorsement of the Washington *Telegraph,* won handily over a score of candidates. In the fourth district Helena's Thomas B. Hanly easily defeated James Patterson. The third district, which included Pulaski County, was the scene of a vigorous battle between Jilson P. Johnson and former delegate A. H. Garland. Johnson "was one of the first to write his name on the roll of these who would run aloft the red flag," while Garland was "too bitter a Unionist." The race was close, and the results rested on the returns from Arkansas County. Governor Rector certified the first return even though the *True Democrat* claimed he knew it was incomplete. Garland was proclaimed elected, Rector had his revenge, and Johnson went to Richmond to protest the election.[53]

Meanwhile on call of the governor the legislature reassembled. The main purpose of this session was the selection of two Confederate senators. Editor Peek made every effort to encourage the legislature to support Governor Rector. He claimed that the "family" wanted this legislature dissolved and a new one elected, and that they sought the disfranchisement of ex-Union men. Peek also attacked the harmony between the *True Democrat* and the *Gazette,* who had "got to billing and cooing with each other like two suckling doves." The net effect of his activities, however, was to draw the two papers closer together.[54]

The legislature opened with an address by the governor. Since the Missouri legislature meeting at Neosho had just declared that state seceded and Price was on the Missouri River, Rector waxed eloquent over the state of affairs. "Arkansas," he said, "has no war, nor is likely to have, unless disaster should overtake the Confederate flag." The war bonds, although now greatly discounted, would be at a premium by January 1. The only legislation he called for was a reforming of the militia system, the abolition of the home guard ordinance, and the authority to raise special companies of Irish and Germans.

Rector took advantage of his opportunity to defend his past conduct, together with that of his associates, in the handling of military affairs. With his infinite capacity for never losing an argument, the governor proved at great length that the legislature now assembled had not been abolished by the convention, that they had the power under the Confederate constitution to elect two senators, that the convention had not possessed unlimited power, and that the creation of the Military Board was an act of "supererogation." Moreover he spoke of his critics in terms rarely if ever found in a gubernatorial address:

> More treason lurks in Arkansas, under the garb of patriotism, than most men conceive of. Libelous 'traduction' of its authorities, gloatingly sought for, and swallowed by snarling cormorants of newspaper filth, well attest this fact. The press—the freedom of the press—once the synonym of liberty,—now, the covert and insidious vehicle for undeveloped treason—the hypocritical defender of public justice—its calling, lowered to the dignity of mercenary avarice—a blessing to the people when guided by enlightened patriotism—a dire curse, when marked by malice and ignorance.

Danley and Johnson let this tirade pass in well-deserved silence, but continued their criticisms. Edmund Burgevin took offense at some of Danley's comments and attacked the editor through the columns of Peek's paper. Not satisfied with this, he challenged Danley to a duel, in violation of state law, with Governor Rector acting as second. "It has seldom, if ever," Danley observed, "been the lot of an editor to receive a challenge from as low a vagabond, or to have it borne by as high a public functionary." Since Burgevin had resorted to print, Danley claimed a violation of the code duello and refused to fight. Burgevin accused Danley of endeavoring "to cover his physical defects" while Danley replied that "no one who knows him, would expect any decent man to meet Burgevin as an equal."[55]

Thus the duel did not take place. Danley charged Rector with instigating the affair. "It was a bullying attempt to attack the liberty of the press, by overawing the editor, and thus preventing a free expression of opinion through the columns of the *Gazette.*" The *True Democrat* refrained from commenting, but the *Ouachita Conference Journal,* a religious papèr, commended Danley for his "noble moral courage in refusing the challenge to mortal combat."[56]

With no incentive from the governor or press to tackle the already present problems of collapse of law and order and civil government, runaway inflation, shortages of necessities, distressed soldiers' families, and war profiteering, the legislature played politics. When Rector found little support for his goals, Peek finally gave up his campaign to convert the legislators declaring that they were "completely Johnsonized." In return, in an alleged effort at economy, they abolished numerous appointive offices including Peek's position as Inspector of the Penitentiary. A bill to abolish the Military Board passed the house but was lost in the senate. On the other hand, the governor was empowered to call out the militia in case of invasion, and $25,000 was appropriated to arm the soldiers in Colonel F. A. Terry's command.[57]

Domestic measures enacted by the legislature were few. For the relief of the sick, wounded, and disabled volunteers, the legislature authorized a paltry $10,000. The economically-minded legislators also repealed the convention's war tax. Only with respect to the war bonds did the legislature take constructive action. Of the two acts passed, the first, "to facilitate the circulation of the Arkansas war bonds," required debtors to accept them at the penalty of not having any suit enforced until two years after the war. The second authorized the state treasurer to issue script ("pictorial promises to pay") in small denominations.[58]

Already peeved, Peek complained that a substantial portion of the legislature's work was "useless," and he was right. Much that needed to be done, and was done in later sessions, could have been accomplished in November. But with no leadership, the lethargy was understandable.[59]

The main action of this session was the election of two confederate senators. Robert W. Johnson and C. B. Mitchel were active candidates, although earlier it was said Mitchel wanted only "the privilege of shouldering his musket and marching with us to share our fate, our triumphs, and, if need be, our sorrows." Earlier it was said David Walker was being considered, while Albert Pike, who was "entirely willing Mitchel should sit in the Senate," allowed his name to be put forward "to please my friends." In the voting Johnson received sixty-seven votes; Mitchel forty-nine; Pike thirty-one; and Rector's friends, Yell and Burrow, thirteen and six respectively. Peek tried to take some credit for Mitchel's election by insisting that he was not a "family" candidate.[60]

Even as the legislature was adjourning, trouble was brewing for Arkansas. In November and December the state was rocked by the discovery that secret societies opposed to the war had formed in at least a half dozen northern counties. In some the militia was called out to deal with the offenders, while in others vigilance groups did the work. Variously known as the Peace Society, the Peace Organization Society, or in one case, the Pro Bono Publico Society, these bodies each had a constitution, an oath, a yellow ribbon or some such for identification, and passwords, one being "It's a dark night," — "Not so dark as it will be before morning." At least one legislator was involved in these potentially treasonous activities. Many were arrested and brought to Little Rock where the governor threatened them with treason trials if they did not enlist in the Confederate army. Estimates of membership in the movement ran as high as 1,700.[61]

Little evidence was presented to indicate that these men intended massive rebellion or jayhawking. One meeting held in Searcy County on November 25, 1861, resolved: "That the charge of conspiracy is a gross and palpable falsehood, and that we are ready at any time to take up arms against any body of robbers, North or South, and to maintain the peace of our country and the liberties of our citizens." A careful student of the movement concluded: "Their brotherhood was indigenous, composed of mountaineers who had no intention of going to war on either side and who wanted to be left alone."[62]

The press tried to hush up the affair by suggesting that the men were merely misled by abolition agents and troublemakers. According to the *True Democrat*, "there was a great deal of mischievous humbuggery in it about the rich and poor, an attempt to array non-slaveholders against slaveholders." But the editor refused to believe that the backwoods men were treasonous: "Most of them were so ignorant that they did not know what the objects of it were." A Little Rock grand jury agreed two months later when those who had refused to enlist were brought to trial.[63]

But the suspicion lingered. One Izard County resident disagreed with the attempts to minimize the significance of the societies or the innocence of their motives:

> When I and several other gentlemen raised the *stars and bars* here, these very men threatened to come and pull them down. When the news came last summer, as it first did, that Price and McCulloch were beaten at Oak Hills, these very men threw up their hats and hurrahed for the United States of America. When I and others were canvassing this country last summer for Col. McCarver's regiment, these men would not come out even to hear us speak nor muster—they swore that they would never muster under the d—d nigger flag, but if any one would just come along with the stars and stripes that they would arise at midnight and go to it, and they would fight for it too when they got there. They plead ignorance now, [*but*] I have traded with these men for six years and I defy any man to overreach them in a trade.[64]

Whatever the motives, the efforts of the Confederates to stamp out the peace societies, although reasonably lenient, converted some Arkansians from neutrality to Unionism. Loyalists forced into the Confederate army were prone to desert. Others, fearing for their lives, took to the woods or fled to Union lines. The discovery of deepseated alienation in Arkansas, the first such discovery in the Confederacy, set the stage for the long, vicious, and brutal war of personal vendettas that followed.[65]

The fall of 1861 was productive of yet another conflict between Governor Rector and the military authorities. In early November, Colonel Solon Borland at Pocahontas feared himself threatened by Union forces located in southeast Missouri. Borland, always excitable, called on the local militia to assist him. Although the Military

Board subsequently renewed the order, Rector protested vigorously that Borland's call was a usurpation of the governor's authority. Borland replied that he had not ordered out the militia, but merely invited their services.[66]

In late November, perhaps emboldened by this first encounter, Borland issued another order, this time proclaiming martial law. Citing as the cause the tremendous inflation (e.g., salt went from $2-5 a sack to $20). Borland's order forbade the exportation or monopolization of necessities. Enforcement would consist in the arresting of violators and the seizing of goods.[67]

Both the *True Democrat* and the *Gazette* supported Borland's move, but they were in the minority. The Washington *Telegraph* led the chorus of complaint, warning that Borland's action was "dangerous as a precedent, however excusable on account of its particular circumstances." Protests were made to the governor, and Rector, as might be expected, was in a high dudgeon. He protested to the Secretary of War and issued his own proclamation to "annul, set aside, revoke, and countervoke," Borland's order. There was an ominous tone in his assertion that "repeated acts of insult, injustice, and wrong have by the subordinate officers of the Confederate States been contumaciously and without provocation insultingly offered to the State of Arkansas." The War Department revoked Borland's order, and the Colonel, on plea of sickness, soon retired to practice medicine in Little Rock.[68]

However Borland's removal did not abate the inflation or retard the speculators. Alive to the situation, the press criticized those Memphis speculators who had been buying up Arkansas produce at pre-war prices, fully aware that since before the war Arkansas had been a food importer, prices were sure to rise. According to Danley, "from the beginning of the war the country has been infested with a set of unprincipled, soulless speculators, who have traversed almost every settlement." The result, Johnson reported in March, 1862, was that "Memphis has drained a portion of Arkansas of her means and subsistence. That city has been a huge leech fastened on the side of our state sucking its life blood and never satisfied." Little Rock felt the pinch. Peek reported:

> Everything in the eating line is unusually scarce in this city, and lamentably high. It is almost impossible to procure sufficient provisions and groceries for the most ordinary demand, and our dealers cannot get anything from other points on account of the suspension of navigation.[69]

As economic woes mounted, military affairs continued to drift. General Hardee, taking many of the Arkansas soldiers, had left the state never to return. McCulloch put his troops in winter quarters and went to Richmond to explain why Confederate success at Wilson's Creek had been followed by retreat. Relations were very strained between Price and President Davis, as the project to appoint West Pointer Harry Heth to command the west was dashed by a combination of Missouri and Arkansas oppositions. Such opposition was only to be expected. Senator Johnson said: "I will support the bitterest enemy on earth I have before I will support a non-resident to take charge of our Arkansas troops." Editorials in a variety of western papers all emphasized the importance of the west in deciding the ultimate outcome of the war, but malignant neglect continued to characterize Richmond's policy.[70]

This neglect fed the fires of Rector's desire to direct the course of the war in Arkansas. No longer having a state army, he now issued orders in January for the militia to muster.

No sooner did the news get out than reports of insubordination began to arrive in Little Rock. In Clark County over two-thirds of the men refused to muster, claiming that by recent law they could not be fined for nonattendance. In the northwest some fled to the mountains. In Van Buren and Fort Smith there was "a flat refusal to turn out." Class antagonisms came to the fore as it was reported that "the more cultivated, polished, and refined are those who avoid militia service." And all through Arkansas there were "a good many long faces," all blaming the governor, not only for the inconvenience, but also for not being able to get in their winter plowing. Rector, the Helena *Southern Shield* decided, "has shown himself a miserable apology for a high public functionary."[71]

By early spring it was clearly apparent that Rector's scheme had failed. Resistance by the men and the inability to provide an organized commissary doomed the effort. In addition Confederate authorities interfered, and conscription, either state or Confederate, was in the offing.

While Rector's militia scheme was hatching, a new general officer, Mississippian Major General Earl Van Dorn, on January 16, 1862, was assigned to command the Trans-Mississippi, a region defined as Indian Territory, Louisiana north of the Red River, Arkansas, and most of Missouri. Van Dorn, who was to bring so much disaster to Arkansas, was a West Point man, a friend of Jefferson Davis, and in the particulars of his person not unlike Arkansas's T. C. Hindman. Both were diminutive and compensated for this supposed deficiency by feats of great daring. Both were extremists before the war; both met violent ends as a result of their indiscretions. Van Dorn's biographer describes him as a "rash young commander with a one-dimensional mind," certainly not the ideal leader or the best kind of mind to control the dashing but frequently impractical Sterling Price.[72]

Upon assuming command, with headquarters again inappropriately placed at Pocahontas, Van Dorn called on Rector for ten regiments: if armed, for twelve months; if not, for the war. To fill this call the Military Board divided the state into districts, each with a prescribed quota. State conscription was threatened if volunteering proved slack. For encouragement the *True Democrat* predicted that the war would end in six months "if the people of the South will rise as one man."[73]

While Van Dorn was organizing his command, the pressure of economic problems prompted Governor Rector to call the legislature into special session. Only five senators and fifteen representatives showed up for the opening session on March 6, 1862; not until the 17th could a quorum be assembled. Despite the tardiness, this session proved the most productive wartime meeting. Among the important items were laws preventing the distillation of liquor, stopping the sale of public lands, authorizing county courts to levy taxes to aid the poor, limiting cotton production to two acres per hand, and defining sedition as any effort to impair volunteering.[74]

The most far-reaching of the new acts was that dealing with cotton. All during the winter the press sought to show planters that excessive cotton production only invited enemy attack, that a short crop would mean high prices when the ports opened, and that the salvation of the army depended on adequate foodstuffs. Even Governor Rector privately stated: "Cereals should be grown exclusively, cotton *abolished.*" But the planters thought otherwise and went about planting cotton as usual. Their response to the new law was not encouraging either. Some were actively planning to resist it, and editor Johnson warned that "infinite mischief" would result from such actions. Others were said to be planning or pursuing trade with the enemy. In Federally occupied New Orleans it was reported that seventy-five bales were received from Bayou Bartholomew.[75]

The legislature also took under advisement the proper organization of the state military effort. Danley, in fact, feared that Rector's motive in summoning the special session was to revive his state army. But even if that had been the case, the legislators showed little regard for Rector's sensibilities. They proceeded to virtually abolish the old militia system and instituted a new one, appropriating $75,000 to finance the change. Rector waited until the legislators adjourned, allowed the bill to die for want of his signature, and took the $75,000 to finance the current system. His move excited considerable comment, but nothing could be done.[76]

While paper bullets were falling on the head of the governor, hot lead rained elsewhere in Arkansas. Upon arrival Van Dorn drew up an elaborate plan to rescue Missouri and turn around the war in the west. McCulloch was to move his force to Pocahontas, leaving Brigadier General Albert Pike's Indians and Price's Missourians to guard southwest Missouri. Van Dorn and McCulloch would drive toward St. Louis, to be joined by Price en route. However before anything could develop along these grandiose lines, Price was rudely driven out of Missouri. Since the battle of Wilson's Creek, Price had moved north, capturing Lexington and picking up many recruits, for whom he still lacked arms. During the winter it proved too difficult to supply his army on the Missouri River, so he returned to Springfield. Here he was attacked by Brigadier General Samuel Curtis with over 12,000 men, and was forced to flee into northwest Arkansas followed by Curtis. Accordingly, Van Dorn ordered Price, McCulloch, and Pike to concentrate in northwest Arkansas.[77]

The combined Confederate army attacked Curtis at Pea Ridge (Elkhorn Tavern) on March 6, 1862. Despite some brave fighting, the Federal army won a notable victory in this the "Gettysburg of the West." Generals Ben McCulloch, James McIntosh and William Slack were killed, adequate munitions were lacking, and most of all, Van Dorn's battle plan (which called for dividing his forces) were defective. Confederate forces fell back toward the Arkansas River, but the Union army showed little sign of wanting to pursue.[78]

The defeat at Pea Ridge signaled the abandonment of Arkansas by the Confederacy. Pike, robbed of supplies and insulted by Van Dorn, returned to Indian Territory; the Confederate army moved down the Arkansas River to Little Rock and on to the Mississippi to aid in stopping Grant. The removal of large quantities of supplies and equipment including the machinery at the arsenal suggested that they might not come back.[79]

This second abandonment of Arkansas did not at first alarm Governor Rector. Writing at the time a "candid" letter to South Carolina Governor Francis W. Pickens, Rector criticized Jefferson Davis for "undertaking an impossibility—a defensive warfare," and of lacking "a systematic and well digested plan" involving cooperation between the states and the general government. But he made no mention of the abandonment of the Trans-Mississippi.[80]

Meanwhile the Federal army turned east following a leisurely route along White River, occupying Batesville on May 4, and foraging further south. The press advised massive guerrilla warfare, but stronger measures were obviously needed. On April 15, the congressional delegation wrote Davis calling attention to the state of affairs, asking that either Bragg or Price be appointed to command in the west, and requesting return of supplies and soldiers that had been moved from Arkansas. Rather than take the requested action, Davis temporized, and in a less than honest move, told Van Dorn to issue a reassuring statement which Price was supposed to endorse. Price, however, perceived the deception and headed for Richmond. Arkansas continued in isolation.[81]

The abandonment of Arkansas gave Rector his opportunity, which the governor used to issue a proclamation. He called for all men to turn out for state service, promising that they would not be transferred to the Confederacy. He also threatened to "build a new ark and launch it on new waters" if Confederate neglect continued.[82]

Reaction to this threat of state secession was immediate and hostile. "We apprehend that few will follow," wrote editor Johnson. The Washington *Telegraph*, which refused to print the message, stated that the idea of picking quarrels with the Confederacy was "hair splitting" and the notion of state secession "ungrateful and foolish." One month later Van Dorn assured Davis that the people indignantly rejected the governor's "pernicious opinions," and that Rector "stood almost alone."[83]

Rector's proclamation did not stop the Union advance for by May Curtis was within fifty miles of Little Rock. Fearing the imminent fall of the capital. Rector conceived it to be his duty to remove the offices of state and the archives. At first he planned to send the latter on board ship via Memphis and Fulton to Washington. He was dissuaded from this plan (which might have led to the capture of the records since the fall of Memphis was pending), and sent them up river to Dardenelle instead, whence they were carried in uncovered wagons to Hot Springs. Meanwhile Brigadier General (and ex-Governor) J. S. Roane, left in command by Van Dorn, stopped some Texas companies headed east and declared martial law. This defense saved Little Rock for the time being and gave editor Johnson a magnificent opportunity to embarrass Rector. "We would be glad if some patriotic gentlemen would relieve the anxiety of the public by informing it of the locality of the State government," Johnson wrote. "The last that was heard of it here, it was aboard the steamer *Little Rock* about two weeks ago, stemming the current of the Arkansas River." When Rector returned at the end of May after the Federal threat had receded and the state archives were safe, he was quite angry, attacking Johnson for "misrepresentations of my acts'' and promised ''to defend the government of this state against its *internal and external foes.*'' Johnson replied that a properly arranged tribunal should investigate this implied charge of treason. After more heated exchanges, Rector challenged Johnson to a duel. Rector's second, the ubiquitous Burgevin, quibbled over the choice of weapons and finally ended the correspondence. Once again the governor got the worst of a confrontation with the press. Editor Johnson, who it was said had also made arrangements for leaving if the Federals occupied Little Rock, concluded: ''Had everyone followed the example set by our governor, Arkansas would now be a Federal province instead of an independent state.''[84]

While the governor and the editor were having their little ''set to,'' Brigadier General Thomas Carmichael Hindman, under orders issued by General Beauregard on May 31, 1862, assumed command in Arkansas. The state needed a savior. Federal troops were still thirty-five miles away from Little Rock. Loyalist recruits were flocking into Batesville, depredations of all kinds were going on throughout North Arkansas, civil government was in collapse, and a critical food shortage existed. If Arkansas was even to remain in the Confederacy, vigorous efforts had to be made immediately. Governor Rector had neither the ability nor the support to fill the need. Hindman, however, was of a different stamp. As Judge Brown noted: ''He is determined to make his mark for weal or for woe.''[85]

7)
The Second
Year of
the War

Arkansas: "A grave of ambition,
energy, and system."
—T.C. Hindman to Braxton Bragg,
February 14, 1863,
O.R., LIII, 848.

It would be pleasing to assume that the appointment of T. C. Hindman to command in Arkansas reflected a realization by Richmond of the significance of the west. But such was not the case. Hindman's appointment was secured by Senator Johnson, who went to Beauregard and got Hindman transferred to Arkansas, even though, as it developed, Beauregard's authority did not extend across the Mississippi. Curiously on the same day that Hindman received his orders, Richmond assigned Gen. J. B. Magruder to the same command, thus laying the foundation for a simmering controversy over the legality of Hindman's subsequent actions.[1]

Hindman was well aware of the need for strong measures. The continued complaints from the Missouri and Arkansas congressional delegations had been met by President Davis with bland assurances that troops fought better away from home, that home defense was "a fatal error," and that the Confederacy must be "one united body"—all perfectly true, but all entirely irrelevant to the pressing needs of Arkansas and Missouri. Such an attitude made it apparent to Hindman that Arkansas could not be saved with letters addressed to the War Department. Moreover the impending fall of Memphis signaled the end of Confederate control of the Mississippi, and make Arkansas's isolation physical as well as spiritual.[2]

Hindman's initial efforts showed that he did not lack enthusiasm or vigor for the task. At Memphis he obtained a few weapons and impressed one million dollars from the banks. Other supplies, some condemned, were appropriated from depots at Grenada, Jackson, and Columbus. At Helena he raided the stores, confiscating medicine, ammunition, and clothing, which he loaded on some steamboats he "captured" (before they could fall into Federal hands), and brought this precious cargo to Little Rock.[3]

When Hindman reached the capital the situation was not encouraging. Federal troops were at Searcy, and General Roane had only 1,200 men, many unarmed, to oppose them. Governor Rector was trying to create another state army, and had issued his proclamation about starting a new ark. Although Hindman did not have the authority to raise an army, that did not stop him. Governor Rector's skeleton state army he took by the expedient of threatening to conscript every man and impress all supplies. Under his orders stores of all kinds were taken from the citizens and even books from the State Library were appropriated to abtain paper for making cartridges. Eight old guns which were planted in the ground as corner posts were dug up and mounted. Manufactures were established to supply deficiencies. Cotton was seized and burned to prevent it from falling into the hands of the enemy.[4]

Hindman knew that he was on dubious legal ground, although as yet he had no reason to suspect the legitimacy of his appointment. Within a few weeks after his arrival he outlined to the War Department both his situation and the powers he needed to save Arkansas. He requested the right to negotiate loans, appoint, promote, and dismiss inferior officers, and to assume extralegal powers. No answer was received, so he continued his policy. Martial law was established throughout the state, including the use of a passport system. The permission of the provost marshal general was required to leave the state. Confederate money was to be received at par, and prices of over thirty-four items ranging from Ipecac to cornmeal were established. All white males not subject to conscription were to be organized as provost guards, and summary punishment would be extended to violators of the new rules, and to draft evaders, gamblers, vagrants, and illegal sellers of liquor. Finally an enrolling officer in each county would collect all the cotton in private hands and store it at least twenty miles from a navigable stream, to be destroyed upon the approach of an enemy.[5]

Meanwhile he still faced the immediate threat of Gen. Curtis. As Hindman slowly collected an army, he used spies and agents to fill Curtis's ears with rumors of considerable Confederate reinforcements. Curtis, harassed flank and rear by partisans, drew back. Although the Federal situation seemed to improve when the fall of Memphis and Helena gave the Union gunboats the ability to reach Curtis, the Confederates succeeded in minimizing this advantage when a lucky shot passed through the boilers of the *Mound City,* killing over half her crew. General Albert Rust was ordered to cut off Curtis's army and burn all cotton which lay within Federal reach. Rust, however, was unsuccessful, his soldiers not always too willing to fight, and Curtis made good his escape to Helena, looting as he went.[6]

With Curtis isolated at Helena, Hindman worked to consolidate his position. He organized the enforcement of the conscript act, established manufactures, including an elaborate chemical plant at Arkadelphia, and attempted to put the state on a war footing. But his abrasive, dictatorial ways created a host of enemies, when "a kindlier course might have resulted more happily."[7]

Hindman also took steps to quiet dissatisfaction within the army. Unpaid, unarmed, unclothed, and occasionally unfed, men had deserted in droves to Curtis. When a small mutiny involving the effort by some sixty men to march off en masse was discovered, nine of those involved were shot without trials on Hindman's orders. Open manifestations of dissatisfaction ceased.[8]

In an attempt to give legal status to the partisans who had so effectively harassed Curtis, Hindman issued his famous Order Number 17, authorizing the formation of independent companies of irregulars. The Confederacy gave sanction to guerilla warfare which characterized the last years of the war. Guerillas, generally without supervision, coordination, or purpose, made life miserable and finally impossible for noncombatants. That the notorious ruffian Quantrill should have been commissioned by the Confederacy, shows how far the ideals of chivalry had been eroded by 1862.[9]

Hindman was less successful in dealing with civilian discontent. Although supported by both the *Gazette* and the *True Democrat,* martial law, the passport system, conscription, and especially the orders for the seizure of all cotton aroused considerable hostility among all classes of citizens. Senator Mitchel made a special trip to Little Rock to get the cotton order modified, but discontent on the other issues rankled. Eakin of the Washington *Telegraph,* a strict constitutionalist and a firm patriot, never criticized Hindman by name, but the drift of editorials entitled "Stability not Tyranny" could hardly be missed. Eventually Eakin consented to print the letters of Gen. Albert Pike which not only mentioned Hindman by name but also contained some of the most violent vilification ever seen in Arkansas. Pike, in command of Indian Territory, had been systematically robbed first by Van Dorn and then by Hindman of the supplies he had accumulated for his Indians. When Hindman ventured to declare martial law in Indian Territory and to issue Pike direct orders, Pike exploded, first to the War Department, and then to the press. Pike pointed out that when Borland attempted martial law in only a limited area, he had been removed and even possibly tried for the offense. Yet nothing had been done about Hindman. "The distance on the road to slavery that we have traveled since then is immeasurable." Pike went on to attack the provost marshals: "Like a triple-headed Deity, he wears the robe of the Senator and the ermine of the Judge, and wields the bloody fasces of the Lector at once." Pike especially denounced violations of due process of law.

> By now a General, seizing in one hand the fortunes, and in the other the lives of loyal men, declares it treason for a loyal citizen to conceal his own lawful property, to prevent its unnecessary and wanton distruction [*sic*], and stamps with both his feet on the whole constitution and all the law at once, and men sneak about and only dare to speak of it in whispers, lest the Provost Marshal should arrest, imprison and punish them for disaffection to the Confederacy.

Pike then sent in his resignation, and issued a circular explaining his action and criticizing the Confederate authorities. Col. D. H. Cooper, claiming Pike was either insane or a traitor, arrested him. Hindman endorsed Cooper's action. The upshot of all this turbulence was a War Department order on July 16, which placed Theophilus Hunter Holmes in command of the Trans-Mississippi Department over Hindman.[10]

Holmes was a North Carolinian and a close personal friend of Jefferson Davis. According to William Preston Johnston, an aide to the president, Holmes had given satisfaction in North Carolina and Davis trusted him not to be taken in by Gen. Sterling Price. Some political maneuvering surrounded his appointment, as Gen. Magruder, who it will be recalled had been appointed to this command at an earlier date, told Davis that Homes did not want to go but that the Missouri delegation had expressed a desire for Magruder. "Yes," answered the President, "because you assured them you would not interfere with Price, but would give him his own way.

They care nothing for *you* General, It is Price they wish for.'' Holmes got the appointment.[11]

This faith in Holmes' abilities proved unjustified. Although he remained in command from August, 1862, until after the fall of Little Rock in September, 1863, criticism of his performance was constant. The most damning indictment came from Bishop Henry C. Lay, who characterized Holmes, his parishioner, as "an easy old soul" who "appreciated soul questions," who cried during religious services, and who at forty-seven was "a very old man" with "memory, will, judgment all debilitated to a degree which incapacitates him for any efficient administration."[12]

Equally uncomplimentary were the appraisals of the soldiers who served "old Granny," as they liked to call him. One Rebel described Holmes as "a poor excuse for a man and a General," while another rated him "the ugliest old mortal in one hundred miles of here." Six months after his arrival in Arkansas, one paper suggested that he "relax his wearied mind by dragging his 'sexagenerian' limbs through the mazy dance. In justice we must add, that Gen. Holmes is a man of most excellent heart, kind disposition and a gentleman in all things, and it is not his fault that he is not a General."[13]

Holmes' mission, as Davis informed him, was to correct Hindman's abuses "as rapidly as is consistent with the defense of the country." Instead Holmes fell under the spell of the dynamic younger man whom he supplanted. To Davis he wrote that the much assailed provost marshal system "had the effect of restoring order."[14]

Thus allied with Hindman, Holmes was unable to resolve peacefully the Pike problem. Upon his arrival in Arkansas, Holmes had given Pike a leave of absence pending the arrival of official acceptance of his resignation. But when the War Department continued to address him as if he were in command, Pike decided to resume command in Indian Territory, and Holmes ordered his arrest for treason, this time by Gen. J. C. Roane, a bitter personal enemy. Pike continued to hammer away at martial law and Holmes' failure to stop it. "What is now called martial law," he wrote on October 25, "is what has been known for many ages as a *favorer* and advocate of High Treason, an apologist for usurpation, and the parasite of odious tyranny." Pike was eventually released, but his string of public letters, pamphlets, and protests continued well into 1863 and did the Confederacy little good. Like Vice President A. H. Stephens, Pike did not believe in the sacrifice of one particle of personal freedom in the name of military necessity.[15]

Militarily new danger threatened the state from the northwest. Although Hindman's initial efforts succeeded in forcing Curtis into relative uselessness at Helena, new Federal efforts followed. Following Curtis's withdrawal, that region together with most of western Missouri, was the battleground between Federal regular and state militia and Confederate irregulars and small detachments. During the fall Hindman reorganized the Confederate forces and prepared for another campaign. The Federals, operating out of Springfield, had two main armies under Generals J. G. Blunt and F. J. Herron. Northwest Arkansas was again reoccupied. While it was claimed that Judge Walker was captured and took the oath of allegiance, it was true that John Ross, the Cherokee chief, and many of his people deserted and went over to the Union side.[16]

In the emergency, Hindman, who remained in Arkansas as Holmes' subordinate, made rapid efforts to improve the Confederate position. Many Indians were fed from government stores, and Indian territory was reorganized in the wake of Pike's departure. By early fall the Union forces were falling back toward Springfield. The Confederate Cherokees met and deposed Ross, electing Stand Watie chief. But Hindman was not content. Competent strategist that he was, he perceived that the best defense of Arkansas could be made in Missouri. Holmes, however, was of another stripe. Hindman got permission from the reluctant Holmes to offer battle only on the condition that he would return to Little Rock regardless of the outcome. This proviso, together with the severe shortage of food, munitions, and clothing including shoes made the Prairie Grove campaign of dubious utility even in the event of overwhelming victory.[17]

Hindman's plan, to defeat Blunt's army before Herron's could come to its assistance, was sound in its conception, but failed in the execution, with the result that Hindman ended up fighting a defensive battle against the combined armies. The Confederate and Union troops fought to a standoff at Prairie Grove, south of Fayetteville, on December 7, 1862. Most of the troops fought well, but shortages of food and munitions gave Hindman no incentive to continue the fighting. The next day the long and laborious retreat down the Boston Mountains began. Initially at least the battle was considered a Confederate victory. One officer wrote: "Had General Hindman one week's supply on hand at the battle of Prairie Grove, he would not have been satisfied with defeating but would have annihilated that whole force." As a result of Hindman's withdrawal and the subsequent dispersion of his forces, the Federals reaped the fruits of a victory which they never earned on the battlefield. For a second time the inability of the Confederate forces to be properly armed and supplied proved to be a bigger obstacle than the enemy.[18]

After Prairie Grove Hindman's army fell to pieces. The depression of morale resulting from the failure of the campaign was enhanced by a Federal raid on Van Buren in which five hundred new Enfield rifles and a large quantity of corn were lost. Only by massive furloughs was Hindman able to maintain even the semblance of an army. His name became for the soldiers a symbol of failure and defeat. Hindman, the *Patriot* said, was

> universally unpopular in the State, and not much loved by the army; uncertain as a politician, and incompetent as an officer; foisted upon us through the favoritism, it is said, of the President and the influence of a former political and private enemy. Hindman has been weighed, and found wanting.[19]

Before Hindman's star began its rapid plunge Arkansas witnessed the tortuous political death of Henry Massie Rector. Following the embarrassing flight of Rector's government, Danley and Johnson carried to the supreme court a *mandamus* proceeding against the sheriff of Pulaski County for failing to list the gubernatorial office in the fall election notice. Although Rector hotly protested this action, and although it was claimed that the majority of the members of the convention had no knowledge or desire to cut two years from Rector's term, the legal decision was a foregone conclusion. A new governor would have to be elected in October.[20]

Undaunted Rector announced his intention of running. A circular supporting his views and attacking those of his critics was distributed. In it Rector claimed that the supreme court decision in the mandamus ruling was known on the streets before being officially announced, that he was "grossly misrepresented" by the press in "their toadyism for everything Confederate, begot by remote expectations of small jobs of public printing from Richmond," and that his removal of the state government saved Little Rock from Federal capture because "there was nothing to come for." Since only the Camden *Herald* supported him, another Rector paper, the *Patriot,* was founded in Little Rock with James D. Butler, a long time job printer, as publisher, but with no editor listed.[21]

Meanwhile the "family" and conservatives caucused, and agreed on the nomination of Colonel Harris Flanagin. Formerly a Whig, Flanagin was a conservative secessionist of unimpeachable political background. His position was strengthened by the fact that he was serving in the army in Tennessee. A public letter, signed by such diverse and previously hostile political antagonists as T. C. Hindman, Elias N. Conway, William E. Woodruff, and C. C. Danley, served as his nomination.[22]

A third candidate, James S. H. Rainey, was offered by his friends at Camden, and supported by the Camden *Eagle*. The *Eagle* attempted (one must suppose) to stir up debate by asking the other candidates "whether, at public elections, should the votes of faction predominate by internal suggestions, or the bias of Jurisprudence?" Colonel Rainey, it added, has "promptly and unqualifiedly endorsed this clause." Nothing came of the *Eagle's* query.[23]

The campaign was waged mostly in the press. "Family" dictation, war expenses, Rector's flight from Little Rock, the transfer problems in 1861, and a few other issues were discussed. The *Ouachita Herald* asserted of Flanagin: "His patronymic is O'Flanagin; and his descent directly from the original Patrick O'Flanagin of Derry, county Connaught, Ould Ireland," and suggested he was a Yankee. Among the prominent political figures, only outcast General Yell announced for Rector.[24]

Although Union forces prevented the holding of elections in Phillips, Monroe, Greene, and Mississippi Counties, the balloting was surprisingly heavy. Flanagin received 18,187 votes to Rector's 7,419 and Rainey's 708. Thus Harris Flanagin, who was said not to have known of his nomination until after the election, was called to the direction of state affairs. Before Flanagin was inaugurated, the new legislature convened and heard an address from the governor culminating in his resignation. Thomas Fletcher, president of the senate, was sworn in on November 4 and served until the 15th.[25]

In another interesting development it was soon discovered that the entire election of the state senate had been in error. Governor Rector in his announcement of the election in the summer had stated that all senate seats were to be filled, whereas the constitution stated that only half were to have been up for election. When Oliver H. Oates, a former member of the senate, was elected secretary of state, it was pointed out that the constitution forbade the senate from electing one of their number to political office. The case went to the supreme court wherein it was resolved that the new constitution had vacated all office holders; therefore Oates was not really a senator, and hence his election was legal. However the *obiter dicta* in the decision suggested that half the senate lacked constitutional sanction.[26]

The election of the conservative Flanagin was matched by conservative gains in the legislature. Although little open campaigning took place, men of conservative leanings found ways to let the public know they were not original secessionists or friends of T. C. Hindman. This conservative resurgence manifested itself strongly after the new legislature assembled in November. One Confederate senator had to be chosen, since the term drawn by Robert Ward Johnson in November, 1861, was for only two years. The year before Johnson had led in the balloting; now he encountered strong opposition. His challenger was A. H. Garland, the dubious winner over Jilson P. Johnson in the contested congressional race the previous year. Rector's former paper, the *Patriot,* launched a bitter attack on Senator Johnson, indicting his complicity in the seizure of the Fort Smith arsenal, his role in getting Hindman appointed, and "his easy, weak, insinuating tone and manner." In the candidates' addresses to the legislature, Johnson was on the defensive, while Garland, with no past sins to defend, echoed Pike with a "manly and patriotic defense of civil law and liberty against military rule and oppression."[27]

On the twelfth ballot Johnson finally won. But the legislature, in an almost unheard of action, took the public printing away from Johnson and Yerkes and gave it to Eakin and Etter of the *Telegraph.* In another strike at Johnson and Hindman the legislature passed a resolution condemning "illegal acts" and asking that they be set aside and annulled. Flanagin, however, refused to sign the resolution on the ground that it promoted disharmony. In another conservative action, the legislature chartered Judge Brown's Camden Merchants and Planters Insurance Company to do business as a bank. Flanagin vetoed this too, on the ground that the charter provided no safeguards and that too much money was already in circulation.[28]

The new legislature sought to alleviate some of the problems caused by war. It declared all able-bodied men liable for patrol duty and authorized the indefinite imprisonment of suspects if conditions made a trial impossible. Furthermore, it suspended all criminal and civil suits until the end of the war and provided that land sold for taxes could be redeemed within two years after the war's end. It appropriated $300,000 to assist persons in manufacturing cotton cards and iron works, and allocated $1,200,000 to aid the indigent and hungry of northwest Arkansas. It also extended the prohibition against distillation of liquor and suspended collection of revenue. Thus the state government recognized its responsibility and enacted legislation to meet it.[29]

The twofold aim of civil government during wartime was to preserve the internal peace and promote the welfare in accordance with military needs. Arkansas did not oppose the general government, as did North Carolina and Georgia, but neither did the state assist the Confederacy by adequately protecting and providing for civilians. The constant pressure put on military authorities to assume extra-legal powers reflected a situation in which, by 1863, in most of the state travel was dangerous, farming hazardous, and county government inoperative.

Equally critical to the law and order problem was the food situation. The military made the only efforts at price control, first with Hindman's tariffs in the summer of 1862, and again in the fall with new orders issued by General Holmes. These were the subject of considerable complaint on both practical and constitutional grounds and appear to have been ineffective. Poor harvests, bad transportation (especially after the Federals gained control of the Mississippi), and high prices for such necessities as salt hurt soldier families at home, whose complaints when relayed to the menfolk lowered morale and led to desertions. The counties had been authorized to aid these families, but county government tended to disappear in the northwest and east after Curtis's invasion. Moreover counties had little money and lacked the power to organize relief on a general basis. The state made large grants on paper to look after the needy, but suspension of revenue collection deprived the state funding while reliance on county officials to carry it out led to a situation which by late 1863 one critic described as "impossible."[30]

In addition, the general welfare was far too often sacrificed to private profit. A spirit of speculation abounded after 1862 and infested the inner sanctums of government. One soldier wrote his wife that the man entrusted with the state appropriation for the indigent was planning to "borrow" the money and buy cotton cards, sell them at a considerable profit, and then replace the money, having made "something thereby." The correspondent added: "The thought of speculation and moneymaking enters into all the calculations of all persons." Perhaps the most amusing instance was the famous Little Rock cotton card swindle. George W. Curtis, a well-known bookkeeper, served as front man for a group who had allegedly smuggled in a large supply of cotton cards. Prospective purchasers were led to a building on the edge of town, into a cellar, and shown boxes of cards. Sales were made, payable in advance, and secrecy was enjoined since the cards were alleged to be liable to confiscation. One man paid $30,000 for his cards. However when Curtis and his associates tried to leave town before delivery, an innkeeper became suspicious, and an investigation was made. The boxes of cotton cards turned out to contain pieces of wood. Thanks to the innkeeper's quick action, part of the money was recovered, and Curtis later was arrested.[31]

The best example of the ineffectiveness of the civil law in opposing private speculation was the attempted ban on the distillation of spiritous liquors. Although the patriotic press, including the *Telegraph, Gazette,* and *True Democrat,* supported the move, such sentiment was not universal. The misnamed *Patriot,* which served as the defender of speculation and trading with the enemy, condemned the action, observing that "the people will use ardent spirits."[32]

And that they did. With mass starvation facing much of Arkansas after the disastrous harvest of 1862, distilling flourished. The *True Democrat* estimated that over 200,000 bushels of corn were plucked from the mouths of starving widows and soldier-families and converted into whiskey during the six months preceding April, 1863. The *True Democrat* stated that even at the center of government, it was no secret "that soldiers procure whiskey whenever they want it." The flow of liquor was injurious to both civilians and soldiers. At Brownstown it was reported that ten stills were in operation, with the result that "soldiers get drunk and molest citizens." Some of the best citizens, not to mention the whiskey-guzzling officers, set a poor example. David Walker, who later became a judge of the Military Court, in 1862 offered to pay "any price in or out of reason" for a keg of whiskey. Baptist preacher Thomas H. Compere wrote Governor Flanagin in 1864: "I have had it said to me, 'your governor loves whiskey too well to get him to stop still houses' "[33]

Arkansas authorities, seeking to protect civilians, had to contend with armed resistance. Partisans, authorized by Hindman on his arrival in Arkansas, were frequently no more than armed bands with "legalized authority to steal." David Walker complained: "A pretty 'bush' business is going on in stealing and plundering." A number of leading citizens, including DeRosey Carroll, were assassinated by these bands, and some of the killings were premeditated. One veteran recalled that "at the bottom of every combat was an intense hatred." And Judge Brown wrote in 1863: "It is well in times like these to be without enemies." Thomas Compere complained:

> We are overrun with wandering reckless soldiers and these independent thieves, who are coming into the country with stolen stock of every description. These characters force themselves upon our best citizens and wantonly waste their scanty supplies and pay when and what they please.

Unless law was restored, Compere warned Flanagin, "you will be deserted by all worth anything to the state, and left with only an host of wandering helpless women and children as citizens of Arkansas."[34]

Citizens suffered almost as much from soldier depredations as from the brigandage of irregulars. Missouri and Texas troops were reported to be the worst offenders. A Tulip resident wrote in 1863:

> Many of my neighbors were badly treated by those dismounted *MO.* troops in passing through our neighborhood. Many of my poor neighbors had their corn taken from them by impressment and in consequence of not being able to get the money for their corn could not buy elsewhere and had to suffer.

Such practices, one farmer complained, made Confederates the "equal terror" of the Yankees.[35]

The military made only spasmodic efforts to correct the situation, and except in areas subjected to martial law these were of little avail. In one instance, General Holmes informed a farmer that "the persons who should make restitution for the damages claimed are now prisoners in the hands of the Federal Government." Soldiers, in turn, complained of "uncertain patriots who swear to the loss of more rails than they ever had and more hogs than they ever owned." Eventually harsh steps were taken, including a few executions, but as one officer observed: "The presence of any army, even of friends, is demoralizing and corrupting beyond your conception."[36]

It was against this background of murder, robbery, desolation, deprivation, and forced evacuation that the martial law controversy had to be examined. Practically every military commander in the state recognized that an urgent necessity for military control existed. But while this necessity convinced Borland, Roane, Hindman, Holmes, and editors Danley and Johnson, it did not succeed with strong libertarians like Pike. Conservative public opinion, especially in the safer regions, was outraged. Judge Brown, for instance, protested:

> How soon our liberties are lost! We are slaves, not to a foreign despot, whose power crushed us, but reduced by our political leaders. We are required in a peaceful city, not within a hundred miles of an enemy to produce a pass to go out of our corporation limits.

Most conservatives took their text from Gen. Pike. Pike, in his letters criticizing Hindman and Holmes, emphasized the oppressive nature of martial law, and warned against "irresponsible and unguarded military despotism." Comparing Hindman unfavorably to the Duke of Alva, Pike found that "such a scene of wickedness and imbecility, tyranny and incapacity, pretension and ignorance, has never been witnessed since Noah emerged from the ark." Pike's claim that martial law was "a more galling and degrading tyranny than that of Abraham Lincoln" appeared treasonous to the authorities. Opponents of martial law nearly unseated Senator Johnson in November. And in December one irate judge of the supreme court resigned and went over to the Federals because the "military authority overstepped their proper line of operations." Many more were only awaiting the opportunity.[37]

Mounting public pressure resulted in the gradual abandonment of the system, "so quietly," according to the *True Democrat*, that few could "fix the date when it was done." Yet even in its heyday (June-December, 1862) martial law had only limited success. No power in Arkansas could force the farmer to bring his produce to market against his will, or restock the merchant's shelves.[38]

After the abandonment of martial law, extortionist ways returned with a vengeance. Just before Prairie Gove, Danley observed that prices had risen from 100 to 300 percent. "The spirit of extortion," he protested, "lives in our midst—it waxes strong in our highways, has its being in the great stores of the emporium, and at the little counter of the village shop." Little Rock was soon described as "the paradise of speculators." Chief among the offenders were the planters. By not selling their produce, and failing to make provisions for soldier families, the majority were charged by the *True Democrat* with "sacrificing their country for lucre."[39]

A second bone of contention with the military was conscription. B. F. Danley (C. C.'s brother), whose career under Hindman began as head provost marshal, became commander of conscripts. His operation was less than completely successful. Everyone attempted to find some excuse to avoid service. The caustic Doctor Bragg commented:

> Those who once wished they were "only men" seem now very glad that they are not. I have done lots of little, mean, disagreeable pieces of work since this war began, but the meanest of the mean is the task of examining Conscripts. Of all the imaginary diseases,

as well as real ones, to which flesh is heir, they have them. I think it must have been in
South Arkansas that Pandarus opened his box of diseases.

There were other problems. In northwest Arkansas it was reported that the conscript
officers "do not desire to get the men out," and the men would not move until the
deserters were taken in. Elsewhere one officer was described as "too good hearted"
to be effective. As might be expected, there were many complaints of injustice. In
one instance it was said that while good doctors were drafted, a quack, who "can
neither read or write as well as many a negro in this county," was in his practice.[40]

In the Ouachita and Ozark mountains, where the war had been considered an alien
imposition from the first, the threat of conscription intruded violently on the culture
of the hill folk. Given the sturdy independence of the mountaineer and his propensity
for violence, conscription gave an added impetus to bushwhacking and guerrilla
warfare. Moreover the mores of this folk culture made it necessary for the mountaineer to seek revenge for each actual or alleged aggression. Thus the need of the
Confederacy for manpower clashed head-on with traditional mountain ways. The
results were murder, robbery, brutality, destruction, and lasting bitterness as mountaineers either hid in the hills, fled to the Federals, or, if taken, sought to desert at the
first opportunity.

The mountaineer's most telling argument against conscription was the exemption
granted owners or overseers of twenty slaves. Under the cry of "rich man's war,
poor man's fight," men used "every equivocation possible to evade the law." In
Texas discontent was so great that armed rebellion broke out, ending in the hanging
of some forty men. Many Arkansans were in sympathy with the revolt, and armed
resistance developed in the southern portion of the state in what was guardedly called
the "Calhoun County Rebellion." At Magnolia the conscripts staged a "demonstration." To lessen discontent General Holmes ordered the enrolling of all exempted
overseers and owners but then sent them back to work.[41]

Irregularity in applying conscriptions was a major cause of complaint. In one area
it was reported that "conscription has been enforced to the very letter almost" with
the result that the community was low on supplies to feed the women and children
left. At Dardenelle there were complaints that the law was not being applied to the
myriad Missouri refugees. Others objected to the provision which restricted the
profits of a mechanic but not those of a farmer. Editor Eakin, himself a lawyer,
confessed he simply could not understand all the exemptions and rules, and could not
interpret what they meant or how they should be enforced. One irate patriot finally
suggested: "I wish our Congress would conscript the entire Confederacy, and while
it takes one part to defend the country, take the rest to support it *and make them
work*." [42]

Conflict between the civil (where they existed) and military authorities was
inherent in enforcing both martial law and the conscript act. The instructions for
enforcing martial law given the provost marshals allowed them to arrest for any
unspecified offense against the community, "avoiding mere technicalities," and to
punish "sufficient to secure order and quiet in the community." The ancient remedy

of the issuance of a writ of *habeas corpus* conflicted directly with these instructions. In spite of the rather violent criticisms of this system by Pike and other conservatives, a head-on clash was avoided. But throughout 1863 criticism mounted, especially after Holmes in January, 1863, suspended the writ of *habeas corpus* on authority of the president. By summer even editor Eakins of the *Telegraph* warned: "We shudder when we think of the lives and liberties of our citizens becoming subject to authorities which our State courts have no right to question." "This," wrote the editor of the *Patriot*, "for Mr. Eakin, the editor of the *Telegraph*, is saying a great deal." Less circumspect was R. F. Garland, the brother of A. H., who expressed the fear that Arkansas was becoming a military dictatorship, in part because of "the great aversion on the part of *nearly all* the journals of the State to giving a true presentation of affairs." In one known case, a man arrested by the military for selling whiskey was turned loose by the civil authorities on a writ of *habeas corpus* only to be arrested again. Other cases of a similar nature occurred.[43]

While enforcement of the conscription acts created problems, it should be emphasized that the state government never made a determined effort to thwart conscription. After June, 1862, all thought of state self-defense by a state army vanished. Nor did the governor liberally bestow draft exemptable positions. Nevertheless the enforcement of conscription posed several interesting constitutional questions. The state had a law on the books requiring one white person to remain on every plantation. However the term plantation was not defined by law. The Confederate conscription act (at first) allowed exemption for one white man for every twenty slaves. At first Holmes asserted that there was no conflict, but the *Telegraph* refused to accept his opinion as final and insisted that only the courts could make that determination. In the absence of a Confederate supreme court, this meant the Arkansas supreme court. The first case, arising in Hempstead county, was a claim for a writ of *habeas corpus* from a man owning ten Negroes. The Confederate law, the judge pointed out, deferred to the states in that the twenty slave provision only applied if the state had no requirement of its own. Arkansas had such a requirement; ten Negroes did constitute a plantation; therefore the Arkansas law governed the operation of the national law. The conscript was released. This one case did not stop the authorities, however, and Holmes then ordered that the enrolling officers continue to apply the twenty slave clause in Arkansas. Apparently they were successful, for by April the *Telegraph* considered the issue dead and noted that "the community has acquiesced in the military orders." This proved premature, however, for the issue came up in the case of Fernando C. Herbert. The county court on a writ of *habeas corpus* discharged Herbert. The conscript officer applied to Judge L. B. Green for a certiorari to review and quash the proceedings on the ground that the county judge had no jurisdiction and that Herbert's petition showed no sufficient cause. The case of *Ferguson on Petition for Mandamus* v. *Green* was carried to the supreme court when Green refused to act. The court held that Green had acted improperly in failing to review the lower court proceedings. The court then went on to declare that the state law was defective in not defining a plantation, and since the Confederacy was not responsible for defective state laws, Herbert had been improperly released from the military authorities. Another case in the Confederate District Court in Little Rock dealt with the question of whether election of a conscript as justice of the peace was grounds for dismissal. No subsequent election can justify a discharge, the court ruled. Thus the legal framework of conscription was unchallenged in Arkansas.[44]

The second controversial case involving conscription raised different problems. In June, 1864, the enrolling officers tried to conscript the clerk of the state supreme court. The chief enrolling officer, B. F. Danley (appointed first by Hindman then by Holmes) insisted that the clerk's appointment was not valid. The court, which now included Albert Pike, retaliated by questioning the validity of Danley's appointment. The whole affair was referred first to the Trans-Mississippi commander of conscripts and then to Kirby Smith. Governor Flanagin rode his constitutional high horse: "The attempt by the Conscript office to decide whether the occupant was legally appointed is unwarranted by law and insulting to the court. It is "the duty of the Executive to ask and *insist* upon those rights of the State which she undoubtedly possesses."[45]

The dawn of 1863 saw the harvesting of the bitter crop of two years of neglect. Although after Prairie Grove both sides "flew in opposite directions to look for food," the North had the wherewithal to continue the fight and the South did not. North Arkansas was desolated: "The country is almsot depopulated and devastated, southern families have been driven off, and the abolitionists have gone north." General Hindman asked to be transferred, complaining that "matters have not prospered since General Holmes came. I am satisfied they will never prosper while he commands." Lawless bands roamed over one third of the state, speculation flourished, and prices rose. By April, 1863, the *True Democrat* recorded, "Civil law, if not dead, is very soundly asleep." [46]

While Holmes sat idle, the first federal assault on Vicksburg got underway. Although this effort failed, the federals on their way back stopped off at Arkansas Post, beseiged the fortifications, and after a brief battle the fort fell when some of the defenders without authorization from the commander, Gen. T. J. Churchill, raised the white flag. The press tried to minimize the fall. "One more gallant stand, such as was made at the Post, and a few more weeks time, and the enemy will be discomfited," asserted the *True Democrat*. But the way to Little Rock was now open anytime the federals wanted to make the effort. The chorus of complaints against Holmes continued. The Arkansas congressional delegation took up the problem with Jefferson Davis. As a result, on January 14, 1863, Edmund Kirby Smith was appointed to command the Department of the Trans-Mississippi. Holmes' jurisdiction was limited to Arkansas. Following this change, Sterling Price was sent west, to bolster morale, but without any troops.[47]

Under these circumstances the situation in the spring of 1863 momentarily brightened, bringing, said the *Patriot*, "new life in the army." Nevertheless the western army remained ill-fed, ill-clothed, and underarmed. Disease took a heavy toll, and men refused to go anywhere near the hospital if they could avoid it. The Little Rock graveyard achieved notoriety as "bones protruded through the thin covering of earth and the stench was almost unendurable." [48]

During the spring the second Vicksburg campaign under General U. S. Grant got underway. In hopes of retarding Grant's efforts, General Holmes was encouraged to launch some sort of demonstration against the Federals along the river. This matured into an attack on Helena on July 3, the day before Vicksburg surrendered. The Confederates, led by Holmes in person, made a gallant but confused assault on the fortifications and were severely repulsed. An "egregious blunder," proclaimed the *Patriot*. "In the first place we had no use for Helena; secondly we could not take it; and thirdly, if given to us to-day, we could not hold it an hour." [49]

The loss of Vicksburg and the defeat at Helena dealt a severe blow to the morale. At Washington, "many of our citizens here refuse to believe it. They think the reports put out in Delhi are by deserters, or by the enemy, or by speculators in cotton." As for the soldiers, "they are becoming tired of the war and disheartened. They have not been paid and the fall of Vicksburg and Port Hudson seems to weigh very heavily on the men and those that are deserting are rather weak on the cause." [50]

This deepseated depression led to a Trans-Mississippi governors' meeting at Marshall, Texas, in August. Rumors were afloat that Texas would hoist the Lone Star and that the Trans-Mississippi ought to go it alone. To Jefferson Davis, brooding in Richmond, the idea seemed "suicidal," and seems to have reinforced his desire to continue control of the department's military and political activities, despite the obvious difficulties involved. Some leading Arkansas Confederates were convinced that only strong measures of self-defense could save the region. Prior to the meeting, George C. Watkins, Senator Johnson, Congressman Garland, and C. C. Danley wrote Governor Flanagin urging the removal of all persons away from the Mississippi, turning the whole country over to guerrilla warfare, enforcing the conscript act, and endowing Kirby Smith with extraordinary powers "without waiting upon the uncertainties and chances of orders from Richmond, where, as we apprehend, the wants and true condition of the department, if not overlooked, have never been fully comprehended." Even the very conservative Jno. R. Eakin admitted, "Gen. Smith must assume a large authority and be sustained in it too, or this department is lost." Governor Flanagin, however, was suspicious of Kirby Smith and insisted to the president that the general did not intend to defend Arkansas. During July and August machinery and supplies were again moved out of Little Rock to points less exposed. Governor Flanagin protested against this implied lack of faith: "If the state be abandoned again, she may well ask to be protected from her friends." But the removals continued. As for Senator Johnson, Davis was amazed at "how far your confidence was shaken and your criticism severe on men who I think deserve to be trusted." [51]

Faced with these suspicions and distrusts, the governors' conference endorsed the formation of Confederate associations to rejuvenate the cause. The Hempstead County association had a pledge (which they mislaid), "to keep alive the loyalty and zeal of our people—to spread correct news—to correct false reports—to encourage the timid—to find out the designs of the enemy, and to keep up public spirit, by frequent meetings and addresses." But these measures could not stop Federal armies. Since the fall of Arkansas Post, no serious military obstacle stood between the Federals and Little Rock. Fort Smith fell to a land army on September 1. Clearly the end of Confederate control of the Arkansas River valley was at hand.[52]

The Federals were not long in exploiting the situation. In late August a Union force commanded by General Frederick Steele and assisted by gunboats headed up the river. Governor Flanagin called for an old men's company which he promised to command, but response was meager. Doctor Bragg concluded "that the great city of Little Rock is doomed to feel the weight of the oppressor's heel":

> If the state would rise as it did two years ago, upon the bare rumor that she was being invaded, the foe would thunder in vain at the gates of her capital. As it is the danger now menacing her kindles no patriotic fire to blaze forth and consume the invader. Dull apathy, sits upon the face of her people. Her chivalry has long since gone from her shores. The wail of distress and supplication lifted up in her borders meets with no response of assistance, no "Campbells are coming" breaks upon the strained ear.

With Price offering little resistance, Little Rock fell on September 10, 1863. In retreat the Confederate army melted away. "I acknowledge," lamented one soldier, "that I have never until since the fall of Little Rock felt the real sting of being an exile." [53]

8) Wartime Conditions

"This wretched war has left its marks upon each of us."—Mrs. Mary B. Eskridge to W. E. Woodruff, May 30, 1866, Worley, *At Home*, p. 35.

The Civil War caused dislocations and hardship throughout the Confederacy. But the testimony of the people of Arkansas suggests that Arkansas suffered more extensive hardship than most. Contributory factors included the poor roads and unusable rivers which isolated communities from sources of supplies and the abandonment of over two-thirds of the state to irregulars. Some persons, in favored locations or with adequate resources, avoided or minimized the difficulties. But others were less fortunate. Circumstances were as varied as the people. As late as September 11, 1862, Judge Brown from the safety of Camden could write:

> I arise early, feed my ducks of which I have about forty, look over the garden, yard, etc., and gather watermelons, say two or three for the day, of which we have a handsome sprinkle, a second growth on the vines—wash and eat a light breakfast, say a light roll of light bread and fresh butter with a cup of coffee—one half parched corn and the other genuine Rio. Then go down to town, see if any business offers, talk about the news, return home, eat fruit, read some poetry or newspapers, take about a tablespoon of good whiskey (raw) and dine. Then a nap of half an hour, up again. Eat our watermelons—go down street—do a little marketing or shopping, discuss the news, talk about elections, which is lately agitated, return to supper, usually a little batter-bread of good sweet corn meal, some fresh butter and plenty of good buttermilk, and then shortly to bed for a profound nights sleep of about eight and one half hours. Such is my usual routine.

On the other hand a rustic woman of the Ozarks described her life:

> Hit shore was mighty hard for us gals endurin' o' th' war. Th' boys had all tuck t' th' hills, an' th' horses was all gone, an' nothin' for we-uns t' eat, nohow. Atter while they got t' killin' ol' men even, so Paw he lit a shuck for th' timber, an' bushed up thar till th' war was plumb done. I warn't full growed then, only jest teenage, but me an' Sis made two craps 'ith a yoke o' cowcritters.
>
> I mind when ol' Sterlin' Price was a-raidin', th' Choctaw Injuns was with him, an' they et up ever' last stalk o' sugarcorn even—jest all set down an' peeled it an' chawed it for th' sweet. We did make a leetle crap o' corn thet year, but th' dang Yankees come an' tuck most of it.
>
> Two o' my own cousins did git kilt right in front of our house. I was a-feedin' 'em, an' they was shot down as they run for th' horses. Th' Yankees they jest laughed an' left 'em a-layin' thar in th' road, so me an' Sis had t' dig graves an' bury 'em. Hit shore was turrible, them days.[1]

All Arkansians, whether rich or poor, rural or urban, soldier or civilian, experienced difficulties in getting enough to eat. The war cut off the traditional sources of flour and bacon from the North, and poor roads and a shortage of wagons limited the ability to obtain these commodities elsewhere. The food shortage was compounded at the start of the war by local crop failures in 1861. Coming on top of a poor harvest of the year previous, a serious food crisis existed as soon as the war began.

Rather than improving the situation worsened. In 1862 the wheat rusted, the oats were diseased, acorns (hog food) were ruined, and the corn was "a remarkable failure." So bad was the harvest that it was said to be "manifest evidence of the displeasure of God." To make matters worse, an epidemic of hog cholera cut severely into the meat supply.[2]

The next year brought some relief. The fields yielded a bountiful wheat crop, although part of it could not be harvested because of the absence of manpower. Nevertheless the price of flour declined from $35–40 a barrel to $20–25.[3]

In 1864 the crops were good, but as much of the state had been abandoned, little harvesting could be done. Field upon field of corn in the Arkansas River valley grew to maturity and rotted. Thus the last year of the war brought the greatest scarcity. "The spring of 1865," one veteran recalled, "was the most trying time. People ate anything they could get to sustain life, and some starved to death." [4]

The experience of Judge Brown in keeping his larder stocked was illustrative. Although amply supplied with money, Brown nevertheless experienced lean times. The soldiers raided his poultry yard, killing the chickens and depriving him of eggs. He finally butchered his hogs because he could get no feed. By the fall of 1864 Brown was down to "hogs and hominy." Many would have been glad to have just that; during the spring of 1865 Brown reported that corn was unobtainable and that people were on the "point of starvation for bread."[5]

The food shortage also reached the army. The absence of a reliable grain supply crippled the Prairie Grove campaign, making impossible a sustained campaign in northwest Arkansas or into Missouri. After the fall of Little Rock and the subsequent loss of the Arkansas River valley, it became impossible to sustain the army on Arkansas foodstuffs. "The bulk of our subsistence," it was explained, "must come from Texas." The already harassed commissariat impressed wagons and teams from the farmers in southwest Arkansas, thus preventing them from raising a crop. Besides sabotaging the generals' plans, the food shortage undermined morale. One soldier noted in his diary late in the war that all "discipline and subordination of a command mainly depends on the commissariat and Q[uartermasters]." The absence of food justified stealing, while bad food made the soldiers sick. "We did well while our flour lasted," wrote one soldier, "but when it came to coarse cornbread with bran in it, it got a great many of us down with diarrhea and fever." The troops on the border were the worst off. "It is contrary to our principles to have anything to eat," one officer wrote.[6]

Closely related to the food shortage was the difficulty in obtaining salt. Salt, an essential item in preserving pork, was not readily available in Arkansas despite the existence of a few salt springs. Prices soon rose, the result, it was said, of deliberate slowness of production. Some public seizures followed, but salt prices remained high throughout the war.

Fortunately Arkansians did not need many manufactured goods, for few were readily available. One of the most sought after items was cotton cards without which the making of clothes would stop. A great demand remained unfilled. One plant at Camden turned out eight to twelve a day, but to increase production the owner reported he would have to go to England to get the necessary machinery. In addition a cotton factory and a thread factory were in operation. The Pike County cotton factory, the only one operative in the state after the accidental burning of the mill at Van Buren, took Confederate notes at a discount. Many citizens were incensed at this lack of patriotism and talked of "taking forcible possession of his factory and using it for the benefit of the community." The prices at the Arkadelphia thread factory were such that only "the feather bed gentry" could afford.[7]

The result of shortages and high prices was a clothing problem nearly as severe as the food shortage. We "will be reduced to a state of nudity," predicted one planter, and he was not wrong. By the fall of 1862 one officer wrote that "clothing is the most serious question." In the emergency carpets were torn up, gowns became the rag supply, and women were encouraged to compete in the production of clothes for the army. Thus the soldiers fared better than the civilians. "The people, men, women and children, go bareheaded, barefooted and almost destitute of clothing," one Reb wrote his wife. A Northern soldier told his wife, "It would indeed be a most refreshing sight to see Calico and Hoops on a tidy woman or a decent suit on a man. All you see is long necked, yellow skined [sic] dirty women, and filthy children. Many of them as innocent of apparel as was Adam and Eve in the days of Paradise." The winter of 1862-63 worked a considerable hardship on the unfortunate. As late as April the Arkansas River was so solidly frozen that men and supplies crossed over the ice; the trees did not leaf until the middle of May.[8]

Medicines were another item in short supply. While the war in cutting off the supply of the ubiquitous patent medicines may have been beneficial, the shortage of quinine and other proven drugs was not. Home remedies, of varying effectiveness, were used. In addition, Arkadelphia was the site of an extensive chemical factory. Here herbs were collected, ground, and processed, with the help of a steam engine, large evaporating pans, and extensive chemical apparatus. Blue mass, castor oil, and other vital remedies were produced. Nevertheless there were outbreaks of measles and smallpox throughout the war years.[9]

The citizens and soldiers also suffered from shortages of shoes, harnesses, needles, writing paper, and coffee. Some effort was made by the government to manufacture leather goods. One man claimed to have discovered a new, quicker, cheaper way to prepare the leather, but the need was never filled. All over the South the shortage of coffee caused discontent, as did the difficulty in obtaining alcoholic drinks. Paper also became scarce as the war went on. People made their own ink.[10]

The greatest suffering, however, came about in the last two years of the war as the result of invasion. Jayhawkers, bushwhackers, Billy Yanks, and Johnny Rebs competed with each other to rob the widow of her last chicken, burn her barn, waste her corn, steal her money, and drive away her slaves. Thus the collapse of the social order brought the greatest hardship to Arkansas.

It is hard to overestimate the lawlessness which resulted. From northwest Arkansas, former schoolteacher Robert Mecklin, a man not given to hyperbole, wrote: "Theft, plunder, arson, murder, and every other crime of the black catalogue have lost their former startling significance of horror by their daily occurrence amongst us. If we hear that one of our neighbors has been murdered, his house burned and family left to freeze and starve to death for want of clothes and food, it is soon forgotten by us." Throughout the state the destruction of property was immense. An amazing lack of Christian charity existed. Both sides cursed each other with a vengeance and exulted in each other's ill fortune. The animosities engendered justifications for the most outrageous brutalities. In one case a soldier accused of horse stealing "thought he had a right to the mare" since its owner was probably in the Union army. The soldier's friends supported him: "We think him a clever worthy young man and a good soldier."[11]

The result of such activities was that the war on the border became a private battle for revenge and retaliation. A Union occupation meant that the "Arkansas Feds" could get even. From Fayetteville in 1862 an Iowa colonel wrote: "Hundreds of Union men are comeing [sic] in from the woods and mountains where they have hid for months. Secesh property melts whenever it comes near them." Regular soldiers, many from Kansas, also excelled in robbery. One soldier gleefully described his raid on the property of Missouri slaveholder John S. Phelps, whom he erroneously believed to be a secessionist. A Billy Yank wrote from Helena: "I will do like other soldiers. I will take everything from them I can and if they put me to guarding their houses, I will burn them up. If ever my hands tuches valufale [sic] I expect they will stick to my fingers." Thus Union families, who had braved so much hostility at home, found little comfort from the army of liberation. A Union general during Curtis's invasion in 1862 warned that the excesses of the Germans in his command would only unite the people into making guerrilla warfare. A boy living in Northeast Arkansas dated Confederate sympathy in his area to a Federal raid in 1864: "We grew up rebels from this cause."[12]

The women bore the brunt of the burden. Their sacrifices, though they cannot be quantified, were extensive. They kept the farms going, made clothes for their families and the soldiers, dealt with bushwhackers, robbers, and invading armies, and were a pillar of strength to the Southern cause. Even their contemporaries recognized their courage. A Baptist preacher wrote: "Southern Arkansas women are the truest patriots that ever trod the soil of the world." Professor Mecklin wrote from Fayetteville, "The Federals here say the Southern women here are the most indsutrious and remarkable women they have ever met with, that they keep their husbands and sons comfortably clad in the army and themselves and children neatly dressed in homespun and seem afraid of no one."[13]

Of course there were exceptions. One woman found the war upsetting because she simply could not get along without six slaves. Another pestered her husband, who would go to his death at Marks Mills, to buy her a piano. But even when overwhelmed by disaster, others did their best to manage and not unduly worry their husbands. One soldier thanked his wife for her cheery letters. "Instead of making one homesick, they cheer one up and make one contented and happy. I think of you and the children every day but I would rather die and never see you any more than to whine around and disgrace us all. The army is a great place to develop character." Probably more typical was the response of the woman whose husband had been gone less than three months. "You must not leave me again," she wrote, but "if worst comes we will burn up our houses and sweep the earth literally."[14]

When left face to face with the enemy, the women proved more courageous and resourceful than the men. One woman living near Helena turned bushwhacker, wore a bowie knife, and was reputed to have killed seven men. She was reported to be "on intimate terms with thieves and desperadoes on both sides." Another woman fought a notable battle for a hog felled by the Federals. "You have killed my hog but you cannot carry it away," Mecklin reported her saying. One soldier then entered her house and started breaking things, but she stood steadfast over the hog with her club. The soldier then returned "as near as it was safe for him, turned his ugly end towards her, pulled down his pants and emptied his bowels of stinking load in her presence. 'Now, sir,' said she, 'You have made a dog of yourself. I am old and not thus to be abashed, for all my life long I have always seen dogs go with _____ .' "[15]

The measure of Confederate success was morale. To a very large extent the internal history of the Civil War in Arkansas was the erosion of the will to win. Since less than one-third of the whites even favored Southern independence, Confederates found it difficult to sustain the public spirit.

Newspapers played a vital role in sustaining morale. "We all live on war news," one soldier wife reported. A Rebel soldier noted that the presence of a newspaper "cheers us up." Bad news was discouraging, but no news was worse than bad news. Throughout the war Arkansians were woefully misinformed, especially after the fall of Vicksburg cut communications with the east.[16]

Most of the press in Arkansas sounded the patriotic note. Criticisms of the president and his conduct of the war, so heated in the east, were muted in Arkansas. Mrs. M. B. Eskridge of the planter class wrote approvingly: "I like the *Gazette* and [*True*] *Democrat* too for they speak to the common sense and virtue of the reader, and they animate us in our retired homes to industry, management, and economy." [17]

Not all the press was so inspired. A preacher found the editor of the *Daily State Journal* to be "alarmist," and complained: "He is always snapping and snarling at the government at Richmond." One subscriber-patriot wanted his subscription stopped because "I am tired of it." The Little Rock *Arkansas Patriot*, another paper sometimes critical of the authorities, defended such dubious activities as liquor distillation and trading with the enemy.[18]

But these papers were the exceptions. Washington *Telegraph* editor Jno. R. Eakin took the position that "nothing could be more destructive to all hopes of success than opposition and dislike on the part of citizens to the military commander of the district." Accordingly he suppressed criticism, even apologizing on one occasion for the appearance of a letter from Rufus K. Garland, soon elected to Congress, critical of the state of affairs. Eakin's twofold aim of "diffusing all reliable information and inspiring proper sentiments amongst the people" led him to become increasingly vague as Confederate hopes declined. But Eakin was honest. When Missouri Governor Thomas C. Reynolds approached him with the letters he had forged purporting to be written by an abolitionist to defector Colonel E. W. Gantt, Eakin refused to publish them.[19]

The effectiveness of newspapers was limited by their unavailability. Suspensions of the county press came first, as editors either went off to war or were unable to purchase paper. One planter, after asking W. E. Woodruff to subscribe to the *Daily State Journal* in the hope that it would prove a "living institution," observed, "I have been badly bit in newspapers this year—having paid in advance for no less than four, all of which have 'died off.' " Eventually the paper shortage became so critical that the leading Little Rock papers became irregular. The Washington *Telegraph*, the only regular paper in the state after the fall of Little Rock, ultimately depended on the bounty of General Kirby Smith for its paper supply. Thus the effectiveness of the press in sustaining morale diminished as the need grew greater.[10]

Of course newspapers had their limitations. News of far-off victories fed no one. At first, however, there was universal euphoria. Judge Brown was almost alone in his pessimism. Brown concluded early in the war that the South suffered from "too much swaggering and braggadocio." The North, he decided, would win. "The only thing that can save us," he wrote on November 9, 1861, "is dissention among them."[21]

Most Confederate Arkansians held out hope until the fall of Vicksburg and the loss of Little Rock. Then morale declined disastrously. The loss of Little Rock was seen as the last hope for Arkansas." In the two remaining years a more realistic attitude emerged. Although reports of foreign recognition persisted, editor Eakin wrote candidly: "We have been deceived in our expectation that the necessity for cotton would force European nations to recognize our independence. This delusion was a very demoralizing one." By the summer of 1863 there was an "almost universal disposition to skulk and hide," and men were "fleeing to Texas to save their property who ought to have a mess kit over their shoulders." Whereas during General Curtis' invasion of the state in 1862, the citizens had hounded his flanks and cut off his supplies, in 1863 the defense of the country was "practically given up so far as those at home are concerned."[22]

Changes in political affairs reflected the times. Before the war started, E. W. Gantt, congressman-elect from South Arkansas, told an audience: "I will bring to her [the Confederacy] all the best energies of my nature, my present and future hopes and prospects, my life, my all, and laying them upon her altar, offer them up freely in defense of her insulted honor, wounded pride, and priceless freedom." Elected colonel of the Twelfth Infantry Regiment, Gantt participated in the disasters of New Madrid and Island Number Ten. "His morals," a friend reported, "have greatly changed. He can outcurse either of us, and as to the women, he is a second Aaron Burr." Unable to obtain a commission as brigadier general, Gantt, in the summer of

1863, went over to the Federals, issuing an address attacking General Hindman and Senator Johnson and counseling surrender. Judge Brown correctly observed: ''Most of those who were so willing to shed the last drop of blood in the contest for separate government, are entirely unwilling to shed the *first*.'' [23]

With the decline of Confederate chances came a shift in politics. Congressional candidate Rufus K. Garland observed, in a criticism of his original secessionist opponent, that ''fulsome and unmeaning jargon about war and blood-shed expressed on paper or in long-winded speeches—all this has 'played out.' '' Garland's victory at the polls Judge Brown felt showed a condemnation of the continuation of the war.[24]

Even county politics were affected. In Chicot county the ''rascals, Yankees, cotton speculators, dogs and cliques'' united behind one candidate for county judge. Although a loyal man won, there was ''more intense feeling and anxiety than any election I have witnessed in the county—all kinds of trickery, falsehoods and combinations were resorted to.'' [25]

As enthusiasm for the war faded, many sought only to be left alone. In the midst of bushwhacker country, Robert Mecklin wrote: ''I am quiet and submissive, take no interest in what is going on, and am looked upon by them as a harmless, inoffensive old dotard.'' Since much of the state was only under nominal control, the population found it necessary to be ''shifty.'' A Texas soldier complained, ''You don't know whether you are talking to a white man or a Yankee, it is the most degraded country I ever saw.'' A woman near Helena admitted to her diary, ''How hard it is to know people now.'' [26]

Some observers noted other changes. A Texas conscript reported on the morals of some of the women:

> As we came along, I can say there is but verry few vertious ones along the road we travailed. There husbands had gone to the ware and they have for saken them. The men would go way on before and some would stay behind and go their houses and get all around them and such talk you never head among straingers. Ile leave a little for you to gess at for fear some boddy sees this. There was so many would croud up on the women that it was enough to scare them to do any thing but such as that was just as lots of them wanted.[27]

People living in the country had much to complain about. It was officially reported that Confederate troops at Camden had plundered the country for miles around. One soldier wrote his wife, ''If you hear of an army about to pass, hide all your corn and bacon for they will steal all you have got.'' The author did not specify whether the army was Federal or Confederate, for by 1863 it would make little difference.[28]

The towns of Arkansas also suffered. From the rural point of view, shared by many soldiers, the towns were strongholds of heartless speculators, ''gold lace and brass buttons.'' ''There is not much love for Little Rock in the soldiers,'' one of them wrote.[29]

For those towns abandoned to the enemy, the picture was bleak. Fayetteville was partially burned by McCulloch in 1862. Van Buren had ''an air of desolation pervading it.'' Napoleon, a Union soldier reported in 1863, was "deserted, the houses—many in ruins; and all untenanted—make it a thing of the past." Hopefield was completely burned to the ground in retaliation against guerrilla activities.[30]

The population of towns under Confederate control often was greatly augmented by the influx of slaves, soldiers, and refugees. Civil government proved too weak to deal with the crisis. Martial law was invoked in and around Fort Smith and Little Rock on several occasions. Even so, corruption flourished. "There is a heap of such pilfering and swindling going on here in this state," one soldier reported. Another observed, "Our army was greatly contaminated by our stay at Little Rock, particularly the officers giving themselves to licentiousness and drunkness, which has a demoralizing effect upon the men." Drunkenness also became a problem among the Indians at Fort Smith. That town, a notorious place which festered on fraud and political jobbery of government Indian affairs, was described by Wiley Britton in 1864 as a "terrible hole of corruption." Britton claimed that if all the prostitutes were sent away, the number of remaining females would be "very small." Confederate observers agreed.[31]

Towns suffered a physical decline. Symbolically, the Little Rock town clock ran twenty minutes late. Streets were a major problem. In Little Rock in January, 1863, a wagon loaded with corpses for the graveyard mired down and could not be removed until the next day. The well-traveled Bishop Lay said of Little Rock, "I never saw such mud in any town." [32]

Morale in the towns, never high, soon declined. As early as December, 1861, the Ladies Soldiers Aid Society was "very poorly attended." Caustic Doctor Bragg noted:

> Last July, a year ago, the ladies of this city could not do enough for the soldiers. [But now there is] no friendly hand to do the last kindly offices, nor no friendly ear to receive the dying messages to a wife or Mother. Do these 'Angels of Mercy' visit the sick, now that their presence and influence is needed, more than at any other time! *Not a bit of it!* But if you will stand on a corner any fine evening, you can see the dear creatures riding on horseback, in perfect *shoals,* each one escorted by a man and eighteen mittens, carrying and thinking as much about the sick soldiers, as if they were so many sheep.

The soldiers did not neglect to complain about this attitude. One wrote: "The rich sit back and seem to regard a wet and hungry soldier as something beneath their notice. They will certainly receive their reward." Soldiers also objected that merchants refused Confederate notes. "When it comes to that," wrote one irate soldier, "I think it is time to quit." [33]

Both country and city folk took part in the most pervasive evil of the times, trading with the enemy. Some were forced to it. A woman outside of Helena explained that it was the only way to get salt. Mrs. Mecklin made gloves which she sold to Federal officers for the same purpose. Although the *Patriot* defended the practice, few others cared to do so. The *Gazette* declared:

> Trafficking with the enemy is, of necessity, demoralizing in its tendency. Besides the corrupting hope of gain which always accompanies it, their agents, pimps, and spies

are admitted among us under its pretexts and pretences. Philip of Macedon made it his boast that he could capture any city whose gates were broad enough to admit a mule laden with gold; in words and practice he was a Yankee.[34]

What happened to the morals of a community so corrupted was recorded by Doctor Bragg:

> Some thirty or forty spools of thread, three or four pairs of scissors and a pocket knife have found their way into the great county of Bradley, and the result is that the people, even to the women, are demoralized. Confederate money is valueless to them when compared to the life of a chicken or a pound of butter. They are the most absurd people in the world.[35]

By 1863 the evil encompassed the whole state. "Post officers," Judge Brown recorded, "get rich out of the Government—whilst the balance of the officers in command are drinking bad liquor whenever they can get it." Doctor Bragg observed, "The people do not sustain the Government, they never have done it, and the result is, we see today, the hated Yankee and his hateful colors, over the fairest portions of our country." [36]

The war adversely affected practically every aspect of social and cultural life. Education suffered. In the region north of the Arkansas River schooling virtually ceased by the spring of 1862. Some schools were continued in towns, or informally at home, but only in South Arkansas did academies continue to eke out a precarious existence. So great was the danger that all formal education would disappear that one soldier urged his eldest daughter to learn rapidly since she might have to teach the younger children herself.[37]

The war produced some significant changes in religion. Army life was not conducive to moral living. Officers and men, of good character at home, in camp fell into habits of drunkenness, card playing, cursing, and debauchery. Civilian life was similarly affected. Bishop Lay, who thought that "scarce one in a hundred of this western population has any practical sense of religious obligation," railed against benefit balls for the soldiers and ordered a church woman who participated in a play denied communion. Many preachers left their trade to join the army. Something of a competition developed to see which regiment contained the most.[38]

Declining Confederate morale also coincided with increased emphasis on religion. An Army Church and the Christian Soldier Association were organized. Both were controversial. "I believe the soldier comes before the Christian," was the comment of one soldier. The Baptists objected that many of the chaplains of the Army Church were Methodists, and their preaching partook of the character of camp meetings, "if we regard noise and confusion as *the* characteristics." [39]

Preachers and religious materials were in short supply. One chaplain stated: "We have not one Army Hymm Book, no Tracts and few Testaments, nor do I know of any command in the Trans-Mississippi District better supplied than we." Nevertheless, for some, religion helped to sustain morale through the hard years of 1864–65. In April, 1863, one soldier noted: "I think I can see a change for the better in the army and the citizens of the country. [We] have one of the greatest revivels [sic] of religion that ever was witnessed.''[40]

Others found little cheer or comfort in God's inscrutable will. The complete loss of hope at the war's end was reflected in the diary of a woman living near Helena. On March 10, 1865, she wrote: "This is a fast day by Jeff Davis's appointment. None of us have regarded it though. The prayers and fastings of one or two will avail nothing.'' [41]

The last resort—and in some instances the first—to the accumulation of woes was flight. Although no statistics exist, it is highly probable that Arkansas lost a greater percentage of her population than any other Southern state. Starting in early 1862, emigration to South Arkansas and Texas increased rapidly. At Paris, Marshall, and other Texas towns wealthy Arkansans and Missourians enjoyed ''lives of perfect ease and indolence.'' Oysters, champagne, and other luxuries were obtainable. Others, arriving with the skin on their backs, were described as living ''in a small and uncomfortable way.'' The population of these towns grew greatly. Little Rock was estimated to have 11,000 souls before it fell; Washington, the makeshift capital thereafter, was described as dreadfully crowded.[42]

Those at home criticized the refugees. Professor Mecklin wrote: ''Those who ran to get out of danger and have left others to fight in a war which they did much to bring upon us, I think ought to have done better.'' But increasingly the fortunes of war, hunger, and lawlessness left little choice. ''Many citizens of this part of the state have gone north,'' Mecklin reported, ''the most of whom are well rid. But many others, with whom we are loath to part, are running away south to save themselves from murder and their property from plunder. There are but few of us now left and we may be driven away or killed.'' Curiously the class with the most invested in a successful outcome of the war was by universal consent the least patriotic and most prone to flee. ''The planters of this region,'' wrote a Chicot countian, ''have no patriotism. It's get all you can, keep all you get and 'devil take the hindmost' with them.'' [43]

The families of Union men suffered just as great distress, and their suffering dated from the discovery of the peace societies in 1861. Many of the men took to the bush and subsequently made their way to Union lines at Cassville, Missouri. They and their family's condition was celebrated in verse by a veteran of the bush business:

Each Union man in Arkansas was driven to and fro
Ruedly into the mountains I then was forced to go.
Now I was forced to be a soldier and leave my native land
Into the lonely mountains in sorrow I did rome.

Very cruel were the people down in that Reble land
And they robed my dear companion of ever thing she had
Now they robed and abused her until she left her home
Proud be the woman that has no husband for whom to mone

(chorus) for we are fedral soldiers and a long way from home.

Yes here we are at Cassvill away from our homes
And the Kansians are making our famleys mourn
They are takeing off our property whilst we in Mo. Rome
For we are fedrals soldiers and a Long ways from home.[44]

At Fort Smith women and children received half rations from the Federals. But the usual Union attitude was that Union refugees merely got in the way. Many were sent to Kansas, while a boat load of 487 persons including thirty orphans was sent to Cairo, Illinois. There, in the dead of winter, they were loaded on open stock cars and carried into the interior. Without food or adequate clothing, four died of exposure from this Yankee generosity. Two books, Baxter's *Pea Ridge and Prairie Grove,* and Bishop's *Loyalty on the Frontier,* sought to tell Northern audiences the tale of woe suffered by Arkansas Unionists. But there never emerged from Arkansas a figure of the national stature of a "Parson" Brownlow or Andrew Johnson to unify the Arkansas Unionists and lobby for them in Washington.[45]

One of the most obscure aspects of the state's Civil War history is the life of the submerged quarter of the population held in bondage. Few surviving letters tell of plantation affairs during the war. The press rarely mentioned slaves or their activities. Yet in their way Negroes played a significant if silent role.

At the start of the conflict whites feared a slave uprising. By the summer of 1861 this concern had apparently vanished. Few signs of any slave conspiracy, revolt, or gross insubordination during the war have come to light. Slaveholders took pains to inform slaves of Yankee atrocities towards blacks. Moreover the Yankees' deliberate exploitation of runaway slaves tended to undermine any extravagant hopes blacks might have. Thus while the slaves undoubtedly hoped for Federal success and while individual acts of resistance occurred, there is little to suggest that Arkansas blacks actively prepared the way for the coming of the Yankees.

As Federal armies moved into Arkansas, planters took precautionary steps to protect their slave property. One delta planter reported in December, 1862: "We have all moved our hands some distance back from the river, but have no work of value to do and meat is very hard to get." A number of planters who owned farms in different counties transferred their Negroes to the one that seemed the safest. Others found moving an "almost impracticable thing to do as most of us are without money to support them when removed a distance from home." [46]

One answer was to send the slaves to town to be hired out. Of the six Mrs. Eskridge sent to Little Rock, three had tried to escape and two "are bent on getting to Memphis." Apparently some owners were satisfied with this arrangement. One planter wrote: "I have no doubt that they are better off than at home (so near Gun boats) as from their accounts they get on quite well, which is decidedly different from the accounts of our neighbors." [47]

The actual test of slave loyalty came when Federal troops arrived in the vicinity. Some masters attempted to hide their slaves in the numerous woods or canebrakes.

That this expedient was not always successful is indicated by the report of one owner that hidden slaves were "found *invariably* through bad faith of some of the neg- roes." Indeed it was Mrs. Eskridge's experience, "that those *I trusted most* have deceived me most and will yet give me trouble on account of their families." Professor Mecklin's cook felt "much inclined to make declaration of their independ- ence" upon the arrival of the Federals, and in about a month found a paying job and left.[48]

Of great concern to all planters was the impressment of slaves by the Confederate government. Beginning in August, 1862, impressments were frequent and heavy. In 1864 Negroes were enrolled for military labor. Judge David Walker claimed such action was not only unconstitutional but "is a thousand times worse than impress- ment because there is no security for the return of property and no remuneration for time."[49]

Planters opposed government use of their slaves on the ground that it was harmful to the Negroes. Reports indicated "great mortality amongst the negroes employed by the government caused by bad treatment and gross neglect of them in sickness for which there can be no reasonable excuse." Service with the army was feared most. "I hope," one Chicot countian wrote, "you have not allowed any of my negroes to go with the marching army. Change is death to them. I have lost so many of my men, I fear the loss of more." Thus one planter reclaimed his slaves. "I feared they would not be cared for and attended to in times of sickness and that I feared they would be more likely to be finally lost to me in the army than if I returned here." Invariably there were complaints of favoritism against the authorities. Those with friends, it was said, "get theirs off when their neighbor's are retained to do work or die."[50]

It is not surprising that some planters put their investment in slaves above the Southern cause. "I have lost all hope," wrote one such, "but at the same time, I deem it my duty to use every effort to save my property." Many planters abandoned threatened plantations, sacrificed their cotton and much other property which could not be hauled away, and moved to Texas. Official sources indicate that as many as 150,000 slaves were removed from Arkansas.[51]

Planters frequently expressed more than an economic interest in their slaves. Efforts were made to keep in touch with absent slaves and see that they were well-treated. Mrs. Eskridge professed "a great desire to do what may be for the spiritual good of my negroes." She instructed her agent to read them a few lines about home affairs and admonished them: "You must be *faithful* converted Chris- tians and *good servants,* then I will never have to doubt you—and you will be returned *gladly* to your home and families. I hope Fagans reads the Bible."[52]

Slaves away from home, whether in military service or civilian employment, caused trouble. Despite military supervision and strengthened patrol laws, the relocation of a significant part of the black population was not effected without problems. Although planters like Mrs. Eskridge urged their slaves to lead a moral life, the lax atmosphere of the towns tended in the other direction. Slaves from various plantations and regions were mixed together, a situation every planter considered "bad."[53]

In July, 1863, it was reported in Little Rock, "in the vicinity of the Sabbath," a "grand quarter-race, on which large sums of money were bet," was held by the slaves. One main street was blocked by the large number of Negroes, estimated at three hundred. The *True Democrat* reported:

> Not withstanding stringent laws and ordinances against negroes hiring their own time, slaves hire houses and have cookshops, beerholes, and other pretended means of support. They are flush of money; buy pistols and horses and get white men to bid for them at auctions. On Markham street, for two or three squares, every third house is a negro brothel, and where it is said, whiskey is sold.[54]

Either by flight or conquest many slaves fell under Federal control. Union soldiers in Arkansas generally approved of the Emancipation Proclamation but doubted the effectiveness of arming the ex-slaves. One Northerner wrote: "They had about as throw the arms away as to give them to the niggers, for not one out of a hundred of such as I have seen would stand fire." Estimating that at least two thousand contrabands were at Helena, he concluded, "I think that [eating rations] is all they are fit for in the army." Nevertheless over five thousand served as Federal soldiers, and on plantations under Union control, others were put to work. Many more were employed to build and maintain fortifications. When the word got around, often with assistance from the planters, that Negroes who went to the Federals were worse off than those who remained on the plantations, "the mania for going to the Yankees subsided." Mrs. Eskridge reported that some of her slaves returned "better servants from their trial of it." By 1863 a Union officer reported that the slaves "hide from us like the dickins." A Southern planter reported that the visiting Federals "talked to them pretty roughly" in order to get them to leave.[55]

In the final stages of the war, the Union army simply took all able-bodied male slaves, leaving the old, the women, and the children for the Confederates to feed. Great hardship resulted. Mrs. Amanda Swink obviously fulfilled the objectives of Federal policy when she asked for the deferment of her son from the army: "I have 18 negroes here. The Feds took two. I have only 7 field hands, the rest are old sickly women and children. I can't make much of a crop." The welfare of the Negro did not influence Federal policy in Arkansas; instead the unfortunate blacks were simply pawns in a white man's war.[56]

In the closing days of the Confederacy, Negro slavery was a topic of debate for the first time in Arkansas history. Proposals were put forward to arm slaves to defend the South, on the promise of eventual emancipation. Arkansas General Patrick Cleburne was among the initial promoters of the idea. General emancipation was also discussed. "It is a peace proposition," wrote one soldier, "and as the people are very tired of war it may take. It is a good deal talked in the camps." The Washington *Telegraph,* on the other hand, opposed ending slavery, stating that "we owe it to God to sustain it." Arkansas Unionists E.W. Gantt and Jesse Turner voluntarily repudiated the institution. Turner wrote in the Fort Smith *New Era* that slavery was "doomed" and that he was "for the Union at all hazards, with or without slavery."

In 1863 a Confederate soldier wrote ''A negro is as certain as Confederate money.'' He was right, for by the end of the war neither was of any value.[57]

9)
The War's
End

"Everything (officially) has gone wrong."

—Kirby Smith to Mrs. Smith, September 10, 1863. Kirby Smith Papers, Southern Historical Collection, University of North Carolina.

The loss of Fort Smith on September 1, and Little Rock on the 10th reduced effective Confederate control to the extreme southwest counties. Only bad roads, burned out houses, and abandoned fields separated Confederate from Union Arkansas. In the vast no-man's land which constituted three fourths of the state, both armies foraged, and bushwhacker bands, with and without legal sanction, operated. Following the loss of the Arkansas River valley, the men desired "to fight alone for their homes." Organization and discipline were lost. One officer complained that the soldiers were "beastly drunk." He added, "I am thoroughly disgusted with affairs here. I am determined to go to leave and go somewhere to find an army of *men*."[1]

Relatively few men seem to have deserted immediately, perhaps remembering the experiences of those who had welcomed Curtis in 1862 and then been abandoned when the Union army moved on. In the places considered safe, however, new converts and old persistent Unionists reaffirmed their support for the stars and stripes. Of Little Rock, one Missouri soldier wrote, "There is a good many Union families in town and has always been called by the rebs an abolition hole." Even before the fall of Little Rock, some of these men, mostly mountaineers, had been formed into regiments in Missouri for service in Arkansas. In Helena and at other points adjacent to the planting region Arkansas regiments were formed out of ex-slaves. Two books, Bishop's *Loyalty on the Border,* and Baxter's *Pea Ridge and Prairie Grove,* gave vent to long suppressed loyalist sentiments. Thus it was made to appear that Arkansas was not being conquered but rather liberated. Even in 1862 a shadowy military government under Missouri Unionist Jno. S. Phelps existed in a St. Louis hotel room. In 1864 Isaac Murphy, who had voted no to secession and refused to change his vote, replaced Phelps. The Union commander, General Frederick Steele, followed a conciliatory policy, which was echoed in his paper, the *National Democrat,* edited by C. Van Meador. Steele, an Arkansas Unionist testified, "has done more and can do more to restore Arkansas to her former relations to the Union than any other man anywhere."[2]

Nevertheless the Unionists were a rather disharmonious group. Meador, in an analysis of the situation, defined four different groups: those who had initially opposed secession and had had to flee or hide; those of "secret sympathies" who had nevertheless gone along with secession to avoid being persecuted; those who had believed in the war at first, but "become disgusted with the selfishness of rich men, at the conduct of the leaders, and the management of the war," and who now repudiated their former involvement; and finally "some without principle," often former followers of T. C. Hindman. Meador, himself a discharged Confederate surgeon, wanted a broad based Union movement, while the radicals, consisting mainly of carpetbaggers and those of the fourth of Meador's classes, wanted strict standards. Moreover the conservatives wanted to defend white supremacy, even if slavery had to be abolished. The radicals were soon criticizing Steele for being too lenient, calling for a larger role for the Negro, and demanding the reorganization of the state government. In this last goal, many conservatives agreed. Thus in early 1864 a convention met in Little Rock to draft a new constitution. On March 14, 1864, the document was submitted to the voters, in a *viva voce* election. Not surprisingly, it was approved: Murphy was elected governor (his inauguration procession was escorted by a battalion of colored troops, whose "quiet and orderly demeanor, were the admiration of almost every beholder"), and a legislature was chosen. At this point cooperation between the two groups ceased to exist. The radicals controlled the legislature, some of whose members were, it was said, elected in the streets of Little Rock. Elisha Baxter, a North Arkansas lawyer and former Hindman supporter, and William M. Fishback, formerly of the secession convention, were elected to the U. S. Senate, but only after a comic opera episode in which the speaker of the house was expelled by less than a quorum majority, his successor refused to serve, and a third man had to be chosen who would sign Fishback's certification papers.[3]

When the two arrived in Washington the radicals in Congress made short work of Fishback. Though supported by Senator Lane, some rather pertinent questions were posed: Why had Fishback introduced the resolution into the secession convention that Arkansas would resist coercion to the last extremity? What had he done to support the Union cause thereafter? Fishback, who could not take the floor to answer these queries, explained in the press that he had been warned that he would be hanged if he even attended the convention, that during the first sitting "my life was frequently threatened, and on my return a mob in the town of Clarksville, through which I had to pass, had provided a half bushel of rotten eggs for my benefit." At the second session he was closely watched, and some wanted to assassinate him. These explanations failed to erase the stain, and the radicals were opposing Lincoln's reconstructed governments on principle, so the delegates were not seated. At home the Washington *Telegraph* asserted that Fishback had fought for the South at Oak Hills before deserting, while the *National Democrat* suggested that Fishy was a political opportunist.[4]

Without Congressional recognition of its legitimacy, hard pressed for money, and with the governor and legislature at odds, only Federal bayonets sustained the movement. With the expansion of Federal power, the prestige of the government rose; with military defeat or withdrawal, it declined. Many Unionists who had fled the state remained refugees either in other states or in the few occupied posts. Nowhere in Arkansas did the Unionists have complete control over the countryside.[5]

As for the Confederates, the demoralized Confederate armies, after abandoning two major posts without fighting a major battle, disintegrated in retreat. Many looked upon the Confederate cause as lost, while others took advantage of the confusion to desert to the enemy. Those from North Arkansas tended to regard the retreat as the abandonment of their homes, and went home to protect their families. "In this retreat," Governor Flanagin lamented, "we lost twice as many men, including sick, as we would have lost in a battle had one been fought."[6]

Following the retreat came a period of reorganization. A report of Inspector General W. C. Schaumburg, dated October 26, 1863, indicated that an overhaul of the army was greatly needed. Widespread laxness in command, which he attributed to "too much familiarity" between officers and men, had caused petty crimes to go unnoticed, "while greater ones go unpunished. I think that they are past appreciating leniency, and moral suasion is lost upon them. Some excuse may be made for the men, but none for the officers." More favorable was the report of Inspector General Jilson P. Johnson. He reported that Holmes was "doing everything that can be done," and that morale was "better than it was." But "the general disregard of all law or sanctity of private rights by the officers and men" had led to "great dissatisfaction" among the civilians. "Generally among the masses our success [is] deemed almost a matter of indifference, and in many localities the advent of the enemy would be hailed as a relief."[7]

The new year, 1864, began with the removal of Holmes. This action was long overdue. The soldiers had no respect for him, and after the battle of Helena it was believed in the camps that Holmes was "sick or crazy or something else." He had feuded with Price, and even Governor Reynolds of Missouri, an inveterate Price-hater, reported that General Smith told him Holmes had softening of the brain. The Arkansas Congressional delegation, reflecting home sentiment, had requested Holmes' replacement, and Price assumed temporary command.[8]

For about six months after the fall of Little Rock, there was considerable agitation in state circles for a campaign to retake the Arkansas River valley. Despite the political and military reasons favoring such an advance, the logistic problems were too great. The troops were underarmed; only broken muskets were arriving from across the river, and without arms, Kirby Smith was loath even to make plans. Moreover, as General J. B. Magruder pointed out, "the country between the Ouachita and Arkansas is almost a desert, without corn or grass or man or beast." In addition the energies of the department had to be used to resist the advance of General Nathaniel Banks up the Red River. For this purpose Confederate troops were concentrated under General Richard Taylor. Two of Price's best divisions, those of Churchill and Parsons, were sent to Taylor at Shreveport, thus practically denuding Arkansas of its defenses.[9]

As part of the Federal plan, General Steele in Little Rock began moving southward with approximately 10,000 men to join up with Banks. Steele entered Arkadelphia on March 29, 1864, and, after pretending to threaten Washington, moved into Camden. Somewhat unexpectedly, Taylor met Banks' advance units at Mansfield (Sabine Crossroads) and soundly whipped them. Banks' retreat left Steele in the lurch.[10]

At Camden Steele's immediate need was supplies. Accordingly a train was sent back toward Pine Bluff. The Confederates ambushed the wagons and escort at Marks Mills. The Southerners, egged on by Indian reinforcements, and maddened by the enemy's use of Negro troops, made short work of the Federals, killing, wounding, and capturing almost 2,000.[11]

With hope of succor removed, Steele was forced to evacuate Camden. The Jewish merchants of the town, who had taken the oath of allegiance on his arrival in the expectation that Federal occupation would prove permanent, were now forced to flee for their lives. On April 27, 1864, Steele left the town and headed back for Little Rock. The gloating Confederates, hoping to cut him off and destroy him, started in pursuit. They overtook him at Jenkin's Ferry and engaged him in a hard-fought battle in which "each side displayed true American grit, though some got a little shaky," but Steele made good his escape.[12]

The battle of Jenkins' Ferry for all practical purposes ended the military campaigning in Arkansas. Later in the summer, Price was finally allowed to make his great raid into Missouri, but the invasion was of short duration, exceedingly costly in men and equipment, and of no lasting benefit to the Confederacy. With Price's return to Arkansas in early December, the war in the West ceased to have any real bearing on the final outcome of events now being played out between Grant and Lee outside of Richmond.[13]

While the Confederate army in Arkansas had its brief moment of glory during Steele's Camden expedition, the state government failed to make even one effective move. Governor Flanagin had in October, 1863, established his office with the remnants of the state government at Washington, and called for a day of fasting. Some leading politicians had defected to the Federals, among them Colonel E. W. Gantt, Orville Jennings (a former law partner of A. H. Garland and wartime mayor of Washington), and Sam Williams, the state attorney general and former member of the military board.[14]

The fall of 1863 witnessed a very heated contest for political office. During the summer, the *True Democrat* suggested that only Royston and Batson should be returned to the Confederate Congress. But the influence of the "family" had "dwindled to a mear [*sic*] cypher." Although Batson seems to have had little opposition, Royston became a symbol for Confederate failure and a stalking horse for anti-"family" elements. His opponent, Rufus K. Garland, brother of Congressman Garland, was loudly critical of martial law and other encroachments on the civil power, had called for the removal of Holmes at an early date, and opposed conscription. In his address to the voters, Garland further implied that he opposed the rejection of any peace move by the North. Although Senator Mitchel made a tour of Royston's district, giving speeches just two days in advance of Garland's canvass, and the *Telegraph* strongly defended Royston's record, the Congressman proved vulnerable. His son, young Charley, six foot three inches, 175 pounds, who "has been riding the fastest horses over the country, attending *stag dances* with his associates," and who had ridden horseback ninety miles in twelve hours time, was exempted from military service, allegedly through his father's influence. Although Eakin of the *Telegraph* rejoined that the exemption was completely legal and justified, the voters rejected Royston, the only Arkansas Confederate Congressman defeated in a bid for reelection. Garland's victory, the *National Democrat* in Little Rock asserted, was a clear sign of Union sentiment in Confederate Arkansas.[15]

As the Union movement in north and central Arkansas gathered strength, it was obvious that something needed to be done to sustain Confederate loyalties. Governor Flanagin urged a campaign against the Arkansas River valley timed to discourage a turnout of voters in the Union elections in March, 1864. On the day of the election a mass meeting was held in Washington, with ex-Governor Rector present, at which it was resolved to continue the war to the end. Governor Reynolds, whose brain teemed with endless schemes, urged the reestablishment of Confederate associations. Editor Eakin warned his readers against Steele's conciliatory policy, and made much of the expulsion from Little Rock of the aged William E. Woodruff, who had written a friend that he had only taken the oath of allegiance to be able to live. The Confederacy received a martyr when David O. Dodd, seventeen, was executed as a spy.[16]

The best way to remind the people that Confederate Arkansas existed would be to have before them evidence of an active civil government. A revived state government, editor Eakin asserted, would end crime and restore law and order.

> If we allow our civil government to go by default, it will not only have a bad effect upon the spirits and patriotism of our people, many of whom may, and already begin to consider our State government defunct, but it will give color abroad to the Federal assumption that we are already conquered.

Therefore, said Eakin, the legislature should be summoned into special session. But Governor Flanagin, whom even Eakin regarded as "too conservative for the crisis," did nothing. An anonymous correspondent in the summer called attention to the need to "revive the drooping energies of our state government," while George C. Watkins privately informed the governor of "an inability to enforce the criminal code." For one thing, certain laws required sending the prisoner to the penitentiary, a manifest impossibility with that building in Federal hands.[17]

Thus prodded, Governor Flanagin issued a call for a general election in October 1864. As difficulties were bound to develop under these circumstances, it was deemed necessary to hold a special session of the old legislature. Supreme court justices E. H. English and Albert Pike assured the governor that the constitution permitted the issuance of writs of election and the summoning of the legislature at any time. With this backing, Flanagin called the old body into session on September 22. When less than a quorum appeared, the justices were again consulted. They decided that while the law required a quorum in all cases, it was obviously unreasonable to permit any enemy to thwart a government by conquering parts of the state and preventing full attendance of the legislators. Thus those who could participate constituted the assembly, and two-thirds of those in attendance comprised a quorum.[18]

In his address to the legislature Governor Flanagin admitted that the state war effort had failed. He cited the following specifics: State relief to soldier families had been stopped after December, 1863; the appropriation for iron and cotton cards manufacture had gone begging because the sum allotted was too small; and the liquor laws had failed because of the irregularity of the courts and the willingness of the defendants to pay the fines and continue operation.[19]

The first business of the legislature was the selection of a new senator to replace C. B. Mitchel who died on September 20. The contest was between Pike and A. H. Garland, with Garland winning by a vote of thirty-eight to fourteen. The legislature also authorized the governor to move the archives out of state if necessary, provided for elections by refugees and soldiers, and reformed the penal code, substituting whipping or the pillory for confinement in the penitentiary. Two other important acts were the appropriation of $35,000 in gold and silver and one million in paper for the purchase of cotton cards and medicine. Another two hundred thousand was voted to purchase salt for the indigent families of soldiers.[20]

On the first Monday in October the state election was held, for the most part in the camps and among refugees. Various county and state officials were chosen, but the newly-elected legislators never assembled, because the war ended before the date fixed by the incumbent legislature for their sitting.[21]

As in previous instances, the results of the legislative enactments fell short of expectations. William Etter, a former editor of the *Telegraph,* was entrusted with procuring the cotton cards and medicine in Mexico. But Etter died at Brownsville, Texas, and most of the supplies eventually fell into Federal hands. Crime, both inside and outside the army continued to make life miserable and farming became increasingly difficult when wagons, food, horses, and slaves were "impressed." A conflict occurred between Circuit Judge A. B. Williams and the provost marshal at Magnolia when the military ignored the judge's injunction. Williams wrote a letter intended for publication, in which he argued persuasively that the army was engaging in illegal search and seizure. Editor Eakin passed the communication to Governor Flanagin.[22]

The demise of the state government did not occur without some protests. Editor Eakin took to print to ask the governor to secure him some paper, as the war governors of Texas and Louisiana had done for their state presses. Flanagin made clear his views of his office in two letters written to Senator Johnson. In the first, Flanagin alluded to "differences of opinion" which had arisen between him and the senator. Apparently Johnson continued to press for an early attack on the Arkansas valley and threatened to "break with the military and civil authorities" unless action took place. Flanagin agreed with General Magruder, who said it was impossible, "the insurmountable obstacle being a want of sufficient transportation to haul corn" and would be "a useless waste of life." [23]

Three months later Flanagin again wrote Johnson to answer charges that he had been inactive. "The clamor that has been raised against me," the governor stated, "arises from disappointed applicants for position." Lacking legislative authorization, Flanagin refused to procure supplies on his own. Governor Allen of Louisiana, frequently lauded for his vigorous actions by editor Eakin, Flanagin characterized as "a governor who acts without or contrary to law," which Flanagin himself said he would never do.[24]

Complaint against the governor was widespread. One man wrote: "The outcry against your policy has been so general, that a careful and scholarlike exposition is necessary to show that your action is in accordance with the law and the constitution of the state." A friend advised him to make efforts to convince the people "that our Governor is not as slow a man as they took him to be." [25]

Thus the burden of sustaining the Confederate cause remained as ever with the military authorities. A Military Court, consisting of Judge B. B. Battle, David Walker, George C. Watkins, and Trusten Polk, sentenced seven soldiers to death under a new law on horse stealing. When in June of 1865 Judge Watkins fell into Federal hands, this court was asserted to have shot a large number of mutinous conscripts and to have kept no records. But the depredations continued. Kirby Smith wrote, "The aged, the infirm, and the lukewarm constitute the mass of the population that remains." Kirby Smith, even though, "he never seems to lose sight of the importance of civil government, and the constitutional and legal rights of the people," managed to protect what was left. Cotton was sold in Mexico for supplies, some efforts were made to limit the exactions of impressments, some factories were established, and the last newspaper in Confederate Arkansas, the *Telegraph,* was sustained in paper courtesy of the general. Congress cooperated by creating separate post, war, and treasury departments. If in the final days of the war the Trans-Mississippi was unable to save Richmond or succor Lee, at least it defended itself.[26]

As 1865 dawned the soldiers and civilians found little cause for hope. There was, said a correspondent in the *Telegraph,* "a degree of nervous weakness and timid shrinking on the part of our people in regard to the discussion of our future destiny." Nearly everyone who could make the trip had gone to Texas, "to get out of the way of our own army." Confederate money continued to decline in value. Although a new issue of notes sought to improve the situation, and a new sub treasury was created, the army still was frequently unpaid and without the ability to purchase supplies. At times the Treasury sent drafts that were too large to cash, and thus useless. Despite official pleas, the situation had not improved by the war's end.[27]

Finally in April came the news of the evacuation of Richmond followed first by Lee's surrender and then Johnston's. For a few weeks there was suspense while the leaders debated what to do. General Smith issued orders for the men to "stand by our colors—maintain your discipline," but the soldiers and people decided for them. The war was over, and the men packed up and went home. As A. H. Garland said, the soldiers "declared that as they had not been paid for a year and a half or two years and had nothing to work with, they would take what they could in settlement of account and go home with it." Anarchy resulted for a brief period as all order broke down. At one depot a trusted guard made off with all the horses and mules. Officers who tried to interfere were roughly handled. Although for the record, some commands and officers surrendered, in essence the Trans-Mississippi merely dissolved.[28]

Governor Flanagin, unlike Louisiana's Governor Allen, had no enthusiasm for continuing the war. His desire was "to restore quiet to the country at the earliest possible day.'' He sent a delegation consisting of Judge Clendenin and Senator Garland to Little Rock to confer with Federal authorities. Flanagin proposed summoning the legislature to repeal all hostile acts, and then resigning. He hoped that Union authorities would recognize the duly elected county governments in South Arkansas. Finally he wanted to deliver the state archives in person to Little Rock. These proposals, which evidenced a desire to restore civil government with participation by all citizens, did not meet with Union approval, and only the delivery of the archives was permitted. These Flanagin surrendered and retired to his home.[29]

The war, sent aloft amid the heady clouds of vapid rhetoric, ended in suffering, death, destruction, and defeat. In Arkansas the end of the war did not even bring peace. A few persons, among whom was T. C. Hindman, fled to Mexico. Most wanted to return home. But the prospects were not pleasing. One woman remembered the trip from Washington to Little Rock:

> Desolation met our gaze; abandoned and burned homes, uncultivated land overgrown with bushes; half starved women and children; gaunt, ragged men, stumbling along the road, just mustered out of the army, trying to find their families and friends, and wondering if they had a home left.

Yet so intense were the hatreds spawned by the war that many feared to return home. In north Arkansas those who had embraced the Confederacy and had persecuted their Unionist neighbors could look for no kind welcome. For a decade thereafter guerrilla bands, now mere outlaws, roamed the Ozarks. Large parts of the region remained desolate and insecure while the original settlers stayed in Texas. For most, however, the recollection of one survivor was valid: ''So there we were like so many of our Southern people, with only our land left.'' And Judge Brown, ever prophetic, noted, ''the greatest trouble is with the negroes.'' [30]

The civil war had wide ranging effects on Arkansas. Economically it set the state back twenty years. A new problem, that of accommodating the two races, would remain unsolved over a century later. Politically, the planter class, as represented by the family,'' would never again rule the state, but the divisions in geography would continue to be the dominant element in shaping the state's politics. Though Arkansas was remote from the centers of the war, the destruction, the ruin, and the hatreds were, if anything, greater than in Virginia or Tennessee. This was the price the state paid for embarking on the Lost Cause. Only after the destruction was repaired, the hatreds forgotten, and the survivors in their old age, could the experience of Confederate Arkansas be romanticized into gallant heroic men, and noble, hardworking patriotic women.

EPILOGUE

A good many years after the war was over, when the nation's wounds were healing, and when the veterans of the blue and the gray were thinning ranks in the last supreme battle, William Quesenbury, broken and decrepit, summoned up his all and gave to the world his epic poem *Arkansas*.[1] This native-born son of territorial Arkansas whose lightning-quick shafts of wit and truth have often brightened these pages was "Old Cush" now. He had seen the day when there were more bears than people in Arkansas. He had fought for the now forgotten Whig party. He had established a newspaper in a town with no railroad and no telegraph. He had opposed secession but fought for the Confederacy. And in the postwar years he had seen the frontier life he knew and loved yield to the onslaughts of land-hungry farmers and Northern capitalists. Yet from this fast moving panorama of change, William Quesenbury stood unmoved, certain of his life and destiny. The conclusion of his poem may well serve as the conclusion for this book:

> The song is sung—if such it may be called
> An unmethodical, rude, backwoods song
> Discordantly discoursed or rather bawled;—
> But be it what it may, it will not long
> Remain in memories amid the throng
> Of busy life pursuits, —a passing flaw
> Upon the stream of time, —and, right or wrong,
> From it one truth, a rock-truth, we may draw,
> 'Tis this: GOD LOVES NOT HIM THAT LOVES NOT ARKANSAS![2]

NOTES

FOREWORD

[1]Walt Whitman, *Specimen Days,* in *The Complete Prose Works of Walt Whitman,* I (New York and London, 1902), p. 140.

CHAPTER 1

[1]Timothy Flint, *The History and Geography of the Mississippi Valley* (Cincinnati and Boston, 1832), p. 277.

[2]Arkansas Post *Arkansas Gazette,* November 25, 1819, July 14, 1821: In 1819 William E. Woodruff strapped his press on a flatboat and got as far as the Post, where he set up shop. In late 1821 he moved his concern to Little Rock, the new capital, editing the *Gazette* off and on until he sold it to C. C. Danley in 1853. A recent history is Margaret Ross, *Arkansas Gazette: The Early Years* (Little Rock, 1969). Although the title varies, the paper will hereafter be cited as *Gazette;* the book as Ross, *Arkansas Gazette.*

[3]*Gazette,* September 1, 1821; February 4, 1823; August 13, 1822.

[4]*Ibid.,* March 25, 1823; October 5, 1824.

[5]*Ibid.,* October 26, 1824; September 16, 1827: For a fuller discussion see Robert B. Waltz, "Migration into Arkansas, 1820–1880," *Arkansas Historical Quarterly,* XVIII (1958), 320. Hereafter cited as *A.H.Q.* G. W. Featherstonhaugh, *Excursion Through the Slave States* (New York, 1844), p. 92. Hereafter cited as Featherstonhaugh, *Excursion.*

[6]*Gazette,* December 9, 1828.

[7]*Ibid.,* May 23, 1827; February 29, 1832.

[8]Washington *Telegraph,* January 13, July 14, 1847. Hereafter cited as *Telegraph.* Batesville *Independent Balance,* July 1, 1858. Hereafter cited as *Balance.*

[9]Mattie Brown, "River Transportation in Arkansas, 1819–1860," *A.H.Q.,* I (1946), 342. "Navigability," however, was determined by the legislature, and the records are full of streams being declared navigable or having their navigability repealed; *Gazette,* January 2, 1839; *Telegraph,* May 30, 1855.

[10]*Gazette,* January 2, 1839: J. T. Knight to Susan E. Knight, February 18, 1865, Tennessee Department of Archives and History.

[11]*Gazette,* June 23, 1823, March 16, 1824, June 19, 1833.

[12]*Telegraph,* April 28, 1852; Letter of Ramrod, Memphis *Daily Avalanche,* February 28, 1861. Hereafter cited as *Avalanche.*

[13]*Telegraph,* June 13, 1849; Powhatan *Advertiser,* December 17, 1857, quoted in *Gazette,* January 2, 1858; Featherstonhaugh, *Excursion,* p. 95. But the German Friedrich Gerstäcker,

Wild Sports in the Far West (Durham, 1968), p. 172, testified: "I have traversed the state in all directions, and met with as honest and upright people as are to be found in any other part of the Union." For an analysis of Arkansas stories, see James Raymond Masterson, *Tall Tales of Arkansas* (Boston, 1953).

[14]*Gazette,* June 4, 1828; July 28, 1835; May 20, 1840; Fort Smith *Herald,* n.d., quoted in Memphis *Daily Appeal,* February 22, 1860. Hereafter cited as *Appeal.* Featherstonhaugh, *Excursion,* p. 87.

[15]Featherstonhaugh, *Excursion,* p. 97; *Gazette,* January 10, 1838. James Anthony proposed, as an amendment to a bounty on wolves bill, that the president of the Real Estate Bank be required to inspect each pelt. James Wilson, the speaker and president of the bank, understood the amendment to imply misconduct on his part. His trial, Anthony supporters said, was a farce.

[16]*Gazette,* August 21, 1844, July 28, August 4, 1835, April 30, 1828, September 29, 1841; Featherstonhaugh, *Excursion,* p. 97. Des Arc had just experienced the work of a local committee, which had "a wholesome effect on the morals of the place," *Appeal,* January 21, 1860. At least a dozen extra-legal bodies were in operation in 1860.

[17]W. B. Flippin, "The Tutt and Everett War in Marion County," *A.H.Q.* XVII (1958), 155–163. During the Civil War, the feud broke out again, with one family for the Confederacy and one for the Union. A.M Haswell, "The Story of an Ozark Feud," *Missouri Historical Review,* XX (1925), 105–107.

[18]Lonnie W. White, *Politics on the Southwestern Frontier: Arkansas Territory, 1819–1836* (Memphis, 1964), pp. 164–182. Later on it was suggested that Arkansas's entry was premature and had contributed to the state's backwardness. See *The Southern States (Condensed from De Bow's Review)* (Washington and New Orleans, 1856), p. 520; *Gazette,* March 27, 1858; Jesse Turner, "The Constitution of 1836," *Publications of the Arkansas Historical Association,* III (1911), 74–166. Hereafter cited as *P.A.H.A.*

[19]Ted. R. Worley's uncompleted history of the banks is contained in "Arkansas and the Money Crisis of 1836–1837," *Journal of Southern History,* XV (1949), 178–191; "The Batesville Branch of the State Bank," *A.H.Q.,* VI (1947), 286–299; "The Arkansas State Bank: Ante Bellum Period," *A.H.Q.,* XIII (1964), 65–74: "Control of the Real Estate Bank of the State of Arkansas, 1836–1855," *Mississippi Valley Historical Review,* XXXVII (1950), 403–426.

[20]*Gazette,* July 18, May 24, 1843; November 10, 1841.

[21]Some of the bonds had been improperly disposed of. These Holford bonds were the cause of a running controversy throughout the rest of the nineteenth century.

[22]Helena *Southern Shield,* August 3, 1860. Hereafter cited as *Shield.*

[23]*Telegraph,* August 25, 1847; Homer Lee Kerr, "Migration into Texas" (Unpublished doctoral dissertation, University of Texas, 1953), p. 69. Arkansas accounted for 13.962 percent of the Texas population. *Gazette,* June 19, 1842, March 20, 1844, September 2, 1845. The decline in revenue resulted in taxes being raised from one-eighth of one percent to one-sixth in 1846. See Elsie Mae Lewis, "From Nationalism to Disunion: A Study in the Secession Movement in Arkansas, 1850–1861" (Unpublished doctoral dissertation, University of Chicago, 1947), pp. 18ff. Hereafter cited as Lewis, "From Nationalism to Disunion."

[24]*Gazette,* March 3, May 12, 1845. Leading Democrats refused to sign.

[25]*Telegraph,* March 30, 1849, April 14, 28, 1852.

[26]*Ibid.,* May 19, March 24, 1852; *Gazette,* July 30, 1852; *Balance,* August 26, 1858.

[27]*Gazette,* November 30, 1850, January 19, 1861; *Shield,* February 26, 1853.

[28]Fletcher Green, "Democracy in the Old South," in George Brown Tindall, ed., *The*

Pursuit of Southern History (Baton Rouge, 1964), p. 188. Josiah Shinn, *Pioneers and Makers of Arkansas* (Little Rock, 1908), *passim*. Hereafter cited as Shinn, *Pioneers and Makers*. John Hallum, *Biographical and Pictorial History of Arkansas* (Albany, 1887), *passim*. Hereafter cited as Hallum, *Biographical History*. Walker L. Brown's forthcoming biography of Albert Pike will shed much light on these matters. At present see Ross, *Arkansas Gazette*.

²⁹*Gazette*, April 2, 1844.

³⁰*Telegraph*, July 21, 1852.

³¹*Gazette*, August 24, 1854; Judge John W. Brown Diary, January 1, 1853. University of Arkansas Microfilm, Hereafter cited as Judge Brown Diary.

³²*Telegraph*, May 26, 1852; *Gazette*, August 22, 1852, August 22, September 8, 1857, November 12, 1859; *Shield*, July 18, 1853; *Inaugural Address of Henry M. Rector* (Little Rock, 1860), p. 6; *Census Table for 1860* (Little Rock, 1860); William Baxter, *Pea Ridge and Prairie Grove* (Cincinnati, 1864), pp. 10–14. Hereafter cited as Baxter, *Pea Ridge*; *Balance*, September 30, 1858.

³³*De Bow's Review*, XXVI (1859), 713.

³⁴Lewis, "From Nationalism to Disunion," pp. 23ff. Much of the real swamp land was not reclaimed until the twentieth century.

³⁵*Gazette*, May 16, June 13, 1857; *Telegraph*, March 30, 1859; Bell Griffith to Ozias Holden, September 16, 1860. Griffith Papers, Department of Archives and Manuscripts, Louisiana State University.

³⁶Bell Griffith to Ozias Holden, September 16, 1860. Griffith Papers, Department of Archives and Manuscripts, Louisiana State University; Orville Taylor, *Negro Slavery in Arkansas* (Durham, 1958). p. 47.

³⁷Lewis, "From Nationalism to Disunion," p. 31; Letter of Ramrod, *Avalanche*, March 2, 1861.

³⁸Bell Griffith to Oxias Holden, April 21, 1861. Griffith Papers, Department of Archives and Manuscripts, Louisiana State University; quoted to John Gould Fletcher, *Arkansas* (Chapel Hill, 1947). p. 125.

Chapter 2

¹Biscoe Hindman, "Thomas Carmichael Hindman," *Confederate Veteran*, XXVII (1930), 97–100. D. Y. Thomas, "Thomas Carmichael Hindman," *Dictionary of American Biography*, V, Part 1, pp. 61–62. Hindman married Mollie Biscoe, the daughter of a wealthy Helena planter speculator, Henry Biscoe, against her father's wishes. Biscoe, a debtor to the Real Estate Bank and trustee from 1852 to 1855, was opposed to the "family" who had wrested control of the bank away from the trustees and who were in 1860 talking of collecting the old bank debts. Biscoe was allegedly a bankrupt at the time of his death in 1862.

²J. N. Bragg to "Miss Josephine," February 11, 1862, in Mrs. T. J. Gaughan, ed., *Letters of a Confederate Surgeon* (Camden, 1960), p. 31. Hereafter cited as Gaughan, *Confederate Surgeon*. Samuel Sullivan Cox, *Three Decades of Federal Legislation* (Providence, 1885), p. 96. David Walker to "Dear Sir," (James David Walker?), April 3, 1860. David Walker Papers, University of Arkansas. Van Buren *Press*, September 30, 1859. Hereafter cited as *Press*. Batesville *Democratic Sentinel*, September 13, 1859. Hereafter cited as *Democratic Sentinel*.

³Arkadelphis *South Arkansas Democrat*, n.d., quoted in the Des Arc *Citizen*, June 8, 1959. Des Arc paper hereafter cited as *Citizen* although the title varies. Sebastian, Robert Ward Johnson testified, was never "consulted by the leading men engaged in the secession

movement.'' John Mula, ''The Public Career of William King Sebastian'' (Unpublished master's thesis, University of Arkansas, 1969), p. 55. Hereafter cited as Mula, ''William King Sebastian,'' Hallum, *Biographical History*, p. 271. *Gazette*, June 13, 1857. *Democratic Sentinel*, September 13, 1859. *Citizen*, June 15, August 31, 1859.

[4]*Democratic Sentinel*, n.d., quoted in Little Rock *Old Line Democrat*, February 2, 1860. Hereafter cited as *Old Line Democrat*. To prepare for its coming, Hindman flooded the country with copies of the prospectus mailed under his Congressional frank. Fayetteville *Arkansian*, July 30, 1859, March 23, 1860. Hereafter cited as *Arkansian*. Rodgers (or Rogers) forged letters of recommendation from Robert Toombs and A. H. Stephens. Little Rock Arkansas *True Democrat*, March 31, 1860. Hereafter cited as *True Democrat*.

[5]*Citizen*, March 21, 1860. Hindman was of course not the first Southern nationalist in Arkansas. Senator Johnson, when a Congressman in 1850, had opposed the famous compromise of that year, and nearly lost his seat as a consequence. But Johnson did not play the role of a demagogue.

[6]*Arkansian*, December 23, 1859. *Citizen*, December 21, 1859. Hindman's father-in-law came to his aid, justifying Hindman's conduct in a public letter.

[7]*Arkansian*, November 25, 1859. Boudinot got a number of leading men to testify that the handwriting was Hindman's. *Old Line Democrat*, November 24, 1859. Letter of W. L. Martin, Helena *NoteBook*, November 1, 1859, quoted in the *True Democrat*, February 29, 1860. *Citizen*, December 7, 1859. *Old Line Democrat*, February 9, 1860. *Arkansian*, February 10, 1860.

[8]*Arkansian*, January 6, February 10, May 25, 1860. *Citizen*, March 21, 1860. *Old Line Democrat*, May 31, 1860.

[9]*Gazette*, February 19, 1860. *Press*, December 30, 1859.

[10]*Gazette*, March 17, 1860.

[11]Magnolia *Magnolian*, n.d., quoted in *Arkansian*, May 25, 1860. Bentonville *Northwest Appeal*, n.d., quoted in *True Democrat*, March 7, 1860. Camden *Eagle*, n.d., quoted in *True Democrat*, February 22, 1860.

[12]Proceedings of the State Democratic Convention, April 2, 1860, in *True Democrat*, April 14, 1860. The leader of the rejected Phillips County delegation was Thomas B. Hanly, at that time considered a close ally of the ''family.'' Thus it is possible that the only reason for this group's existence was to offset the Benton County contest.

[13]*Ibid. Press*, April 13, 1860.

[14]*True Democrat*, April 14, May 5, 1860. It should not be automatically assumed that the ''family'' was responsible. The act was too blatant and too easily exposed. Furthermore forged instructions would not have been voted by a man as closely associated with Johnson as Yerkes. Since Van Buren County was in Hindman's district, it is not impossible that he was responsible.

[15]*Citizen*, March 21, April 21, 1860. *Old Line Democrat*, April 5, 1860. Pine Bluff *Jefferson Independent*, n.d., quoted in the *Citizen*, May 12, 1860. It is probable that the paper wanted the convention business for Pine Bluff as much as it did another nominee.

[16]Camden *Southern Star*, n.d., quoted in the *True Democrat*, April 21, 1860. *True Democrat*, April 28, 1860.

[17]Letter of William Quesenbury, *Gazette*, June 2, 1860, *Gazette*, April 7, May 12, 1860. *Telegraph*, n.d., quoted in the *True Democrat*, April 28, 1860. Apparently an early attempt to organize at Camden on April 1 failed. In addition a Union meeting in Hot Springs in June deliberately refused to endorse a candidate in any state race, feeling that the internecine struggle within Democracy could best be furthered by their staying out of it. Some confusion

surrounds their one possible candidate, Judge Hubbard. Quesenbury included Hubbard in his satire on the candidates in the *Gazette*, June 2, 1860.

[18]*True Democrat*, May 5, 1860.

[19]*Arkansian*, May 25, 1860. Camden *Eagle*, n.d., quoted in the *True Democrat*, May 19, 1860.

[20]*Old Line Democrat*, May 17, 1860. *Arkansian* May 25, 1860. Fort Smith *Times*, June 7, 1860. Hereafter cited as *Times*. Boudinot, it was said, "seems to have been singled out above all others by the *partisan* Demagogues of the state for their slanderous and low contemptible abuses," said the Pocahontas *Advertiser and Herald*, n.d., quoted in the *True Democrat*, June 9, 1860. "An Observer" wrote that the attack was motivated by Boudinot's taking charge of the *True Democrat*. "It was necessary to disgrace him in advance and thus destroy the force of his arguments." *True Democrat*, June 2, 1860. Boudinot insisted that the convention never endorsed the *Old Line Democrat* over the *True Democrat* and that the minutes were in error. *Ibid*.

[21]*Telegraph*, November 2, 1853. Pocahontas *Advertiser and Herald*, n.d., quoted in the *Arkansian*, August 4, 1860. *Times*, May 31, 1860. Letter of William Quesenbury, *Gazette*, June 2, 1860.

[22]*Old Line Democrat*, May 24, 1860. *True Democrat*, May 26, 1860. Quesenbury had some fun with Peek's verbal extravagance: "Always at the close of any public duty he rushes to the handles of his plough and holds on to them until the people drag him away." Letter of William Quesenbury, *Gazette*, June 16, 1860.

[23]Charles E. Nash, *Biographical Sketches of General Pat Cleburne and General T. C. Hindman* (Little Rock, 1898), p. 153. Hereafter cited as Nash, *Biographical Sketches*. This section cited was contributed by Sam Williams, a *sub rosa* editor of the *Old Line Democrat* during June and July. *Old Line Democrat*, July 24, 1860. Boudinot further charged that Hindman regretted bringing Rector out. *True Democrat*, July 21, 1860. A Unionist suggested: "Hindman and the Johnsons are at odds, but in this struggle they will come together because they are both extreme disunionists." James David Walker to David Walker, May 9, 1860. Walker Papers.

[24]Memphis *Enquirer*, May 28, 1860, quoted in *Gazette*, June 2, 1860. *Old Line Democrat*, June 7, 1860.

[25]*Gazette*, June 9, 1860.

[26]*Address of Richard H. Johnson to the People of Arkansas* (Little Rock, May 31, 1860).

[27]*Old Line Democrat*, June 14, 1860. Hallum, *Biographical History*, p. 408. *Balance*, July 6, 1860, quoted in the *Gazette*, July 21, 1860. *True Democrat*, July 14, 1860.

[28]Shinn, *Pioneers and Makers*, p. 402. *Times*, June 21, 1860. *Gazette*, July 28, 1860.

[29]For instance the *Times*, June 21, 1860, said that the cry of "family" was "mere political bosh" and the forgery, while "villainous," was too stupid to be the "family's" work.

[30]*Gazette*, June 9, 1860. *Old Line Democrat*, June 21, 1860. *Democratic Sentinel*, n.d., quoted in the *True Democrat*, July 14, 1860.

[31]*Gazette*, June 9, 1860.

[32]*Democratic Sentinel*, n.d., quoted in the *True Democrat*, July 14, 1860. *Old Line Democrat*, August 30, 1860. *Journal of the Senate for the Thirteenth Session of the General Assembly* (Little Rock, 1861), pp. 324–238.

[33]*Gazette*, July 8, 1860.

[34]*Ibid.*, July 7, 1860. *Old Line Democrat*, July 24, August 2, 1860.

[35]*Old Line Democrat*, July 20, 1860. *True Democrat*, July 20, 28, 1860.

[36]*Ibid.*, July 27, 1860. *True Democrat*, July 28, 1860. *Gazette*, July 28, 1860.

[37]J. W. Woodward to David Walker, August 19, 1860. *Arkansas Gazette* Foundation Library.

[38]W. H. Rector to Governor Rector, November 8, 1860. Kie Oldham Collection, Arkansas History Commission.

[39]Judge Brown Diary, August 4, 1860. J. W. Woodward to David Walker, August 19, 1860. *Arkansas Gazette* Foundation Library. The 1856 Know-Nothing gubernatorial candidate James Yell was an example of a Rector supporter.

[40]*True Democrat*, August 18, 1860. *Old Line Democrat*, August 30, 1860. *Gazette*, October 13, 1860. John M. Harrell, "Arkansas," in Clement A. Evans, ed., *Confederate Military History*, X (Atlanta, 1899), p. 3. Hereafter cited as Harrell, "Arkansas."

[41]J. Wm. Demby, *The War in Arkansas, or, A Treatise on the Great Rebellion of 1861: Its Progress, and Ultimate Results Upon the Destinies of the State. A Defense of the Loyalty of the People, Their Wretched Condition Considered; A Review of the Policy of the Government Towards Union People and the Rebels* (Little Rock, 1864), p. 56. Hereafter cited as Demby, *The War in Arkansas. Old Line Democrat*, December 20, 1860.

[42]James S. Wade to Governor Rector, October 8, 1860. Oldham Collection. Wade reported that all the lately arrived Whigs had voted for Rector.

[43]*Times*, August 16, 1860.

CHAPTER 3

[1]Granville Davis, "Arkansas and the Blood of Kansas," *Journal of Southern History*, XVI (1950), 431–456. William Quesenbury to "Friend Wheeler," n.d., Arkansas History Commission. Lewis, "From Nationalism to Disunion," pp. 294ff.

[2]*Gazette*, December 17, 24, 1859. Danley had to apologize for the fact that the largest advertisement in his paper was from a New York liquor merchant. His program came to fulfillment in January when the *Shylark* arrived in Arkansas waters from St. Louis loaded with 650 tons of freight for Little Rock and Fort Smith. *Ibid.*, January 28, 1860. William Quesenbury attributed Danley's dislike of Cincinnati to the editor's preference for rot gut instead of good Cincinnati whiskey! Fayetteville *Southwest Independent*, June 16, 1855. *Gazette*, November 6, 1858. *Press*, October 21, 1859.

[3]Elsie M. Lewis, "Robert Ward Johnson: Militant Spokesman of the Old South-West," *A.H.Q.*, XIII (1954), 16–30.

[4]*Appeal*, May 11, 1860. Memphis *Eagle and Enquirer*, n.d., quoted in *Appeal*, May 9, 1860. Letter of Thomas Drew, *Appeal*, February 3, 1860.

[5]Helena *State Rights Democrat*, n.d., quoted in the *Arkansian*, February 10, 1860. *Old Line Democrat*, January 12, 1860.

[6]*Arkansian*, February 10, 1860. Pine Bluff *Jefferson Independent*, n.d., quoted in the *Citizen*, February 29, 1860. *True Democrat*, March 24, 1860. *True Democrat*, n.d., quoted in the *Old Line Democrat*, October 13, 1859. *True Democrat*, January 4, 1859, quoted in *Old Line Democrat*, January 12, 1860.

[7]*True Democrat*, March 21, February 22, 1860.

[8]*Citizen*, March 28, February 15, 1860. *Gazette*, April 7, 1860. *Old Line Democrat*, April 12, 1860. *True Democrat*, April 14, 1860.

[9]Proceedings of the State Democratic Convention, April 2, 1860, in *True Democrat*, April 14, 1860.

[10]*Ibid. Ibid.*, May 10, 1860.

[11]*Ibid.*

[12]*Ibid.*

[13]*Ibid.,* May 19, 1860.

[14]James Ford Rhodes, *History of the United States from the Compromise of 1850,* 8 vols. (New York, 1872–1919), II, 445–454. Closing Proceedings of the Seceding Minority, *True Democrat,* May 12, 1860.

[15]*Gazette,* May 19, 1860. *True Democrat,* May 19, 1860. The *Old Line Democrat,* May 24, 1860, was blunter still: "Arkansas will never support Stephen A. Douglas for the Presidency whether nominated by a convention or not."

[16]*Avalanche,* May 10, 1860, quoted in *True Democrat,* May 19, 1860. *Appeal,* May 10, 1860. Letter of John I. Stirman, in *True Democrat,* May 24, 1860. *True Democrat,* May 19, 26, 1860.

[17]*True Democrat,* May 24, 1860. It was dishonest not only because of Stirman's previous revelation, but because the editor himself observed parenthetically in the Closing Proceedings (fn. 14) that Burrow's resolution never passed. *Press,* May 25, 1860. *Arkansian,* May 18, 1860.

[18]*True Democrat,* May 19, 1860. Gould and Johnson were the radicals; Gould would be a secessionist in the state convention one year hence. Hempstead, a senior "family" politician for many years, was nevertheless a Unionist even after Lincoln's election; Hobson, a Unionist in the 1861 convention, was afterwards a colonel in the Confederacy.

[19]Democratic Convention of the First Congressional District, in *ibid.,* June 2, 1860.

[20]Address of Albert Rust, in the *Gazette,* June 9, 1860.

[21]An Address to the National Democracy in the *True Democrat,* June 2, 1860.

[22]Proceedings of the Regular Delegates from Arkansas, in the *Old Line Democrat,* July 11, 1860.

[23]*Press,* August 10, 31, 1860. It was rumored in early August that Hindman would sell the *Old Line Democrat* to Rust. *Old Line Democrat,* August 6, 1860. Camden *Star,* November 1, 1860, quoted in the *Appeal,* November 14, 1860. *Old Line Democrat,* August 30, 1860.

[24]Judge Brown Diary, October 27, 1860.

[25]*Gazette,* October 27, 1860. R. F. Kellam Diary, October 23, 1860. Hereafter cited as Kellam Diary. Judge Brown chaired the meeting. Judge Brown Diary, October 23, 1860.

[26]*Old Line Democrat,* July 18, 21, August 30, 1860. *True Democrat,* July 7, 14, 20, 1860.

[27]*Gazette,* September 8, 1860. Camden *Ouachita Herald,* July 21, 1860, quoted in the *Gazette,* August 4, 1860.

[28]*Old Line Democrat,* September 13, October 4, 1860. *True Democrat,* August 18, 25, 1860.

[29]Address of Albert Rust, *Gazette,* June 9, 1860. *Gazette,* September 15, November 3, 1860.

[30]*Gazette,* September 29, 1860.

[31]*Ibid.,* September 8, 1860. *Citizen,* September 5, 1860. "Philander" complained in the Searcy *Eagle,* n.d., quoted in the *Citizen,* September 19, 1860, that editor Morrill "cuts it too fat."

[32]*Old Line Democrat,* August 30, October 4, September 13, 1860.

[33]Judge Brown Diary, November 6, 1860.

[34]Letter of William Quesenbury, *Gazette,* November 17, 1860. Judge Brown Diary, October 10, November 6, 1860. *Gazette,* November 17, 1860.

[35]Wiley Britton, *Pioneer Life in Southwest Missouri* (Kansas City, 1929), p. 341.

Chapter 4

[1]*Gazette,* November 10, 1860. *Arkansian,* November 24, 1860. Des Arc *Constitutional Union,* November 30, 1860. Hereafter cited as *Constitutional Union. Shield,* n.d., quoted in the *Appeal,* November 21, 1860. *True Democrat,* n.d., quoted in the *Press,* November 23, 1860. Ollinger Crenshaw, "Governor Conway's Analysis and Proposed Solution of the Sectional Controversy, 1860," *A.H.Q.,* II (1943), 12–19. A.W. Bishop, *Loyalty on the Frontier, or Sketches of Union Men of the South-West; With Incidents and Adventures in Rebellion on the Border* (St. Louis, 1863), p. 9. Hereafter cited as Bishop, *Loyalty on the Frontier.* Judge Brown Diary, November 11, 1860.

[2]Inaugural Address of Henry M. Rector, *Gazette,* November 24, 1860.

[3]Letter of J. H. Quisenberry, in *ibid.,* January 12, 1861. Judge Brown Diary, December 4, 1860. *True Democrat,* December 22, 1860.

[4]J. H. Haney to Jesse Turner, December 13, 1860. Jesse Turner Papers, Duke University. G. J. Clark to Jesse Turner, November 29, 1860. Jesse Turner Papers, University of Arkansas. *Gazette,* November 24, 1860.

[5]*Gazette,* November 24, 1860.

[6]Letter of Robert W. Johnson, *ibid.,* December 22, 1860. G. J. Clark to Jesse Turner, November 29, 1860. Turner Papers, University of Arkansas. *Appeal,* December 9, 1860. Thompson B. Flournoy, the other leading Douglas figure, also became an early secessionist. See Letter of Thompson B. Flournoy, *Appeal,* January 2, 1861. Apparently he was welcomed back into the "family," for the *True Democrat* manifested great disappointment when the regiment he and brother James B. Johnson raised failed to elect them officers. See page 71.

[7]*Special Message of the Governor on Federal Relations* (Little Rock, n.d.). Immediately after the August election Rector supporter E. A. Warren had written to the governor suggesting that work be begun on selecting a suitable Senate candidate, but apparently little success attended the effort. E. A. Warren to Henry M. Rector, August 26, 1860. Oldham Collection.

[8]*Old Line Democrat,* December 13, 1860. *Journal of the House of Representatives,* 1860 (Little Rock, 1861), pp. 296–297.

[9]*Gazette,* December 1, 22, 1860.

[10]*Ibid.,* January 5, 1861.

[11]*Arkansian,* December 15, 1860

[12]*Old Line Democrat,* December 20, 1860.

[13]*Gazette,* December 29, 1860. *Arkansian,* February 8, 1861.

[14]*Gazette,* December 19, 22, 1860. Judge Brown Diary, January 6, February 9, 1861. On the latter date he observed: "the Baptist Church is a Democratic association [and] equals in extremes with the Northern fanatics."

[15]*Gazette,* January 5, 12, 1861.

[16]Judge Brown Diary, January 10, 18, 1861. *Gazette,* January 5, 12, 1861.

[17]*Gazette,* December 15, 22, 1860. David Walker to D. C. Williams, January 29, 1861, in W. J. Lemke, ed., *Judge David Walker—His Life and Letters* (Fayetteville, 1957), p. 44. Hereafter cited as Lemke, *Judge David Walker.*

[18]S. J. Howel to D. C. Williams, February 28, 1861; A. W. Dinsmore to D. C. Williams, January 24, 1861. D. C. Williams Papers, Arkansas History Commission. David Walker to D. C. Williams, January 28, 1861, in Lemke, ed., *Judge David Walker,* p. 43. Letter of Bishop Lay, February 4, 1861, in *Phillips County Historical Quarterly,* I (1962), 34.

[19]Letter of William Quesenbury, *Gazette,* March 2, 1861. [D. C. Williams Broadside] (Van Buren, January 29, 1861). Eno Collection, Arkansas History Commission.

[20]James Grieg to D. C. Williams, February 9, 1861. Williams Papers. *General Thomason's Letter, January 29, 1861.* Eno Collection.

[21]*Gazette,* January 19, 1861. *To A. W. Dinsmore and Haley Jackson.* Eno Collection.

[22]*Gazette,* January 5, 12, 1861. *Constitutional Union,* January 25, 1861.

[23]However the subject had come up in the private correspondence of the governor. Jno. Macon to Governor Rector, January 8, 1861. Oldham Collection. *Journal of Both Sessions of the Convention of the State of Arkansas* (Little Rock, 1861), p. 48. Hereafter cited as *Journal of Both Sessions*. Harrell, "Arkansas," p. 8. This was not the exact wording, said Harrell, but was "in something like these words." *True Democrat,* February 8, 1861, quoted in the *Press,* February 15, 1861. C. V. Meador, an eyewitness to these events, later claimed also that Burgevin sent the telegram to Pine Bluff and other points, but that Rector "was not fully aware of what was being done." See Little Rock *National Democrat,* June 11, 1864. Hereafter cited as *National Democrat*. Evidence implicating Rector consists of a letter from Camden editor George Turner who reported some eight hundred men were gathering in Eldorado (Union County) preparatory to moving on Little Rock. "The leaders of the movement are men of the highest respectability." George Turner to Governor Rector, January 23, 1861. Oldham Collection.

[24]Governor Rector to Captain Totten, January 29, 1861, in United States War Department, comp., *The War of the Rebellion: A Compilation of the Official Records of the Union and Confederate Armies* (Washington, 1880–1901), Series 1, I, 638–639. Hereafter cited as *O.R.* All quotations are from Series 1. Captain Totten to Governor Rector, January 29, 1861, *ibid.,* 639. Captain Totten to S. Cooper, January 29, 1861, *ibid.,* 638.

[25]*Journal of Both Sessions,* pp. 48–49. *Gazette,* February 9, 1861.

[26]*Gazette,* February 9, 1861. Resolution of the Little Rock City Council, February 5, 1861, in *O.R.,* I, 641. R. W. Johnson and W. K. Sebastian to Governor Rector, February 7, 1861, in *ibid.,* 681. R. W. Johnson to R. H. and J. B. Johnson, February 7, 1861, in *ibid.,* 681–682. Albert Pike and R. W. Johnson to John Pope, February 7, 1861, in *ibid.,* 682.

[27]Resolution of Citizens Meeting, February 6, 1861, in *O.R.,* I, 642. Governor Rector to Captain Totten, February 6, 1861, in *ibid.,* 640. Resolution of City Council, February 6, 1861, in *ibid.,* 641–42.

[28]Memorandum, February 8, 1861, in *ibid.,* 644. Orders No. 6, February 12, 1861, in *ibid.,* 646. *Gazette,* February 16, 1861. Virtually every prominent Little Rock family subscribed to the sword. One later regretted the action: "Totten is in Missouri wielding the *Sword* we have given him, *against us!*" Mrs. M. E. Weaver to Omer Weaver, July 5, 1861, in Ted R. Worley ed., *At Home in Confederate Arkansas—letters to and From Pulaski Countians, Pulaski County Historical Society,* Bulletin No. 2 (Little Rock, 1955), p. 4. Hereafter cited as Worley, ed., *At Home*. Captain Totten to S. Cooper, February 9, 1861, in *O.R.,* I, 645. Edmund Burgevin to C. B. [sic—really R. W.] Johnson, February 8, 1861, in *ibid.,* LIII, 617.

[29]James Yell to Jefferson Davis, June, 1861. Letters Received by the Confederate Secretary of War, 1861–1865. Record Group 109, National Archives. Hereafter cited as Yell Letter. R. W. Johnson to R. H. Johnson, February 8, 1861, in *O.R.,* I, 683.

[30]Albert Rust to D. C. Williams, February 7, 1861. D. C. Williams Papers, Arkansas History Commission. A month before these events, L. D. Evans, formerly an anti-Dynasty politician who removed to Texas and served a term in Congress, suggested in the Washington *National Intelligencer,* January 11, 1861, that the seizure of the various arsenals was planned at a meeting of senators from Florida, Georgia, Alabama, Mississippi, Texas, Louisiana, and Arkansas. See Henry Wilson, *History of the Rise and Fall of the Slave Power in America,* III

(Boston and New York, 1877), p. 133.

[31]*Press,* February 15, March 1, 1861. Albert Rust to D. C. Williams, February 7, 1861. Williams Papers. *Constitutional Union,* February 8, 1861. W. F. Holtzman to D. C. Williams, February 10, 1861. Williams Papers. Holtzman was unable to get a letter of Williams' in print because all the journeymen were on military duty.

[32]*Gazette,* February 16, 1861.

[33]*Ibid.,* February 2, 1861. In Letter of Robert W. Johnson, in *ibid.,* December 22, 1861, the senator explained why the idea of being a submissionist struck at the heart of Southern manhood: "Await overt acts! It is a paltry device of the submissionist." *Press,* January 25, 1861.

[34]*To the People of Washington County, February 5, 1861.* Eno Collection. *Correspondence—The Hon. Jesse Turner's Position,* February 4, 1861. Eno Collection. *Gazete,* February 2, 1861.

[35]William Wilcox to G. Wilcox, February 26, 1861. Duke University. *Gazette,* February 2, 1861.

[36]*An Appeal to the Voters of Benton County, Jno. Smith, Osage Mills, February 12, 1861.* Eno Collection.

[37]Camden *Eagle,* n.d., quoted in the *Gazette,* February 16, 1861. *To the Citizens of Benton County! February 8, 1861.* Eno Collection.

[38]*Address to the People of Arkansas by the Honorable R. W. Johnson* (Washington, 1861). Eno Collection. *Gazette,* February 9, 1861. Washington *Courier,* January 3, 1861, quoted in *ibid.,* January 26, 1861.

[39]The *Gazette,* which kept irregular weather charts, accidentally omitted a week which included the 18th. The weather before and after the election day, though, was in the thirties and forties. Given the backward nature of the country and the poverty of the inhabitants, good weather was essential if a large turnout was to be expected. *Gazette,* March 9, 1861. Ben T. Du Val to Governor Rector, February 20, 1861. Oldham Collection. According to Meador, Rector was controlled by Du Val and Edmund Burgevin. "Burgevin was a loud-talking, swaggering, unscrupulous yet free-hearted man. Du Val was a quiet, long-headed schemester; vindictive, ambitious and avaricious. Burgevin was a fire-eater; Du Val would eat anything to make money." *National Democrat,* June 11, 1864.

[40]John Smith to D. C. Williams, February 18, 1861. Williams Papers. D. C. Williams to Jesse Turner, March 11, 1861, Turner Papers, Duke University. *Constitutional Union,* March 15, 1861. H. F. Thomason to D. C. Williams, March 7, 1861. Williams Papers. *Gazette,* February 16, 1861. *Constitutional Union,* January 25, February 8, 22, March 1, 1861.

[41]*Alfred E. Mathews, Interesting Narrative; Being a Journal of the Flight of Alfred E. Mathews, of Stark Co., Ohio* (n.p., n.d.), pp. 24, 30.

[42]Judge Brown Diary, February 18, 1861. Henry C. Lay to Mrs. Lay, February 20, 1861. Henry C. Lay Papers, type copies, *Arkansas Gazette* Foundation Library.

[43]Judge Brown Diary, February 19, 21, 1861.

CHAPTER 5

[1]For profiles of the delegates, compare the *True Democrat,* April 18, 1861, and Ralph Wooster, "The Arkansas Secession Convention," *A.H.Q.,* XII (1954), 175–194. Hereafter cited as Wooster, "Secession Convention." C. Armitage Harper, ed., *Historical Report of the Secretary of State* (Little Rock, 1967), *passim.* Hereafter cited as Harper, *Historical Report.*

[2]Hallum, *Pictorial History*, pp. 303–308. Alfred Holt Carrigan, "Reminiscences of the Secession Convention," in *Publications of the Arkansas Historical Association*, I, 308–313. Hereafter cited as Carrigan, "Reminiscences." Jesse Cypert, "Reminiscences of the Secession Convention," *P.A.H.A.*, I, 315–321. Hereafter cited as Cypert, "Reminiscences."

[3]Wooster, "Secession Convention," 174. *True Democrat*, April 18, 1861.

[4]*Ibid.*

[5]Wooster is seriously inadequate in his figuring. One of his six unidentified delegates was Jilson P. Johnson. Robert B. Waltz, "Arkansas Slaveholdings and Slaveholders in 1850," *A.H.Q.*, XII (1953), 61, found that in 1850 Cousin Jils, although only twenty-three years old, owned forty-six slaves. Other unidentified probable slaveholders include Josiah Gould and B. F. Hawkins, both listed as planters by the *True Democrat*, G. P. Smoote and I. C. Wallace (whose address was in Lousiana!)

[6]S. H. Tucker to D. C. Williams, March 7, 10, 1861. Williams Papers. Carrigan, "Reminiscences," 306. *Avalanche*, March 11, 1861. *Gazette*, March 2, 1861.

[7]H. F. Thomason to D. C. Williams, March 7, 1861. Williams Papers. *True Democrat*, April 18, 1861. *Appeal*, January 3, 1861.

[8]H. F. Thomason to D. C. Williams, March 7, 1861. Williams Papers. *Journal of Both Sessions*, pp. 10–11.

[9]Address of I. H. Hilliard, *True Democrat*, April 18, 1861.

[10]*Press*, March 13, 1861. *Gazette*, March 9, 1861. *Avalanche*, March 9, 1861.

[11]*Arkansian*, March 15, 1861.

[12]John J. Walker to W. W. Mansfield, March 12, 1861. Mansfield Papers, Arkansas History Commission. D. C. Williams to W. W. Mansfield, March 15, 1861. Mansfield Papers.

[13]*True Democrat*, February 28, 1861, quoted in the *Appeal*, March 3, 1861. *Avalanche*, March 9, 1861. Yell Letter. *Appeal*, March 13, 1861. Carrigan, "Reminiscences," p. 307. *Journal of Both Sessions*, pp. 16–55.

[14]*Avalanche*, March 12, 1861.

[15]Jesse Turner to Mrs. Turner, March 7, 1861. Turner Papers, Duke University. The *Journal of Both Sessions*, p. 26, reported that Totten "spoke for some time." *Press*, March 13, 1861. *Gazette*, March 23, 1861 Carrigan, "Reminiscences," p. 306. *True Democrat*, March 11, 1861.

[16]*True Democrat*, March 15, 1861. *Journal of Both Sessions*, p. 108. Cypert, "Reminiscences," p. 316.

[17]James Z. Rabun, "Alexander H. Stephens and Jefferson Davis," *American Historical Review*, LVIII (1953), 293–94. *True Democrat*, March 9, 1861. *Avalanche*, March 14, 1861. *Journal of Both Sessions*, p. 31. In 1864 when confronted by this resolution by the U. S. Senate, Fishy claimed that secessionist threats forced him to offer the resolution.

[18]*Journal of Both Sessions*, pp. 41–49, 24–27, 36–37, 56–58. *Gazette*, March 9, 16, 1861. Yell Letter.

[19]*Gazette*, March 16, 1861. *Journal of Both Sessions*, p. 58. *True Democrat*, March 11, 1861.

[20]*Journal of Both Sessions*, pp. 51–54. *Gazette*, February 2, 1861. *True Democrat*, March 16, 1861.

[21]*True Democrat*, March 12, 1861. *Avalanche*, March 14, 1861.

[22]*Avalanche*, March 16, 1861. *True Democrat*, March 13, 1861.

[23]*Journal of Both Sessions*, p. 62. *Appeal*, April 5, 1861. The *Sage of Monticello*, February 26, 1861, wanted South Arkansas to establish its own independence or be annexed to

Louisiana in the event secession failed. *Appeal,* April 14, 1861. *Avalanche,* March 16, 1861. *Appeal,* March 19, 1861. As for Sebastian, the *True Democrat,* March 15, 1861, solemnly intoned, "his position on the great question of the day is too well known to require mentioning." Actually Sebastian never publicly endorsed secession, and some of his constituents knew it. The Osceola Minute Men, on February 16, 1861, condemned his "weak and vacillating course." "His policy of 'non-committal' meets with our hearty disapproval and censure." *Avalanche,* February 26, 1861.

[24]*Appeal,* March 21, 1861.

[25]*Ibid. True Democrat,* March 15, 1861.

[26]*Ibid. True Democrat,* March 16, 1861.

[27]*Gazette,* August 2, 1843. *Journal of Both Sessions,* pp. 77–78.

[28]*Appeal,* March 23, 1861.

[29]*Ibid.* Jesse Turner to Mrs. Turner, March 19, 1861. Turner Papers, Duke University.

[30]*Press,* March 20, 1861. E. P. Lene to D. C. Williams, March 19, 1861. Williams Papers. Monticello, *The Sage of Monticello,* March 19, 1861. *True Democrat,* March 9, 1861. *Gazette,* March 16, 1861.

[31]H. F. Thomason to D. C. Williams, March 20, 1861. Williams Papers. *Journal of Both Sessions,* pp. 107–108.

[32]In no state in the lower South did a popular referendum take place; a referendum was required by law in Virginia and Tennessee. As to the willingness of the secessionists to accept less than unconditional secession, the *Gazette,* March 16, 1861, commented: "Finding their blandishments unavailing, they have changed their tactics, and now pretend to be very conciliatory, very reasonable, very willing to trust the people, and they ask the Union men, who now have control of the Convention, to pass an ordinance of secession and refer it back to the people."

[33]*True Democrat,* April 13, 1861. H. F. Thomason to D. C. Williams, March 7, 1861. Williams Papers. James Grieg to D. C. Williams, March 25, 31, 1861. Williams Papers. William Fishback to D. C. Williams, March 23, 1861. Williams Papers.

[34]S. H. Tucker to D. C. Williams, March 23, 1861. Williams Papers. James Grieg to D. C. Williams, March 31, 1861. Williams Papers.

[35]William Fishback to D. C. Williams, April 10, 1861. Williams Papers.

[36]J. M. Tebbetts to D. C. Williams, March 25, 1861. Williams Papers. S. H. Tucker promised, "I will see that every poor man gets one." S. H. Tucker to D. C. Williams, March 23, 1861. Williams Papers. William Fishback to D. C. Williams, April 10, 1861. Williams Papers. A. W. Hobson to Jesse Turner, April 16, 1861. Turner Papers, Duke University.

[37]*True Democrat,* April 11, 1861. *Gazette,* March 30, 1861. David Walker answered Senator Johnson at Fayetteville, H. F. Thomason answered him at Batesville, and Jesse Turner was petitioned to answer him at Van Buren. James Moore, *et al,* to Jesse Turner, April 12, 1861. Turner Papers, Duke University. Letter of William Quesenbury, in *Gazette,* May 4, 1861.

[38]Address of I. H. Hilliard, *True Democrat,* April 18, 1861. Lake Village *Chicot Press,* n.d., quoted in the *Gazette,* April 13, 1861. *Gazette,* April 13, 1861. Such was the conclusion of Jack B. Scrogg, "Arkansas in the Secession Crisis," *A.H.Q.,* XII (1953), 217.

[39]Alexander Harding to Governor Rector, June 19, 1861. Oldham Collection. *Arkansas Veteran,* I (October, 1913), 1–2.

[40]*Sage of Monticello,* March 19, 1861, Fort Smith *Thirty-Fifth Parallel,* February 23, 1861. Hereafter cited as the *Thirty-Fifth Parallel.*

[41]S. L. Griffith to D. C. Williams, March 30, 1861. Williams Papers. Fort Smith *Times and*

Herald, March 25, 1861, quoted in the *Press,* April 3, 1861. The other paper, the *Thirty-Fifth Parallel,* pursued, said Griffith, a "manly and dignified" course. *Press,* April 3, 1861. Bishop, *Loyalty on the Frontier,* pp. 7–8: "A lamentable confusion of terms, and a mistaken impression of the character of Northern sentiments, made every opponent an Abolitionist. 'He's no better nor a nigger,' said one; 'He's a nigger thief,' said another; 'He wants to put niggers into office over us,' would chime in a third; and so on through a long diatribe of senseless and vindictive calumnies."

[42]Bishop, *Loyalty on the Frontier,* pp. 148–163. In 1850 Pike penned a poem entitled Disunion: "For nothing that time has upbuilt / And set in the annals of crime, / So Stupid and senseless, so wretched in guilt, / Darkens sober tradition or rhyme."

[43]*Gazette,* February , 1861. *True Democrat,* April 18, 1861. manuscript copy in private possession.

[44]S. H. Tucker to D. C. Williams, March 2, 1861. Williams Papers. W. W. Mansfield to Jesse Turner, April 15, 1861. Turner Papers, Duke University. Rust's defection was reported in the *True Democrat,* April 18, 1861, not necessarily a reliable source. Colonel Warren, a sometime congressman (1853–1855; 1857–1859), was a respectable man's Gantt. "His election to the Border Conference was exceedingly unwise," wrote W. W. Mansfield to Jesse Turner, April 15, 1861. Turner Papers, Duke University.

[45] N. Bart Pearce, "Price's Campaign of 1861," *P.A.H.A.,* I V, 332—33. Hereafter cited as Pearce, "Price's Campaign."

[46]James Grieg to D. C. Williams, May 9, 1861. Williams Papers. S. G. Stallings to Jesse Turner, April 19, 1861. Turner Papers, Duke University. Marginal notation written on *To the People of Arkansas, April 18, 1861,* Eno Collection. James Grieg to D. C. Williams, May 9, 1861. Williams Papers.

[47]C. F. Jackson to David Walker, April 19, 1861. State Historical Society of Missouri. Thomas B. Hanly to David Walker, April 17, 1861. Walker Papers. Hanly added: "In the counties of Phillips, Monroe, St. Francis, Poinsett, Craighead, Green [sic], Crittenden, and Mississippi, the secession sentiment is nearly unanimous since the recent events." *Gazette,* April 20, 1861. Governor Rector to Simon Cameron, April 22, 1861, *O.R.,* I, 687.

[48]*Gazette,* April 20, 27, 1861. *Independent Balance,* n.d., quoted in *ibid.*

[49]Bishop, *Loyalty on the Frontier,* pp.178–181.

[50]D. Y. Thomas, *Arkansas in War and Reconstruction* (Little Rock, 1926), p. 79.

[51]Jesse Turner to Mrs. Turner, May 2, 1861. Turner Papers, Duke University. Symbolic of public sentiment, the Brass Band of Van Buren, the second best in the state, serenaded Senator Johnson; almost one month before it was Jesse Turner who received the compliment. *Press,* March 27, April 24, 1861.

[52]C. C. Danley to David Walker, April 15, 1861. Walker Papers, *Arkansas Gazette Foundation Library.* C. C. Danley to W. W. Mansfield, April 23, 1861. Mansfield Papers. D. C. Williams to Jesse Turner, May 7, 1861. Turner Papers, Duke University.

[53]Bishop, *Loyalty on the Frontier,* p. 23. Jesse Turner to Mrs. Turner, May 8, 1861. Turner Papers, Duke University. James J. Johnston, ed., "Letter of John Campbell, Unionist," *A.H.Q.* XXIX (1970), 179. The *True Democrat,* May 9, 1861, reported that Tennessee had left the Union, although this act was not officially consummated until the ordinance was approved in a popular referendum on June 8, 1861.

[54]Bishop, *Loyalty on the Frontier,* p. 23. Cypert, "Reminiscences," pp. 318–19.

[55]Cypert, "Reminiscences," pp. 318–19. For a slightly different version, together with the remarks of Frank Desha, William Stout, and H. F. Thomason, see the *True Democrat,* May 9, 1861. For Murphy's persistence, a different version to the same effect is in Bishop, *Loyalty on*

the Frontier, pp. 25–26. *Journal of Both Sessions,* p. 124. Cypert, "Reminiscences," p. 319, and Hindman (T. C. Hindman to Jeff. Davis, May 6, 1861, O. R., I, 690) state that the time was four o'clock; the *True Democrat,* May 9, 1861, placed the time at three o'clock.

[56]W. E. Woodruff, *With the Light Guns in '61–65* (Little Rock, 1903), p. 11. Jesse Turner to D. C. Williams, May 8, 1861, Williams Papers, Jesse Turner to Mrs. Turner, May 8, 27, 1861, Turner Papers, Duke University. Demby, *The War in Arkansas,* p. 20.

[57]Hiram A. Whittington to W. E. Woodruff, May 15, 1861, in Worley, ed., *At Home,* p. 12. Judge Brown Diary, April 21, 1861.

[58]A. V. Carrigan to Mrs. Carrigan, May 4, 1861. Carrigan Family Papers, Duke University. This Carrigan was a distant cousin of the conservative delegate A. H. Carrigan. Judge Brown Diary, April 23, 1861. *Citizen,* May 10, 1861. Letter of William Quesenbury, *Gazette,* May 4, 1861.

[59]Ordinances of the Convention (Little Rock, 1861), p. 93. Hereafter cited as *Ordinances.* The 1861 constitution may be found in the *Ordinances* and in the *Journal of Both Sessions.* The 1836 constitution is in *Revised Statutes of the State of Arkansas adopted at the October session of the General Assembly* (Boston, 1838). Changing the date for holding the state elections was a Whig reform because in August, "the Democrats could all get out and vote whether they had shoes or not." *Address of L. B. Woodside, Before the Bar Association of the Nineteenth Judicial Circuit, Held at Salem, Missouri, June 17, 1920.*

[60]R. C. Gatlin to L. Thomas, April 14, 1861, *O.R.,* I, 650. *True Democrat,* April 25, 1861.

[61]*True Democrat,* May 2, 1861. *Gazette,* April 20, 1861.

[62]Jesse Turner to D. C. Williams, May 19, 1861. Williams Papers.

[63]Note of Henry M. Rector, April 7, 1861. Oldham Collection. *True Democrat,* July 25, 1861.

[64]*Gazette,* May 18, 1861.

[65]Yell letter.

[66]*Ibid.* A. B. Greenwood to Governor Rector, May 23, 1861. Oldham Collection.

[67]*True Democrat,* May 23, 1861. *Journal of Both Sessions,* pp. 298, 303.

[68]Hallum, *Biographical History,* p. 409. *Journal of Both Sessions,* p. 449.

[69]Carrigan, "Reminiscences," p. 308. *Citizen,* May 31, 1861. Washington *Courier,* n.d., quoted in *Citizen,* June 14, 1861. Judge Brown Diary, July 6, 1861.

[70]Shinn, *Pioneers and Makers,* p. 234. *Journal of Both Sessions,* pp. 444–473.

[71]Demby, *The War in Arkansas,* p. 52.

CHAPTER 6

[1]Albert Pike to R. W. Johnson, May 11, 1861, *O.R.,* III, 572–74.

[2]Thompson B. Flournoy *et al,* to L. P. Walker, April 3, 1861, *ibid.,* I, 688.

[3]*Arkansian,* December 1, 1860. *Times,* May 31, 1860. Albert Pike to R. W. Johnson, May 11, 1861, *O.R.,* III, 572–74. Annie Heloise Abel, *The American Indian as Slaveholder and Secessionist* (Cleveland, 1915), pp. 121ff. Hereafter cited as Abel, *The American Indian.*

[4]W. H. Heroman to "Dear Father," June 18, 1861. George M. Heroman and Family Papers, Department of Archives and Manuscripts, Louisiana State University. *Citizen,* May 28, 1861.

[5]Dorothy Stanley, ed., *The Autobiography of Sir Henry Morton Stanley* (Boston and New York, 1937), pp. 164–65. For a curious footnote on Stanley in Arkansas, see W. J. and J. F. Weaver, "Early Days in Fort Smith," typescript in the Fort Smith Public Library, where correspondence and testimony is assembled to show that H. M. Stanley was really one J. C.

Stanley, tutor of Elias Rector's children, lieutenant in the Confederate cavalry, and deserter (along with the company payroll of $2,000). Ted Worley, ed., *They Never Came Back—The War Memories of Captain John W. Lavender, C.S.A.* (Pine Bluff, 1956), pp. 4, 152. Hereafter cited as Worley, ed., *They Never Came Back.* Frank P. Peak, "A Soldier's View on the Civil War: Narrative or Sketches Written While in Prison as a Prisoner of War, 1863." Typescript, Louisiana State University. Hereafter cited as Peak, "A soldier's view."

[6]J. W. House, "Constitution of 1874 and its Reminiscences" A paper read by J. W. House at the Bar Association in Hot Springs, June, 1910. Fort Smith Public Library.

[7]William Oliver to Governor Rector, June 11, 1861. Oldham Collection. *Gazette,* May 4, 1861.

[8]For instance, militia General Benjamin P. Jett reported his brigade "all officered and ready for action except in arms and munitions of war." Benjamin P. Jett to Secretary of War, April 27, 1861, *O.R.,* I, 689. One month later, T. D. Merrick complained to Governor Rector that he was "a Major General only in name." T. D. Merrick to Governor Rector, June 6, 1861. Oldham Collection. Furthermore the convention authorized home guards, membership in which exempted men from militia duty. Some used this subterfuge to avoid all duty. Governor's Message, *True Democrat,* November 7, 1861.

[9]Little Rock *Daily State Journal,* November 24, 1861. Hereafter cited as *Journal.*

[10]Kellam Diary, April 30, May 6, 1861. *Gazette,* May 4, 1861. Worley, ed., *They Never Came Back,* p. 5. Marcus J. Wright, *Arkansas in the War,* 1861–1865 (Batesville, 1963). pp. 51–55.

[11]B. F. J. Hyatt to D. C. Hyatt, June 14, 1861. Same to same, July 29, 1861. B. F. J. Hyatt Letters, private possession. Jeff Jobe Diary, June 9, 15, July 2, 3, 20, 25, 1861. Arkansas History Commission. Nash, *Biographical Sketches,* pp. 132–33.

[12]*True Democrat,* May 16, 1861. *Gazette,* May 18, 1861.

[13]Judge Brown Diary, summer, 1861, *passim.* N. Bart Pearce to Jefferson Davis, May 13, 1861, *O.R.,* III, 576.

[14]T. C. Hindman to L. P. Walker, May 29, 1861, *O.R.,* III, 588. G. W. Whittington to W. E. Woodruff, July 24, 1861, in Worley, ed., *At Home,* p. 16.

[15]Rev. Wheat to Maj. Wheat, May 30, 1861. John T. Wheat Papers, Southern Historical Collection, University of North Carolina, Wheat's address was probably delivered by Sandford C. Faulkner's daughter, a well-known Arkansas Belle. *Citizen,* July 24, September 4, 1861. R. F. Kellam Diary, April 29, 1861.

[16]John Seay to Leonidas Polk Wheat, July 21, 1861. John T. Wheat Papers. Letter of a Western Arkansian, *True Democrat,* July 18, 1861. David Walker to D. C. Williams, August 29, 1862, in Lemke, ed., *Judge David Walker,* p. 46. G. McKinney to Governor Rector, November 30, 1861, Oldham Collection. W. H. Foster to "Mr. Henry M. Rector, governor of the state," October 14, 1861. Oldham Collection.

[17]*True Democrat,* August 22, 1861, February 20, 1862.

[18]Mrs. Mary B. Eskridge to W. E. Woodruff, May 6, 1861, in Worley, ed., *At Home,* p. 23. Judge Brown Diary, January 24, March 3, December 9, 1861. John S. Hornor to W. E. Woodruff, March 12, 1861. Woodruff Papers, same to same, June 15, 1861. James Touchstone to W. E. Woodruff, January 20, 1862. Woodruff Papers. *True Democrat,* October 24, 1861. Freeman H. Mooring to W. E. Woodruff, April 6, 1862. Woodruff Papers.

[19]*Journal,* November 10, 12, 1861. Governor Rector to J. P. Benjamin, October 14, 1861, *O. R.,* III, 719

[20]S. C. Turnbo, "History of the Twenty-Seventh Arkansas Confederate Regiment", pp. 55—57. Typescript, *Arkansas Gazette* Foundation Library. Hereafter cited as Turnbo, "The

Twenty-Seventh Arkansas.'' *Press,* October 2, 1861. *Journal,* November 6, 10, 21, 1861.

²¹Hodges to William Crawford, July 4, 1861. William Crawford Letters, Arkansas History Commission. *Gazette,* August 24, 1861.

²²Peak, ''A Soldier's View.'' *True Democrat,* July 4, 1861. *Citizen,* May 10, 14, 21, 31, July 6, 10, 1861. Jacksonport *Herald,* May 4, 1861, quoted in *Citizen,* May 14, 1861. *Shield,* May 11, 1861, quoted in *Citizen,* May 21, 1861. Judge Brown Diary, May 16, 1861. Kellam Diary, May 4, 1861. At Hickory Plain the vigilance measures met with less than overwhelming approval. It was said that the confessions were extorted and the slaves inhumanely whipped. The committee was thus forced to justify its conduct in the press. Probably untold minor investigations were numerous. J. W. Felts to W. E. Woodruff, July 28, 1861, in Worley, ed., *At Home,* p. 10.

²³*Gazette,* May 18, 25, 1861. Mathews, *Interesting Narrative,* p. 30. Brownsville *Prairie Democrat,* n.d., quoted in *Gazette,* May 11, 1861.

²⁴Mathews, *Interesting Narrative,* p. 30. *Gazette,* May 25, 1861.

²⁵*Journal of Both Sessions,* pp. 423–24. *Citizen,* June 4, 1861, *True Democrat,* July 4, 1861. *Press,* July 17, 1861.

²⁶*Press,* June 26, 1861. A. B. Greenwood to Governor Rector, May 23, 1861. Oldham Collection. F. A. Rector to Governor Rector, May 26, 1861. Oldham Collection. *True Democrat,* October 10, 1861.

²⁷For instance, ''Our people have no confidence in such as we have,'' A. H. Garland to Secretary of War, June 5, 1861. Letters Received by the Confederate Secretary of War. The visiting Indian commissioner wrote, ''I have never yet saw people who appeared to know so little about commanders, who seemed so utterly devoid of confidence in any one faction or leader of a faction in the state. My belief and conviction is that but little can be done among these factions, and that a military leader from without the state is needed.'' David Hubbard to L. P. Walker, *O.R.,* III, 589–90. Cherokee chief John Ross wanted no Confederate protection. See Abel, *The American Indian,* pp. 149–50. Letter of James Yell. Ben McCulloch to L. P. Walker, May 20, 1861, *O.R.,* III, 579–80.

²⁸C. C. Danley to Jefferson Davis, June 13, 1861, *O.R.,* LIII, 698–99. *True Democrat,* July 4, 1861.

²⁹*True Democrat,* June 20, 27, 1861. On the later date the paper published the board's ''Rules and Articles for the Government of the Army of Arkansas,'' a clear indication of the intended permanence of the army. Governor Rector to L. P. Walker, June 12, 1861, *O.R.,* III, 590–91. L. P. Walker to Governor Rector, June 22, 1861, *ibid.,* 597.

³⁰S. Cooper to W. J. Hardee, June 25, 1861, *O.R.,* III, 598. W. J. Hardee, General Order Number 1, July 22, 1861, *ibid.,* 612.

³¹Ben McCulloch to L. P. Walker, July 3, 1861, *O.R.,* III, 600. *True Democrat,* July 4, 1861. *Gazette,* July 20, 1861. *Press,* July 10, 1861.

³²John A. Jordan to L. P. Walker, July 3, 1861, *O.R.,* III, 602. Ben McCulloch to L. P. Walker, July 9, 1861, *ibid.,* 606–608.

³³W. J. Hardee to Governor Rector, July 25, 1861, *ibid.,* 614–15. W. J. Hardee to Sterling Price, July 27, 1861, *ibid.,* 616.

³⁴Articles of Transfer, July 15, 1861, *ibid.,* 609–610. *Gazette,* July 20, 1861. T. C. Hindman to S. Cooper, June 19, 1863, *O.R.,* XIII, 31. W. J. Hardee to Leonidas Polk, July 28, 1861, *ibid.,* III, 618.

³⁵For two recent accounts, see Albert Castel, *General Sterling Price and the Civil War in the West* (Baton Rouge, 1968), pp. 25–47. Hereafter cited as Castel, *Sterling Price,* and Robert E. Shalhope, *Sterling Price—Portrait of a Southerner* (Columbia, 1971), pp. 170–78.

Hereafter cited as Shalhope, *Sterling Price*. McCulloch explained his withdrawal with the public excuses of shortage of ammunition, the disbanding of the Arkansas troops (which left him only 2,500 men), and his orders to defend Indian Territory and Arkansas. But privately McCulloch had serious reservations about the quality of the Missouri army. See Ben McCulloch to J. P. Benjamin, December 22, 1861 *O.R.,* III, 734–49.

[36]Governor's Message, *True Democrat,* November 7, 1861. Rector's memory was very selective. Ben McCulloch to L. P. Walker, August 31, 1861, *O. R.,* III, 716.

[37]N. Bart Pearce to the Secretary of War, October 10, 1861, *O.R.,* III, 715–16. Letter of a Private, *True Democrat,* September 12, 1861. The delay was occasioned by the inability to print the war bonds fast enough.

[38]W. J. Hardee to Sterling Price, July 27, 1861. *O.R.,* III, 616. Ben McCulloch to L. P. Walker, August 31, 1861, *ibid.,* 691–92. N. Bart Pearce to the Secretary of War, October 10, 1861, *ibid.,* 715–16.

[39]Governor Rector to Leonidas Polk, July 30, 1861, *ibid.,* 621. W. J. Hardee to S. Cooper, August 7, 1861. *ibid.,* 638.

[40]*Press,* September 11, 1861. *True Democrat,* September 26, 1861.

[41]*Press,* September 4, 1861. Ben McCulloch to J. P. Benjamin, December 22, 1861, *O.R.,* III, 743–49. Castel, *Sterling Price,* pp. 48–49. Ben McCulloch to J. P. Benjamin, November 8, 1861, *ibid.,* 734. Shalhope, *Sterling Price,* p. 187. Relations between Price and McCulloch had so deteriorated that they had to meet halfway between their respective camps, as neither would condescend to visit the other.

[42]L. P. Walker to Ben McCulloch, September 4, 1861, *O.R.,* III, 694. L. P. Walker to Governor Rector, September 5, 1861, *ibid.,* 697–98. Governor Rector to L. P. Walker, August 9, 1861, *ibid.,* 639. W. J. Hardee to Ben McCulloch, September 9, 1861, *ibid.,* LIII, 737–38. *True Democrat,* October 31, 1861.

[43]W. J. Hardee to Leonidas Polk, September 17, 18, 19, 24, 1861, *O.R.,* III, 702–707.

[44]T. C. Hindman to Ben McCulloch, September 20, 1861. Thomas C. Hindman Papers, Record Group 109–121, National Archives. Hardee had originally ordered the arms removed to Pocahontas. McCulloch protested that this was tantamount to abandoning the northwest. Ben McCulloch to Governor Rector, September 25, 1861. Photocopy, University of Arkansas.

[45]Governor Rector to Secretary of War, September 30, 1861, *O.R.,* III, 710–11.

[46]J. P. Benjamin to Governor Rector, November 19, 1861, *ibid.,* 742. Of course while Rector was unable to get arms, Hindman and McCulloch were arming their twelve month volunteers with the transferred state arms! Jno. D. Kimball to Secretary of War, November 12, 1861, *ibid.,* 738.

[47]*Press,* October 16, 1861. Edmund Burgevin to Governor Rector, October 8, 1861. Oldham Collection. C. C. Dawson to Governor Rector, August 31, 1861. Oldham Collection.

[48]Governor Rector to L. P. Walker, September 4, 1861, *O.R.,* III, 695–96. Stanley recalled seeing Burgevin as a general later in China. In the Civil War it was Senator Johnson who influenced appointments. An example of his power may be seen in his letter to D. H. Reynolds: "You are appt. at last by dint of your merits, and the devotion, and esteem, and perseverance of your friends." R. W. Johnson to D. H. Reynolds, March 14, 1864. Daniel Harris Reynolds Papers, University of Arkansas.

[49]Ben McCulloch to Governor Rector, September 35, 1861. Photocopy, University of Arkansas. *Message to the Senate,* November 11, 1862 (Little Rock, 1862). *Journal,* November 5, 12, 1861.

[50]Historians of the war on the border have always stressed this significance, but additional

support can be found in Allan Nevins, *The War for the Union* (New York, 1959), I, 119–129; and James Rawley, *Turning Points of the Civil War* (Lincoln, 1966).

[51]Judge Brown Diary, December 13, 1861. Letter from Chicot County, *True Democrat*, October 31, 1861. *Ibid.*, September 5, 1861. Mansfield and Walker were former Unionists; Cross, president of the Cairo and Fulton Railroad, was an ex-Democratic congressman from South Arkansas.

[52]*True Democrat*, December 12, 1861. The *True Democrat* said the three were absent; the *Journal*, December 12, 1861, charged that they had resigned. *Journal*, December 13, 1861. As part of the bitter persecution, editor Peek lost his appointment as Military Storekeeper at the Arsenal to "family" friend Sandford C. Faulkner.

[53]*True Democrat*, November 7, 14, December 19, 1861. Napoleon *Planter*, n.d., quoted in *ibid.*, April 18, 1861. Letter of Virgil, *Ibid.*, October, 31, 1861. Rector rather than Garland was the object of the *True Democrat's* criticism. The *Journal*, December 20, 1861, defended Rector. Johnson contested the election, but the contested elections committee decided on narrow grounds that it had no authority to look beyond the certified returns. See *Confederate Congress, Arkansas Contested Election, Johnson v. Garland, Exposition and Argument by the Counsel of Mr. Johnson* (Richmond, 1862).

[54]*Journal*, December 4, 1861, January 5, 1862.

[55]Governor's Message, *True Democrat*, November 7, 1861.

[56]*Ibid.* Arkadelphia *Ouachita Conference Journal*, n.d., quoted in *ibid.*, January 2, 1862.

[57]*Journal*, November 29, 1861. Journal of the Senate of the Special Session of the General Assembly, November 4, 1861. (Ms), pp. 69, 85. Microfilm Collection of Early State Papers, Emory University. Hereafter cited as Senate Journal.

[58]*Acts of Arkansas, Passed at the Special Session* (Little Roc, 1861), pp. 43, 48, 55, 78. Hereafter cited as Acts of Arkansas. Uriah M. Rose, "An Episode During the Civil War," (Ms), p. 3. University of Arkansas.

[59]*Journal*, November 19, 1861. One legislator apparently agreed and offered a resolution: "that both houses organize into a military company and repair immediately to Pocahontas, to aid in the defense of our State." *Ibid.*, November 12, 1861.

[60]Extract from a letter, *True Democrat*, August 15, 1861. *Thirty-Fifth Parallel*, n.d., quoted in *ibid.*, October 31, 1861. Albert Pike to John C. Peay, November 22, [1861]. Microfilm, Arkansas History Commission. *Journal*, November 7, 10, 1861. The best evidence that supports Peek comes from the assertion of the *True Democrat*, November 14, 1861, that Pike's name was used "without his knowledge or consent." Pike, a good friend of Johnson and his future law partner, had been moving toward Democracy during the 1850s and had become an early secessionist. Indeed his record was more consistent than Mitchel's. Yet in the nature of things, if the Johnsons wanted Pike elected, they did not dare admit it. To the public, Pike's name was linked to that of Robert Crittenden and the creation of the Whig party.

[61]Ted. R. Worley, "The Arkansas Peace Society of 1861: A Study in Mountain Unionism," *J.S.H.*, XXIV (1958), 445–56. Hereafter cited as Worley, "The Arkansas Peace Society." Ted. R. Worley, ed., "Documents Relating to the Arkansas Peace Society of 1861," *A.H.Q.*, XVII (1958), 82–111. Hereafter cited as Worley, ed., "Documents."

[62]Bishop, *Loyalty on the Frontier*, p. 135. Some who signed this protest soon fled to Union lines. *Ibid.*, pp. 136ff. Worley, ed. "Documents," 82.

[63]*True Democrat*, December 5, 19, 1861, March 6, 1862.

[64]*Ibid.*, March 6, 1862.

[65]Worley, "The Arkansas Peace Society," 445–56.

[66]Solon Borland to Leonidas Polk, November 10, 1861, *O.R.*, VIII, 683–86. Proceedings

of the Military Board of the State of Arkansas, November 8, 1861, *ibid.*, LIII, 889. Solon Borland to Governor Rector, December 6, 1861, Oldham Collection.

[67]General Order, November 29, 1861, *Gazette,* December 14, 1861. *Telegraph,* January 22, 1862.

[68]J. H. Foster to Governor Rector, December 11, 1861. Oldham Collection. Governor Rector to J. P. Benjamin, December 12, 1861. Oldham Collection. *True Democrat,* December 26, 1861. *Journal,* January 23, 1862. Borland's card appeared in the *Gazette,* June 14, 1862.

[69]*True Democrat,* October 24, 1861, March 13, 1862. *Gazette,* December 14, 1861. *Journal,* November 12, 1861.

[70]*Journal,* November 28, 1861. *Telegraph,* January 15, 1862. *Gazette,* March 1, 1862.

[71]C. N. Paisley to Governor Rector, January 4, 1862. John Burrows to Governor Rector, March 2, 1862. N. B. Burrow to Governor Rector, March 9, 1862. John A. Beck to Governor Rector, March 7, 1862. For more complaints, see A. L. Withington to Governor Rector, January 26, 1862. Burton Hallbrooks to Governor Rector, February 13, 1862. James F. Baston to Governor Rector, February 16, 1862. Oldham Collection. The file of letters to the governor breaks off in March and does not resume until 1863. *Shield,* n.d., quoted in *True Democrat,* February 20, 1862.

[72]Robert G. Hartje, *Van Dorn–The Life and Times of a Confederate General* (Nashville, 1967), p. 12, Hereafter cited as Hartje, *Van Dorn.*

[73]Special Orders Number 6, January 16, 1862, *O.R.,* VIII, 734. General Orders No. 1, January 29, 1862, *ibid.,* 745. Governor Rector to J. P. Benjamin, February 6, 1862, *ibid.,* 748. *True Democrat,* February 6, 13, 1862.

[74]*True Democrat,* March 6, 20, 1862. *Acts Passed at the Thirteenth or Special Session* (Little Rock, 1862). pp. 3–24.

[75]Governor Rector to Governor Francis W. Pickens, April 11, 1862. University of Arkansas. *True Democrat,* January 27, April 24, 1862. *Telegraph,* June 25, 1862.

[76]*True Democrat,* March 27, 1862.

[77]Earl Van Dorn to Sterling Price, February 7, 1862, *O.R.,* VII, 749. Sterling Price to C. F. Jackson, February 25, 1862, *ibid.,* 756–57. Van Dorn rode across north Arkansas to reach the other army; the cold which he caught hindered him at Pea Ridge. Hartje, *Van Dorn,* pp. 115ff.

[78]Accounts of the battle may be found in Hartje, *Van Dorn,* pp. 115–161. Shalhope, *Sterling Price,* pp. 197–209. Castel, *Sterling Price,* pp. 66–83. Walter Brown, "Pea Ridge: Gettysburg of the West," *A.H.Q.,* XV (1956), 3–16. There is general agreement that given a little luck, a better plan, etc., the Confederacy could have won an important victory. But they did not.

[79]R. W. Johnson, *et al,* to Jefferson Davis. *O.R.,* XIII, 814–16.

[80]Governor Rector to Governor Francis W. Pickens, April 11, 1862. University of Arkansas.

[81]*True Democrat,* May 1, 1862. R. W. Johnson, *et al,* to Jefferson Davis, *O.R.,* XIII, 814–16. Jefferson Davis to Earl Van Dorn, May 20, 1862, *ibid.,* 828–3̇2. Shalhope, *Sterling Price,* pp. 211–12.

[82]Proclamation of Governor Rector, *True Democrat,* May 8, 1862.

[83]*True Democrat,* May 8, 1862. *Telegraph,* May 14, 1862. Earl Van Dorn to Jefferson Davis, June 9, 1862, *O.R.,* XIII, 831.

[84]*Gazette,* June 28, 1862. *True Democrat,* May 22, 1862. Letter of Governor Rector in *ibid.,* May 29, 1862. T. C. Hindman to S. Cooper, June 19, 1863, *O.R.,* XII, 30. Letter of R. H. Johnson, *True Democrat,* May 29, 1862. *True Democrat,* July 17, 1862. *Patriot,* October 2, 1862.

[85]T. C. Hindman to S. Cooper, June 19, 1863, *O.R.*, XII, 30. Judge Brown Diary, June 11, 1862.

CHAPTER 7

[1]*Patriot*, November 13, 1861. For the confusion surrounding Magruder's appointment, see *O.R.*, Series IV, II, 73.

[2]Jefferson Davis to the Senators and Representatives from Arkansas, March 30, 1863, *O.R.*, LIII, 863.

[3]T. C. Hindman to S. Cooper, June 19, 1863, *ibid.*, XIII, 28–29.

[4]*Ibid.*, 29–40.

[5]*Ibid.*, 833; 29–40.

[6]*Ibid.*, 37.

[7]Harrell, "Arkansas," p. 102.

[8]T. C. Hindman to S. Cooper, June 19, 1863, *O.R.*, XII, 38.

[9] Very illuminating is the correspondence between Gen. Sherman and Gen. Hindman. Sherman wrote to Hindman (*O.R.*, XIII, 742–43): "If we allow the passions of our men to get full command then indeed will this war become a reproach to the names of liberty and civilization." But Sherman wrote Gen. Carr (*ibid.*, 748–49): "to reach rightful parties will be an impossibility, and we must do something, even if every farm and plantation on the river is destroyed."

[10]*Telegraph*, July 2, 1862. Letter of Albert Pike in *ibid.*, September 17, 1862. Other letters followed. See the *Patriot*, October 2, 1862; February 10, 1863. Special Orders Number 164, *O.R.*, XIII, 855.

[11]William Preston Johnston to Mrs. Johnston, August 15, 1862, William Preston Johnston Papers, Tulane University.

[12]Henry C. Lay to Mrs. Lay, February 18, 24, 1863. Lay Papers.

[13]George W. Guess to Mrs. Sarah H. Cockrell, April 8, 1863. Department of Archives and Manuscripts, Louisiana State University. Robert C. Gilliam to Mrs. Gilliam, March 15, 1864, in James J. Hudson, ed., "From Paraclifta to Marks' Mills: The Civil War Correspondence of Lieutenant Robert C. Gilliam," *A.H.Q.*, XVII (1958), 297. Hereafter cited as Hudson, "From Paraclifta." *Patriot*, January 8, 1863.

[14]Jefferson Davis to General Holmes, August 3 (?), 1862, *O.R.*, XIII, 874. T. H. Holmes to Jefferson Davis, August 28, 1862. Theophilus H. Holmes Papers, Duke University.

[15]R. C. Newton to General Roane, November 4, 1862, *O.R.*, XIII, 981. Letter of Albert Pike, *Telegraph*, December 17, 1862. This type of behavior is called "Failures that were Fatal" in Bell I. Wiley, *The Road to Appomattox* (Memphis, 1956), pp. 77–104.

[16]E. B. Brown to General Schofield, June 27, 1862, *O.R.*, XIII, 451. Annie Heloise Abel, *The American Indian as Participant in the Civil War* (Cleveland, 1919), p. 192. Hereafter cited as Abel, *The American Indian as Participant*.

[17]Report of Major General Thomas C. Hindman, December 9, 1862, *O.R.*, XXII, part 1, 139.

[18]Major Thomas Lanigan to Charles B. Johnson, December 26, 1862. Charles B. Johnson Papers, University of Arkansas.

[19]Jas. G. Blunt to T. J. Weed, December 30, 1862, *O.R.*, XXII, part 1, 168. *Patriot*, January 8, 1863. Hindman's retreat was popularly known as the "skedaddle from Fort Smith." Thomas H. Compere to Governor Flanagin, February 8, 1863. Oldham Collection.

[20]*Danley and Johnson, ex part*, in *Reports of Cases as Law and in Equity* (Little Rock, 1889), pp. 1–7. Letter of "Justice," *Telegraph*, July 30, 1862.

[21]*Telegraph,* September 17, 1862.

[22]Farrar Newberry, "Harris Flanagin," *A.H.Q.,* XVII (1958), 3–21. Hereafter cited as Newberry, "Harris Flanagin." Flanagin wrote Senator Johnson, "nor have I ever felt any but the kindest feelings toward you. I have never taken part in the cry against 'the family,' nor made any effort to defeat you in any except for supporting and voting for members of my own party." Governor Flanagin to Robert W. Johnson, December 20, 1864. Oldham Collection. *True Democrat,* August 27, 1862.

[23]Camden *Eagle,* September 17, 1862, quoted in the *Gazette,* September 27, 1862.

[24]Camden *Ouachita Herald,* n.d., quoted in the *True Democrat,* September 24, 1862. The *Patriot,* October 2, 1862, urged Rector as the soldiers' friend, and in the next issue (October 9) made fun of the wedding of C. Columbus Danley to Miss Nancy Conaway, the cake being a pot pie dough head of Governor Rector mounted on a pedestal. *Gazette,* September 13, 1862.

[25]*True Democrat,* November 5, 1862. *Patriot,* November 6, 1862. Flanagin noted in his diary: "I heard of the result of the election and resigned and returned home." Harris Flanagin Diary, October 28, 1862. Arkansas History Commission.

[26]*State v. Clendenin, Reports of Cases at Law and Equity* (Little Rock, 1889), pp. 78–91.

[27]*Patriot,* October 30, November 13, 1862.

[28]*True Democrat,* December 3, 10, 1862. The editor made light of the loss, saying that the high price for paper would make the work money-losing. Judge Brown complained in his diary, December 9, 1862, that Flanagin was "sold to the click of Demagogues."

[29]The *Telegraph* printed the laws from December 23, 1862, to January 21, 1863. They were not collected and bound until 1896: *Acts Passed at the Fourteenth Session of the General Assembly of the State of Arkansas* (Washington, D.C., 1896).

[30]W. K. Patterson to Governor Flanagin, November 20, 1863. Oldham Collection.

[31]Asa Morgan to Mrs. Morgan, May 19, 1863. Morgan Papers. The man in charge of the money was identified as "Mr. Harrell," undoubtedly John M. Harrell, "a sort of easy, good for nothing fellow named Harrell, commonly called Lord Mortimer," and subsequently the author of the Arkansas volume in the *Confederate Military History* series. *National Democrat,* June 11, 1864. *True Democrat,* April 8, May 6, 1863.

[32]*Patriot,* November 20, 1862.

[33]*True Democrat,* April 22, 1863. George Pettigrew to Governor Flanagin, June 10, 1864. Oldham Collection. David Walker to D. C. Williams, August 29, 1862. Williams Papers. Thomas H. Compere to Governor Flanagin, November 21, 1864. Oldham Collection.

[34]Asa Morgan to Mrs. Morgan, September 10, 1863. Morgan Papers. David Walker to Governor Flanagin, June 9, 1863. Oldham Collection. Dandridge McRae manuscript, Arkansas History Commission. Judge Brown Diary, November 24, 1863. Thomas H. Compere to Governor Flanagin, November 21, 1864. Oldham Collection.

[35]Maurice Smith to W. E. Woodruff, August 10, 1863. Woodruff Papers. Leroy Montgomery to General Holmes, January 7, 1863. Woodruff Papers.

[36]Endorsement written on W. E. Woodruff to General Holmes, March 10, 1863. Woodruff Papers. F. G. Walker to G. W. Sampson, October 30, 1862. Woodruff Papers. Asa Morgan to Mrs. Morgan, June 8, 1863. Morgan Papers.

[37]Judge Brown Diary, September 1, 1862. Letter of Albert Pike, *Telegraph,* September 17, 1862. *Address to the senators and Representatives of the State of Arkansas in the Congress of the Confederate States by Albert Pike* (Louisiana, 1863). H. F. Fairchild to Governor Flanagin, December 12, 1863. Oldham Collection.

[38]*True Democrat,* February 18, 1863.

[39]*Gazette,* November 29, 1862. *True Democrat,* January 7, 21, 1863. President Davis did

not believe in price control. To Holmes on January 28, 1863, he wrote: Prices "must always be regulated by the relation of supply and demand." Rowland, *Jefferson Davis,* V, 424–25.

[40]J. N. Bragg to "My Dear Josephine," July 6, 1862; same to same, March 1, 1863, in Gaughan, ed., *Confederate Surgeon,* pp. 76, 120. N. B. Burrow to Governor Flanagin, August, 1863, Oldham Collection. T. D. Kingsberry to Governor Flanagin, August 8, 1863. Oldham Collection. H. H. Coleman to Governor Flanagin, July 9, 1864. Oldham Collection.

[41]Turnbo, "The Twenty-Seventh Arkansas," p. 227. S. M. Scott to Governor Flanagin, April 27, 1863. Oldham Collection. *Telegraph,* January 7, 1863. Gazette, February 7, June 27, 1863. L. C. Ross *et al,* to Governor Flanagin, January 17, 1863. Oldham Collection.

[42]R. H. Powell to Governor Flanagin, May 5, 1863. Oldham Collection. *Telegraph,* December 24, 1862; April 15, 1863. Thomas H. Compere to Governor Flanagin, June 19, 29, 1863. Oldham Collection.

[43]*Telegraph,* July 30, 1862. *Gazette,* June 27, 1863. *Patriot,* May 9, July 4, 1863. Letter of R. K. Garland, *Telegraph,* April 15, 1863. At the end of February the President's special power expired and was not renewed. Davis' ignorance of Arkansas affairs and especially of Holmes' policies led the President to naively write Holmes on January 28, 1863: "Many complaints were made against the attempt to subject the people of Arkansas to a military police. The effort was certainly unwise, and no doubt much of your embarrassment has resulted from the necessity of restoring things to their normal condition." Rowland, *Jefferson Davis,* V, 424–25.

[44]*Telegraph,* December 24, 1862, January 28, April 15, June 3, 1863.

[45]E. H. English and Albert Pike to Governor Flanagin, June 29, 1864. Oldham Collection. Governor Flanagin to Kirby Smith, July 11, 1864. Oldham Collection.

[46]T. H. Holmes to Jefferson Davis, March 6, 1863, *O.R., XXII,* part 2, 797. Letter of Trooper, *True Democrat,* April 22, 29, 1863. T. C. Hindman to Braxton Bragg, February 14, 1863, *O.R., LIII,* 848. The state law suspending the courts came under review in *Burt, et al, v. Williams, Reports of Cases at Law and in Equity* (Little Rock, 1889), pp. 92–96. The court held the law unconstitutional on the twofold ground that it betokened interference with the sacred obligations of contract, and that it denied the right to a speedy trial. The philosophy of the military was "if the *civil authorities* will *not* take charge of the matter, the *military must.*" B. F. Danley to J. T. Elliot, December 3, 1862. The Records of the Confederate States of America, War Department, Library of Congress.

[47]Report of Brig. Gen. Thomas J. Churchill, *O.R., XVII,* part 1, 780–81. *True Democrat,* January 14, 1863. Special Orders, January 14, March 30, 1863, *O.R., XXII,* part 2, 772, 808.

[48]*Patriot,* March 28, 1863. Turnbo, "The Twenty-Seventh Arkansas," p. 224.

[49]Attack on Helena, Arkansas, *O.R., XXII,* part 1, 383–442. *Patriot,* July 28, 1863.

[50]*Telegraph,* July 15, 1863. W. W. Garner to Mrs. Garner, August 7, 1863, D. C. McBrien, ed., "Letters of an Arkansas Confederate Soldier," *A.H.Q.,* II (1943), 177. Hereafter cited as McBrien, ed., "Confederate Soldier."

[51]Jefferson Davis to T. H. Holmes, July 15, 1863, Rowland, *Jefferson Davis,* V, 555. No doubt the letters Governor Reynolds wrote the President's aide, William Preston Johnston, played on Davis' fears. Reynolds was always reporting various schemes of a separate confederacy while at the same time denying that these rumors had any substance. George C. Watkins, *et al,* to Governor Flanagin, July 25, 1863, *O.R., XXII,* part 2, 945–47. *Telegraph,* August 19, 1863. Governor Flanagin to Kirby Smith, June 15, 1863, Oldham Collection. Jefferson Davis to R. W. Johnson, July 14, 1863. Jefferson Davis Papers, Tulane University.

[52]*Telegraph,* September 2, 1863.

[53]Note of Agreement, August 10, 1863, *O.R., XXII,* part 2, 962. J. N. Bragg to "My dear

Josephine,'' August 25, 1863, Gaughan, ed., *Confederate Surgeon,* pp. 180–81. W. W. Garner to Mrs. Garner, November 5, 1863, McBrien, ed., ''Confederate Soldier,'' 273.

CHAPTER 8

[1]Judge Brown Diary, September 11, 1862. Vance Randolph, *The Ozarks–An American Survival of Primitive Society* (New York, 1931), pp. 19–21.

[2]Judge Brown Diary, October 29, 1862; July 9, 1863.

[3]*Gazette,* June 13, 1863.

[4]Thomas Jerome Estes, *Early Days and Wartimes in Northern Arkansas* (Lubbock, 1928), p. 9.

[5]Judge Brown Diary, November 31, 1864; ʻMarch 17, 1865.

[6]W. H. Crawford to ''Dear Cousin,'' May 2, 1864, Mrs. W. A. Fletcher Papers, University of Texas Archives. James T. Wallace Diary, Southern Historical Collection, University of North Carolina. William Clinton Chambers to Mrs. Burrilla Chambers, July 18, 1862, University of Texas Archives. A. S. Morgan to ''Dear Josephine,'' July 28, 1863, Morgan Papers.

[7]John T. Barber to W. E. Woodruff, March 6, 1863, Woodruff Papers, Arkansas History Commission. *Telegraph,* June 4, 1862. Arkadelphia *War Times,* April 29, 1863.

[8]H. Hayes to D. H. Reynolds, February 8, 1862, Reynolds Papers, University of Arkansas. Clara B. Eno, ''Activities of the Women of Arkansas during the War Between the States,'' *A.H.Q.,* III (Spring, 1944), 5–27. George W. Guess to Mrs. Cockrell, Civil War Letters of Col. George W. Guess, Department of Archives and Manuscripts, Louisiana State University. William G. Thompson to Mrs. Thompson, October 14, 1862, in Edwin C. Bearss, ed., *The Civil War Letters of Major William G. Thompson* (Fayetteville, 1966), p. 38, hereafter cited as Bearss, ed., *Letters.* Turnbo, ''27th Arkansas,'' p. 235. *The Heritage,* VI (April, 1963), 23.

[9]A. S. Morgan to ''Dear Josephine,'' September 14, 1862, Morgan Papers. H. R. Broudriff to ''Gents,'' May 7, 1863, Henry E. Huntington Library. David M. Ray to ''Dear Mother,'' March 8, 1863, David M. Ray Papers, University of Texas Archives. *Arkansian,* January 25, 1862.

[10]John S. Hornor to W. E. Woodruff, January 8, February 14, June 23, 1862. Woodruff Papers. The government shops making shoes, saddles, and clothes were described as ''not very extensive,'' in Trusten Polk Diary, April 4, 1865, Trusten Polk Papers, Southern Historical Collection, University of North Carolina. Texas exile William Quesenbury, who made his own ink from a prairie weed, complained, an ''almost intolerable monotony prevails. I have not tasted one drop of any beverage whatever but coffee and water for more than ten days.'' William Quesenbury to C. B. Johnson, May 28, 1864, February 20, 1865. C. B. Johnson Papers, University of Arkansas.

[11]W. J. Lemke, ed., *The Mecklin Letters Written in 1863–64 at Mt. Comfort by Robert W. Mecklin* (Fayetteville, 1955), 26. Hereafter cited as Lemke, ed., *Mecklin Letters.* James Abraham to Governor Flanagin, October 8, 1864, Oldham Collection.

[12]Bearss, ed., *Letters,* p. 38. *O.R.,* XIII, 86. Stockard, *History of Lawrence,* p. 71.

[13]Thos. H. Compere, to Governor Flanagin, November 21, 1864, Oldham Collection. Lemke, ed., *Mecklin Letters,* p. 29. Another tribute to Arkansas women is *Confederate Women of Arkansas* (Little Rock, 1907).

[14]Johnson Chapman to W. E. Woodruff, December 5, 1862, Woodruff Papers, Hudson, ed., ''From Paraclifta,'' *A.H.Q.,* XVII (1958), 279. E. P. Becton to Mrs. Becton, March 27, 1863, Becton Letters, University of Texas. Mrs. Thompson to Tom D. Thompson, August 15,

1861, Thompson Letters, Camden Public Library.

[15]Charles E. Nash, *Bottom Rail on Top, or Thirty Years Ago* (Little Rock, 1895), p. 11. Lemke, ed., *Mecklin Letters,* p. 25.

[16]Mrs. Thompson to Tom D. Thompson, August 15, 1861, Thompson Letters, Camden Public Library. W. C. Chambers to Mrs. Burrilla Chambers, July 28, 1862, University of Texas Archives.

[17]Worley, ed., *At Home,* p. 27.

[18]J. J. Wheat to ?, November 22, 1861. J. T. Wheat Papers, Southern Historical Collection, University of North Carolina. J. G. Robbins to W. E. Woodruff, January 9, 1862. Woodruff Papers.

[19]*Telegraph,* October 8, 1862, March 25, 1863, May 11, 1864. Castel, *Sterling Price,* p. 266. Robert Freeman Smith, "John R. Eakin: Confederate Propagandist," *A.H.Q.,* XII (1953), 317.

[20]J. C. Robbins to W. E. Woodruff, November 13, 1861. Woodruff Papers.

[21]Judge Brown Diary, April 30, November 9, 1861.

[21]Turnbo, "The Twenty-Seventh Arkansas," p. 295. *Telegraph,* November 2, 1864. A. S. Morgan to "Dear Josephine," September 10, 1863; August 20, 1863. Morgan Papers. Judge Brown Diary, August 15, 1863.

[23]Washington *Courier,* n.d., quoted in *Gazette,* January 26, 1861. Eugene A. Nolte, "Downeasterners in Arkansas, Letters of Roscoe G. Jennings to His Brother," *A.H.Q.,* XVIII (1959), 23. Judge Brown Diary, July 31, 1863.

[24]*Telegraph,* October 21, 1863. Judge Brown Diary, July 31, 1863.

[25]H. Hayes to Daniel H. Reynolds, October 9, 1864. Reynolds Papers.

[26]Lemke, ed., *The Mecklin Letters,* p. 9. B. C. Robertson to J. M. Robertson, August 6, 1862. G. L. Robertson Letters, University of Texas Archives. "Diary of Susan Cook," *Phillips County Historical Quarterly,* IV, 42. Hereafter cited as "Diary," *P.C.H.Q.*

[27]Robert W. Glover, "The War Letters of a Texas Conscript in Arkansas," *A.H.Q.,* XX (1961), 364.

[28]McBrien, ed., Confederate Soldier," 70.

[29]J. P. Blessington, *Campaigns of Walker's Division* (New York, 1875), p. 39. Mrs. Laura Ewing to "My Dear Tom," September 14, 1863, in *Independence County Chronicle,* V (1963), 6.

[30]A. S. Morgan to "Dear Josephine," August 16, 1863. Morgan Papers. Johnstown (Pa.) *Democrat,* May 27, 1863.

[31]William C. Chambers to Mrs. Chambers, July 28, 1862, William Clinton Chambers Papers, University of Texas Archives. R.A.S. Park, ed., *"Dear Parents:" The Civil War Letters of the Shibley Brothers of Van Buren* (Fayetteville, 1963). n.p. Hereafter cited as Park, ed., *"Dear Parents"* Wiley Britton to Mrs. Britton, June 18, 1864. *Arkansas Gazette* Foundation Library. A. S. Morgan to "Dear Josephine," August 16, 1863, Morgan Papers.

[32]*Journal,* January 10, 1862. Gazette, January 31, 1863. Henry C. Lay to Mrs. Lay, February 18, 1864. Lay Papers.

[33]*Journal,* December 13, 1861. Gaughan, *Confederate Surgeon,* pp. 120–21. Park, ed., *"Dear Parents."* A. O. McCollom to "Dear Friends," December 25, 1862. McCollom Letters, University of Arkansas.

[34]Unknown woman's diary from near Helena, December 8, 1863, Arkansas History Commission. Lemke, ed., *The Mecklin Letters,* p. 31. *Gazette,* June 20, 1863.

[35]Gaughan, *Confederate Surgeon,* pp. 246–47.

[36]Judge Brown Diary, October 13, 1863. Gaughan, *Confederate Surgeon,* pp. 246–47.

[37]Hudson, ed., "From Paraclifta," *A.H.Q.,* XVII (1958), 288.

[38]Henry C. Lay to Mrs Lay, February 24, May 23, 1863, December 29, 1862. Lay Papers.

[39]Tom D. Thompson to "Dear John," August 24, 1862, Thompson Letters, Camden Public Library. Mount Lebandon (La.) *Louisiana Baptist,* September 14, 1864.

[40]Mount Lebandon (La.) *Louisiana Baptist,* September 14, 1864. Hubert L. Ferguson, ed., "Letter of John W. Dunan," *A.H.Q.,* IX (1950), 301.

[41]"Diary of Susan Cook," March 10, 1865, *P.C.H.Q., V (1957),* 38.

[42]Mrs Francena Martin Sutton, "A Civil War Experience of Some Arkansas Women," typescript (1914), p. 29. University of Texas Archives. Selene W. Seay to "Dear Parents," August 11, 1864, John T. Wheat Papers, Southern Historical Collection, University of North Carolina. Trusten Polk Diary, May 30, 1865. J. P. Blessington, *The Campaigns of Walker's Texas Division* (New York, 1875), p. 39. R.B. Tyms to W. W. Mansfield December 14, 1864, Mansfield Papers.

[43]Lemke, ed., *The Mecklin Letters, pp.* 7-9. H. Hayes to D. H. Reynolds, October 9, 1864, Reynolds Papers.

[44]Poem by Albert H. Moffatt, dated August 16, 1865, in private possession.

[45]Wiley Britton to Mrs. Britton, June 18, 1864. *Arkansas Gazette* Foundation Library. Clipping, C. C. Bliss Papers, Arkansas History Commission.

[46]Worley, ed., *At Home,* p. 39. R. M. Campbell to W. E. Woodruff, May 15, 1863 Woodruff Papers. Johnson Chapman to W. E. Woodruff, September 29, 1862, Woodruff Papers.

[47]Worley, ed., *At Home,* p. 28, 39.

[48]Johnson Chapman to W. E. Woodruff, September 29, 1862, Woodruff Papers. Worley, ed., *At Home,* p. 31 Lemke, ed., *The Mecklin Letters,* p. 38.

[49]Lemke, ed., *The Walker Family Letters,* n.p.

[50]Johnson Chapman to W. E. Woodruff, December 5, 1862, August 31, 1862, Woodruff Papers. Worley, ed., *At Home,* pp. 36, 41.

[51]Johnson Chapman to W. E. Woodruff, December 5, 1862, September 29, 1862, Woodruff Papers. *O.R.,* XLI, pt. 4, 1030.

[52]Worley, ed., *At Home,* pp. 31, 33. That slavery was no bed of roses for the conscientious owner was also indicated by Mrs. Eskridge: "I have tried to do my part to my negroes—it is truly a trial of uprightness to own them—make *no mistakes." Ibid.,* p. 30.

[53]R. M. Gaines to W. E. Woodruff, April 24, 1863, Woodruff Papers.

[54]*Gazette,* July 4, 1863. *True Democrat,* July 8, 1863.

[55]Henry M. Newhall to Sister and Brother, September 22, 1862. Henry Newhall Letters, University of Arkansas. Worley, ed., *At Home,* p. 32. Minos Miller to Mrs. Miller, June 12, 1863, Minos Miller Letters, University of Arkansas. Clara Dunlap to "Dear Sister," July 24, 1864, Fred J. Herring Collection, Arkansas History Commission.

[56]Amanda Swink to Governor Flanagin, June 5, 1864, Oldham Collection.

[57]The rights and wrongs of slavery with reference to Arkansas were dismissed by William E. Woodruff in the *Gazette* on August 4, 1830: "We can see no good that can result from a discussion of the slave question in Arkansas, which will, beyond all doubt, be a slave state. We apprehend that it would lead to mischievous consequences [to discuss the matter further]. Not until the "oppostiion" press just before the war took up slavery in order to out-Yancey Yancey and thus embarrass the Democrats did slavery reappear in the press. Mc Brien, ed., *Confederate Soldier,* 182, 280. *Telegraph,* March 5, 1865. Fort Smith *New Era,* November 21,1863.

CHAPTER 9

[1]W. K. Patterson to Governor Flanagin, November 20, 1863. Oldham Collection. J. D. C. (?) to Dandridge McRae, 1864. McRae Papers, Arkansas History Commission.

[2]F. M. Emmons to "dear Sister," September 16, 1863. Emmons Letters, State Historical Society of Missouri. Bishop, *Loyalty on the Border, passim*. Not all the men and few of the officers were native Arkansians. The author's great-great-uncle, a Wisconsin man, was chaplain of the First Cavalry Regiment, organized at Springfield, Mo., from July 10 to October 5, 1863. Jno. S. Phelps, Missouri Unionist, was appointed governor on July 19, 1862, and removed on July 9, 1863. Thomas S. Staples, *Reconstruction in Arkansas* (New York, 1923), pp. 9–11. Hereafter cited as Staples, *Reconstruction*. Phelps' penetration into Arkansas affairs was not acute. "Rector," he said, "does not belong to the ultra and extreme men of this state; Flanagan [sic] does." Jno. S. Phelps to Hon. E. M. Stanton, October 20, 1862, *O.R.*, XIII, 751–53. General Steele was the de facto military governor until January, 1864, when Isaac Murphy was installed. C. P. Bertrand to A. Lincoln, December 12, 1864, *O.R.*, XLI, part 4, 835.

[3]*National Democrat*, May 28, October 4, 1864. Staples, *Reconstruction*, pp. 15–100. Little Rock *Unconditional Union*, April 29, May 13, 1864. Hereafter cited as *Unconditional Union*.

[4]Letter of William Fishback, *National Democrat*, July 16, 1864. *Telegraph*, July 23, 1862. *National Democrat*, May 28, 1864.

[5]*Unconditional Union*, May 6, 1864.

[6]H. F. Flanagin to Jefferson Davis, August 11, 1864, *O.R.*, XLI, part 2, 1054.

[7]W. C. Schaumberg to W. R. Boggs, October 26, 1863, *ibid.*, 1050. J. P. Johnson to Jefferson Davis, November 6, 1863, in Rowland, ed., *Jefferson Davis*, VI, 78–9. Thos. E. Adams to S. Cooper, January 29, 1864, *O.R.*, XXXIV, part 2, 921–2. Adams reported the secret part of Johnson's report.

[8]W. H. H. and J. S. Shibley to "Dear Parents," July 30, 1863, Parks, ed., *Dear Parents*, Thomas B. Hanly to Governor Flanagin, December 19, 1863, in Willard E. Wight, ed., "Letters of Thomas B., Hanly," *A.H.Q.*, XV (1956), 163–65. Hanly wrote: "I believe it is the settled purpose of the President to retain Holmes in your Department, Every[thing] has been done which can be done to induce him to relinguish this purpose." Thomas C. Reynolds, Memorandum, August 27, 1863, Johnston Collection, Tulane University.

[9]E. Kirby Smith to Jefferson Davis, September 5, 1864, Jefferson Davis Papers, Tulane University. J. Bankhead Magruder to Jefferson Davis, November 5, 1864. Jefferson Davis Papers, Tulane University. Joseph Howard Parks, *General Edmund Kirby Smith, C.S.A.* (Baton Rouge, 1954), pp. 369ff. Hereafter cited as Parks, *Kirby Smith*.

[10]Parks, *Kirby Smith*, pp. 370–93.

[11]*Ibid.*, p. 399. Separate accounts of the battles involved are Ira Don Richards, "The Battle of Poison Spring," *A.H.Q.*, XVIII (1959), 338–49; "The Engagement at Marks' Mills," *A.H.Q.*, XIX (1960), 51–61. "The Battle of Jenkins' Ferry," *A.H.Q.*, XXX (1971), 193–213.

[12]Judge Brown Diary, April 27, 1864. Turnbo, "The Twenty–Seventh Arkansas," p. 353.

[13]Castel, *Sterling Price*, pp. 188–255.

[14]*Address of E. W. Gantt, of Arkansas, in Favor of Re-Union in 1863*, (New York, 1863). *Telegraph*, February 24, August 24, 1864. In Williams' case, the Supreme Court held his office vacant in *State ex rel. the Attorney General pro tem v. Samuel W. Williams*.

¹⁵*Patriot,* July 11, August 11, 1863. To the Voters of the Second Congressional District, *Telegraph,* October 21, 1863. *Telegraph,* September 23, 1863. *National Democrat,* December 26, 1863.

¹⁶*Telegraph,* January 27, March 2, 16, 1864.

¹⁷*Telegraph,* February 15, May 18, 1864. Letter of W. W., *ibid.,* July 6, 1864. George C. Watkins to Governor Flanagin, July 25, 1864. Oldham Collection.

¹⁸*Telegraph,* July 27, August 10, September 28, 1864.

¹⁹Governor's Message, *ibid.,* September 28, 1864.

²⁰*Acts Passed at the Special Session of the General Assembly of the State of Arkansas* (Washington, 1896), pp. 1–23.

²¹*Ibid.,* p. 15. The new legislature would have assembled in October, 1865.

²²J. W. McConaughy to Governor Murphy, August 10, 1865; B. F. Askew to Governor Flanagin, April 1, 1865; A. B. Williams to Jno. R. Eakin, January 19, 1865, Oldham Collection.

²³*Telegraph,* March 1, 1865. H. Flanagin to R. W. Johnson, December 20, 1864 (draft), Oldham Collection. J. B. Magruder to R. W. Johnson, November 5, 1864, *O.R., XLI,* part 4, 1029.

²⁴H. F. Flanagin to R. W. Johnson, February 14, 1865 (draft). Oldham Collection.

²⁵H. H. Coleman to Governor Flanagin, May 10, 1865; J. N. Smith to Governor Flanagin, October 18, 1864. Oldham Collection.

²⁶*Unconditional Union,* June 15, 1865. E. Kirby Smith to Jefferson Davis, September 2, 1863. Davis Papers. *Telegraph,* January 6, 1864. A recent study is Robert L. Kerby, *Kirby Smith's Confederacy* (New York, 1972).

²⁷*Telegraph,* January 18, 1865. Judge Brown Diary, November 22, 1864. J. P. Johnson to S. Cooper, November 6, 1863, *O.R., XXII,* part 2, 1050. The Treasury sent drafts that were too large to cash, and thus useless. Despite official pleas, the situation had not improved by the war's end. E. Kirby Smith to R. W. Johnson, March 16, 1865, *ibid.,* XLVIII, part 1, 1428.

²⁸*Soldiers of the Trans-Mississippi,* April 21, 1865. Trans-Mississippi Papers, Tulane University. Conversation of Garland, reported by J. J. Reynolds to Adjutant General, May 27, 1865, *O.R.,* XLVIII, part 2, 627. T. A. Faris to Sam T. Flower, May 18, 1865. Trans-Mississippi Papers. In their haste to seize supplies, many records were burned or lost. Some of the papers in the Trans-Mississippi Papers show water or fire marks. Brigadier General Stand Watie in Indian Territory was the last command to surrender.

²⁹H. F. Flanagin to J. J. Clendenin, May 19, 1865. Oldham Collection. J. J. Reynolds to Adjutant General, May 27, 1865, *O.R.,* XLVIII, part 2, 626–31.

³⁰Mrs. Henry Lewis Fletcher manuscript, University of Arkansas. Quoted in Boyd W. Johnson, *The Civil War in Ouachita County* (n.p., n.d.), p. 60. Judge Brown Diary, June 10, 1865.

Epilogue

¹Wm. Quesenbury (Bill Cush), *Arkansas: A Poem* (Little Rock, 1879). Cush's poem was delivered before the editorial convention at Hot Springs, July 2, 1878. The only known copy in possession of the Arkansas History Commission was bound with the *Proceedings of the Arkansas Press Association* for that year.

²*Ibid.,* p. 39.

Index